Dive

For Reference

Not to be taken from this room

Diversity Pedagogy

Examining the Role of Culture in the Teaching-Learning Process

Rosa Hernández Sheets

Texas Tech University

PEARSON

Boston New York San Francisco
Mexico City Montreal Toronto London Madrid Munich Paris
Hong Kong Singapore Tokyo Cape Town Sydney

Series Editor: *Traci Mueller*
Series Editorial Assistant: *Janice Hackenberg*
Senior Marketing Manager: *Krista Groshong*
Senior Production Editor: *Annette Pagliaro*
Editorial Production Service: *Walsh & Associates, Inc.*
Composition Buyer: *Linda Cox*
Manufacturing Buyer: *Andrew Turso*
Cover Administrator: *Linda Knowles*
Electronic Composition: *Galley Graphics*

For related titles and support materials, visit our online catalog at www.ablongman.com.

Between the time Website information is gathered and then published, it is not unusual for some sites to have closed. Also, the transcription of URLs can result in unintended typographical errors. The publisher would appreciate notification where these errors occur so that they may be corrected in subsequent editions.

Library of Congress Cataloging-in-Publication Data
    Sheets, Rosa Hernández
        Diversity pedagogy : examining the role of culture in the teaching-learning process / Rosa
    Hernández Sheets.
        p. cm.
    Includes bibliographical references and index.
    ISBN 0-205-40555-X
        1. Multicultural education—United States. 2. Teaching—Social aspects—United States. 3.
    Learning—Social aspects—United States. I. Title.

    LC1099.3.H48 2005
    370.117—dc22

                                                                    200453155

Printed in the United States of America

10 9 8 7 6 5 4 3 2   09 08 07 06 05

Dedication

To Joseph David Sheets, my beloved husband, and to Miguel, our darling grandchild. Joe is the most amazing golfer, as well as the most brilliant, kind, honest, and incredible man. Joe, I love you for always! Joe, completion of this book literally depended on your love, time, and support. Miguel, you are just about the most perfect human being on the planet! You provide your grandfather and grandmother continual inspiration, hope, and expectations of great things to come.

CONTENTS

FOREWORD

Making Better Sense of Multicultural Education: Principles to Practice

Geneva Gay

Educational excellence for too many students of color continues to be an illusive goal. Disproportionately, rates of school failure among them have reached crisis proportions, and the need for reform strategies to reverse these conditions is urgent. Some educators are diligently searching for different explanations for why the failure rates persist and how to correct them. They are convinced that reasons and practices stemming from pathological orientations and placing the blame on children themselves or their families are not viable solutions to the dilemma of promoting educational equality and excellence for underachieving African, Asian, Native, Latino, and European American students. Nor is continuing to impose middle class, Eurocentric norms, structures, methods, and materials as the only acceptable sources of knowledge and ways of knowing.

The search for more equitable methods for improving the school performance of underachieving students of color is producing some scholarship, research, and practice that exemplify the ideology of multicultural education. The efforts vary somewhat in magnitude, focus, and effect, but at a fundamental level they share some common features. One of these is removing the burden of school failure and reform from individual students (and their families) and placing the responsibility on an educational system that ignores or demeans the cultural experiences and funds of knowledge of ethnically diverse students. Children of color and poverty are seen as being neglected and victimized by schools, and the opinion exists that schools and teachers should be doing everything possible to facilitate their intellectual, social, cultural, and personal development. Another common theme in these multicultural education reform proposals is identifying specific values, traits, and habits of African, Asian, Native, Latino, and European Americans that can be scaffolds or obstacles to successful teaching and learning. Understanding how these operate, how they can be used constructively, and how to avoid the cultural collisions that could occur is contingent upon educators having a thorough knowledge of the cultures of different ethnic groups and genuinely accepting their instructional validity and viability. Therefore, the educational enterprise, rather than children, needs to be transformed if the achievement crisis is to ever be resolved. A critical element of this transformation is making the educational process more representative of, inclusive of, and responsive to the cultural heritages, contributions, experiences, and perspectives of a much wider variety of ethnic, racial, and cultural groups than currently exists in school programs and practices.

This is a major undertaking for everyone concerned. Its execution requires understanding the complexities, potential, and power of multicultural education by school teachers, administrators, and policymakers. This volume makes some noteworthy contributions to facilitating this understanding. It makes it abundantly clear that multicultural education (that is, teaching to, about, and through ethnic, racial, and cultural diversity) is not merely a cosmetic facelift, a transitory diversion, or a quick fix. Educators who have only superficial knowledge of cultural, racial, and ethnic differences cannot address them sufficiently in instructional programs and policies. Additionally, multiculturalism, multiethnicity, and multiracially are complex issues that are deeply ingrained in every fabric of U.S. society. They require corresponding deep thought and carefully executed actions to enhance the educational development of different ethnic individuals and groups. This potential can be realized by using techniques or paradigms for making sense of a powerful, confusing, transformative, and sometimes intimidating field of study. The challenge for multicultural education scholars is to facilitate this sense-making by creating systematic mechanisms to make these analyses, and their related instructional practices, more manageable.

In this volume, Rosa Hernández Sheets offers a conceptual paradigm for characterizing and organizing different approaches to multicultural teaching. Her contributions are both unique and common. While many other multicultural education scholars have developed different ways to systematically organize various dimensions of the field, none of them has created any clearly defined pedagogical typologies. This is Sheets' unique contribution. Other scholars are creating paradigms for explicating the underlying value assumptions and key principles of multicultural education. Some are identifying its major goals and objectives and related pedagogical mandates as they move from simplicity to complexity, from cognitive awareness to social transformation, from selective compensation to widespread necessity. Some scholars are defining criteria for determining the quality of multicultural curriculum, instruction, research, policy, administration, and assessment. Others are developing techniques for how to systematically shift multicultural content and pedagogy from the margins to the center of the educational mainstream. Still others are creating conceptual frameworks for analyzing the historical developments that have occurred in the field and extrapolating lessons learned from them for present and future educational practices.

Sheets' specific contribution to improving the conceptual understanding of multicultural education is a portrait of "diversity pedagogies" for classroom action. It has eight different dimensions, or expressive manifestations, which include developing consciousness of cultural differences, ethnic identity development, interpersonal relations, self-regulated learning, language learning, cognitive content about diversity, high order reasoning skills, and assessment. Although these elements of multicultural education ar endorsed by most scholars in the field to various degrees of emphasis and priority, Sheets packages them differently. In so doing she constructs a comprehensive view of multicultural teaching, and thereby increases its empowerment potential for pre- and in-service teachers. Her diversity pedagogies demonstrate that multicultural education, in its entirety as well as its component parts, is a multidimensional enterprise that can (and must) be addressed on different fronts simultaneously. The pedagogical approaches described provide teachers with a wide range of options and entrees (in both types and magnitudes of significance) for activating multicultural teaching in actual classroom practice.

The diversity pedagogies dispel some common misconceptions surrounding multicultural education. Among them: Multicultural education is monolithic; everyone involved has to do it the same way at the same time; and multicultural education is limited to special occasions, selected subjects, and school settings. Instead, the message is conveyed graphically within and across the chapters of this book that pluralism, multiplicity, and habitually are fundamental features of multicultural education, whether in ideology, content, or pedagogy, and irrespective of the ethnic composition of student populations. Sheets demonstrates how these multiplicities are complementary and reciprocally related in multicultural teaching. The result is some valuable modelling and guidance for teachers to avoid falling victim to the assumption that teaching anchored in multiple ethnic, racial, cultural, and developmental differences is automatically fraught with chaos, confusion, incoherency, and ineffectiveness. Not only is it feasible, but it is viable, and a highly plausible alternative means (if not the only one) for achieving educational equity, excellence, and justice for marginalized, underachieving, poor, and underrepresented groups.

Some notable patterns have emerged in the development of multicultural education since its inception in the earlier 1970s. These differ according to whether the unit of analysis is theory or practice, curriculum or instruction, educational improvement or transformation. The field began as primarily a curriculum enterprise, but quickly shifted to a pedagogical focus. This shift of emphasis has continued over time such that currently multicultural education scholarship deals primarily with pedagogical issues. The content of this book is consistent with these developmental trends in that it is concerned foremost with modifying classroom instruction to make it more reflective of and responsive to the ethnic, racial, cultural, and social diversities that characterize U.S. society.

More growth is evident in multicultural education curriculum and instruction theory than practice. It is apparent in increasing conceptual clarity, complexity, depth, and sophistication. This growth has generated some heightened tensions between theoretical principles and classroom practice. Ironically, as theoretical developments in disciplines mature, it is not uncommon for practitioners to accuse them of being esoteric and having little or no practical value. This widening gap is both a challenge and an invitation to multicultural educators to imagine ways to translate theory into practice without compromising its integrity. In this book Sheets addresses both sides of the gap simultaneously by extending the theoretical conceptualizations of multicultural education and providing some vibrant practical strategies that symbolize them.

Sheets uses two well-crafted techniques to show what theoretical principles of diversity pedagogies look like in practice. She then invites the readers to engage in interpretative and analytical discourse on these illustrations to further crystallize their "theory translated to practice" understandings. One technique is summary charts of pedagogical behaviors of teachers, with corresponding cultural displays of students. The message here is that when teachers use instructional strategies that are compatible with specified aspects of ethnic, racial, and cultural diversity and the attributes of students in different developmental stages, they produce increased levels of cultural competence and academic performance in students. The second tool is a wide variety of vignettes, situations, and scenarios that embody the principles of cultural diversity being discussed. These are little slices of teaching and learning realities that occurred in actual classrooms and involved students from different ethnic groups, instructional issues of varying significance, and multiple means of intellectual engagement. These visualizations of "multicultural education theory in practice" respond to the dilemma frequently faced by teachers new to the field who lament that they do not understand "how to do it in practice even if they understand and accept it in principle."

A strong indicator of the growing sophistication of multicultural education theory is demonstrating how it parallels, is closely connected to, or exemplifies other highly esteemed premises and principles of good quality education. This is an epistemologically, pedagogically, and politically powerful strategy, especially for an endeavor that is as contentious as multicultural education. It demonstrates that multicultural education has its own inherent integrity, as well as value-added utility for making general educational principles meaningful to the particular needs of ethnically, racially, and culturally diverse student populations and learning contexts. In exploring these relationships, other scholars have established conceptual and ideological connections between multicultural education and teaching citizenship for democracy; educational equity, excellence, and equality; social justice, reconstruction, and transformation; education for empowerment and liberation; and closing the achievement gaps among Asian, Native, Latino, African, and European American students. Sheets adds to this scholarly discourse by placing principles and practices essential to multicultural education into the human growth and development paradigm familiar to many educators, but most often not filtered through lens of ethnic, racial, and cultural diversity. The conceptual and pedagogical linkages she makes between these two paradigms for understanding, respecting, and responding to children of color are insightful and enlightening. They offer exciting possibilities for crafting learning opportunities and experiences that can make their school experiences more successful.

Many pre-service and in-service teachers are reluctant to embrace or outright resist multicultural education. They seem mystified, intimated, or overwhelmed by it. These reactions are prompted, in part, by a lack of knowledge about and genuine lived experiences with ethnic, racial, and cultural diversity. The little knowledge they have is tainted by the stereotypes or superficial presentations of ethnic groups obtained largely through mass media, popular culture, and other transitory contacts. Those who do have substantial knowledge about groups of color still may find it of limited value in classroom teaching because it is often not contextualized in pedagogy appropriate for K-12 students. Regardless of the level of their knowledge and prior experiences, most mainstream European American teachers are uncomfortable talking and trying to teach about race-based oppression. Their inclination is to avoid dealing with these difficult issues among themselves, as well as with their students. Many multicultural education scholars have not yet succeeded in convincing teachers to accept, unequivocally, the mandate to confront and combat racism, ethnic exploitation, marginalization, invisibility, and powerlessness. These unmet needs can quickly become frustration that, in turn, leads to alienation and resistance, if not outright rejection.

This book succeeds where others have not. It uses techniques of analysis, explanation, illustration, and transformation that diffuse some of the threat surrounding racism and cultural diversity without avoiding the issues or minimizing their significance in the educational process. This accomplishment is especially worthy, given that much of the text is devoted to teaching young children in the elementary grades. After reading it, teachers will understand that very complex and troubling concerns related to diversity and inequalities can (and must) be included in elementary and secondary school curricula. They will find a wide variety of practical examples for how to do this kind of teaching, and will receive persuasive reasoning for why powerful multicultural teaching is imperative for all students in different chronological and developmental ages. Teachers have many opportunities to *see* theory personified as practice and to witness how ideas move from conceptual abstraction to instructional action. This is a compelling accomplishment that should be empowering to multicultural education novices, as well as affirming to the more experienced advocates. This book is a significant contribution to the field of multicultural education scholarship, and is a worthy addition to the collection of all educators involved in multicultural teacher preparation and K-12 classroom practice.

PREFACE

It is highly likely that you, as a teacher, will encounter children different from yourself in race, ethnicity, culture, language, socioeconomic status, and sexual orientation in your classroom. You will be challenged both as an individual and as an educator to recognize the ways in which your teaching may advantage or disadvantage some children. The complex act of teaching expects you to apply your knowledge about culturally diverse children in ways that enable more students to gain new knowledge. How will you accomplish this task? What knowledge and skills do you think are most critical? What attitudes, values, and experiences will help you develop into a competent teacher? Diversity pedagogy is a developmental approach to the teaching-learning process that can help you advance cultural competency in your classroom.

This book, designed for use in teacher preparation courses, unites developmental psychology and diversity. It helps teachers recognize that success in culturally diverse classrooms often depends on their ability to perceive diversity as the norm and to view it as fundamental to all aspects of schooling. In planning this book, the intention was to produce a volume grounded in scholarship but written in a language that helps teachers understand why the experiential histories of racially, ethnically, linguistically, and culturally diverse teachers and students shape the teaching-learning process. An assumption is made that all teachers can begin and most can evolve into culturally competent educators. However, being conscious of the journey from novice to expert and taking ownership of the hard work, relentless commitment, and high investment of time and energy is also required.

Research on teacher learning shows that teachers learn from interactions with others (Putnam & Borko, 2000; Resnick, 1991). Resources that encourage dialogue provide teachers with opportunities to share learning and performance. These encounters increase the likelihood that new insights about the teaching-learning process will be incorporated into practice. Therefore, the substantive content and the structural design of this text is organized as a resource to increase cultural knowledge and to encourage discussion on specific pedagogical issues, while simultaneously advancing exposure to diverse perspectives needed to reframe teaching-learning events to serve more children.

Three major goals guide this text.

1. To help teachers acknowledge their responsibility to create and sustain social, emotional, and cognitive conditions in classrooms where children from different ethnic, linguistic, and cultural groups can learn what is intended.
2. To heighten teachers' understanding of the role of culture and language in schooling and to acknowledge the significance of ethnicity in the social and cognitive development of students.
3. To instill in teachers cognitive attitudes or patterns of thinking and skills needed to guide culturally inclusive teaching decisions.

Each chapter opens with a powerful quote to stimulate interest and encourage reflection. Classroom vignettes and research in diverse K-12 classrooms demonstrate theoretical positions. These classroom events invite dialogue and focus on specific pedagogical elements based on the current literature on how teachers and students learn. Teaching suggestions are provided in each chapter to further clarify the chapter's purpose. Operational definitions of new terms and definitions of key concepts are embedded within the text. Each chapter concludes with a suggested reading list for further exploration.

The theoretical foundation for this text is found in Part I: Introduction to Diversity Pedagogy. Chapter 1 connects culture and schooling. It examines culture as a socialization process, discusses the power of culture, and explores how culture is sustained and maintained in a society. Chapter 2 introduces Diversity Pedagogy. This new ideology views the relationship between culture and cognition as essential to understanding the teaching-learning process. It focuses on the ways teachers' and students' behavior influences the co-construction of new knowledge. This chapter begins an explanation of the structural components of the ideology, description of its components, and discussion of how diversity pedagogy is conceptualized. The relationship among culture, cognition, teaching, and learning is also examined.

Part II: Diversity Pedagogy Dimensions is the heart of the text. This section positions students and teachers as powerful participants in the teaching-learning process. Grounded in the current research on cognitive and social development, these chapters describe specific teacher pedagogical behaviors and their complementary student cultural displays. Diversity Pedagogy is conceptualized within two paired, interconnected dimensional elements in eight dimensions addressing teacher and student behaviors. In the classroom, these dimensions intersect with each other and rarely occur in isolation. They are not hierarchal in nature. The chapter order and grouping are thematic. A chapter is devoted to each dimension. The first four dimensions—Diversity/Consciousness of Differences, Identity/Ethnic Identity, Social Interactions/Interpersonal Relationships, and Culturally Safe Classroom Context/Self-Regulated Learning—are grouped together in Chapters 3 through 6 because they specifically relate to social and cultural development. The last four dimensions, discussed in Chapters 7 through 10, focus on learning and knowledge acquisition—Language/Language Learning, Culturally Inclusive Content/Knowledge Acquisition, Instruction/Reasoning Skills, and Assessment/Self-Evaluation.

In this section, each dimension is introduced and defined in the first table of each chapter. These tables are designed as reference tools. The tables first describe the dimensional elements. Teacher behaviors, presented as teaching principles or guidelines, are listed in the left column of each table. These guidelines correspond with and encourage the expression and development of the student cultural displays described in the right column. It is theorized that if the teacher behavior in the classroom reflects what is on the left side of each table, then students will have opportunities to display the corresponding cultural behaviors listed on the right side of each table. For example, in Dimension 3: Social Interactions/Interpersonal Relationships, if the teacher *Creates classroom conditions through curricular planning, instructional strategies, and interpersonal relationships where students can openly express aspects of their ethnic identity* (teacher pedagogical behavior), then students have more opportunities to display *Signs of developing a psychological, social, and cultural dimension of self, as an individual and group member of a particular ethnic group or groups* (student cultural display).

The final section of the book, Part III: Classroom Applications, includes research on the high school level: Chapter 11, Cultural Strengths of African American Children, and Chapter 12, Linguistic Strengths of Mexican American Students. These chapters describe selected culturally influenced behaviors, attitudes, and knowledge that students disclose in classroom settings. As theorized, complex developmental processes, involving both student cultural displays and teacher pedagogical behaviors, show that these dimensions rarely occur in isolation and that some dimensions may be more prominent than others depending on the classroom event.

I believe that effective teacher preparation helps teacher candidates explore the ways successful teachers recognize, interpret, and respond to children's cultural displays of competency resulting from their socialization process. My experiential background, fifteen years of successful teaching in high-poverty, low-performing urban schools; six years of teaching in state institutions with the explicit purpose of preparing teachers; a sustained line of inquiry in diversity pedagogy; solid academic preparation; and extensive mentoring from leading scholars in the field of diversity unite to give me a useful and realistic perspective of the knowledge and skills novice teachers need to succeed with more students. This book explores multiple layers of feeling, knowledge, and skill that underlie equitable, culturally sensitive work with children.

ACKNOWLEDGMENTS

I wish to thank Geneva Gay (University of Washington) for her continual support and mentoring. I am also thankful for the time, effort, and insightful comments made by the six reviewers, Barbara Applebaum (Syracuse University), Adrienne Fong (San Francisco State University), Etta R. Hollins (University of Southern California), Kristi P. Johnson (Marymount University), Shane P. Martin (Loyola Marymount University, Los Angeles), and Sharon Thomas (Miami-Dade Community College); and the two editors, Kimberly Hollins and Traci Mueller. I am most appreciative of their assistance.

I am also deeply indebted to Margaret Graham, my friend and gifted copyeditor at Texas Tech University. Her help throughout this entire process made completion of this task possible, especially when facing tight deadlines. Often, with minimal lead time, she always managed to find time to work on this project. I also recognize the invaluable work of my research assistants at Texas Tech University, Gregory D. Gonzales and Vanessa M. Sikes. These two new scholars willingly put in many extra hours. Unfortunately, I experienced computer issues during the hectic last month. I could not have completed this manuscript on time if TTU's computer support staff had not given my laptop priority. Thank you Jesse Trevino, Joe Gonzaga, and Shane Hammontree! I also wish to thank Karissa Greathouse, who helped with the tables.

A special thank you to my colleagues at Texas Tech University: Susan Myers and Judy Simpson, who willingly shared their research assistants during the final weeks of this project; Connie Anderson, for her heartfelt encouragement; and Gerald Skoog, Dean of the College of Education, and Peggy Johnson, Department Chair, for their constant support. I am also indebted to the following individuals at San Francisco State University: Laureen Chew, Department Chair, and Jacob Perea, Dean of the College of Education, for their assistance in time and resources during the early stages of this book; and Robert A. Corrigan, President, for awarding me a sabbatical that was devoted to the development of this work.

PART ONE

Introduction to Diversity Pedagogy

1 Student Learning and Culture

Cultural diversity is strength—a persistent, vitalizing force in our personal and civic lives. . . . It is then, a useful resource for improving educational effectiveness for all students. Just as the evocation of their European American, middle-class heritage contributes to the achievement of White Americans, using the cultures and experiences of Native Americans, Asian and Pacific Islander Americans, Latino Americans, and African Americans facilitates their school success.

—Gay, 2000, p. 14

Teachers are the single most important resource in any classroom. As a result, few professionals hold as much potential and responsibility for improving the schooling experiences of children as teachers in classrooms. Students' success or failure and acceptance or rejection often depend on the ways teachers behave in classrooms. Complex, interpersonal teaching-learning events require teachers to create **equitable** (fair and impartial) learning conditions.

The purpose of this chapter is to help teachers recognize the critical connection between culture and schooling. The first part examines culture as a socialization process, discusses the power of culture, and explores how culture is sustained and maintained in a society. This is followed by classroom applications.

The word culture generally conjures different ideas about what it means in peoples' minds. Understanding a concept such as culture may be challenging due to its complexity and to the tendency to personalize or simplify its meaning. In this section, three aspects of culture are discussed: (a) its role in the socialization process, (b) the powerful influence it has in children's human developmental processes, and (c) the ways that it is maintained and sustained. These views of culture can help teachers acknowledge its significant role in the teaching-learning process.

Culture as a Socialization Process

Anthropologists use the term **enculturation** to describe the process of being socialized to a particular culture. The **socialization process** can be defined as the ways human infants, born without any culture, acquire the **cultural knowledge** of their parents and caregivers. During this transmission of culture, children gain the cultural knowledge of their social group. **Cultural knowledge** includes the language, values, belief systems, and **norms** (concepts of appropriate and expected behaviors). The ways children display and internalize the cultural knowledge learned in their homes and communities influences the development of self and establishes a sense of belonging (Knight, Bernal, Garza, & Cota, 1993).

Pai and Adler (2001) define culture as:

> [Culture is] a system of norms, standards, and control mechanisms with which members of society assign meanings, values, and significance of things, events, and behaviors; culture includes patterns of knowledge, skills, behaviors, attitudes, and beliefs, as well as material artifacts produced by human society and transmitted from one generation to another. (p. 245)

Some scholars maintain that adults, in a purposeful and systematic manner, impose on their children culturally determined ways of seeing, feeling, and acting (Barrett, 1984; Geertz, 1973). As a result, the knowledge and responses learned by children in their socialization process are not spontaneous in nature; rather, they are deliberate and intended. For example, children by the age of 2 or 3 speak a particular language and share the complex norms and belief systems from their homes that guide their thinking and behavior. Children do not choose to speak Navajo if reared in a Vietnamese speaking home anymore than they can determine which modes and styles of communication and etiquette to emulate.

Kluckhohn (1949) describes the socialization process as a blueprint with distinct cultural patterns, which determine certain predictability of cognitive and social actions. In classrooms, some of the students' skills and competencies learned in their cultural group will differ from the behaviors and skills of their teachers who may be socialized in a different cultural group. Some teachers may not be aware of this cultural mismatch. Differences in teachers' and students' cultural strengths, norms, and values can be problematic in classrooms that operate with a single culture model.

Vignette 1.1 and 1.2 demonstrate how diverse cultural norms may produce various assumptions and expectations among teachers, parents, and students.

Vignette 1.1
Mothers and Children

In Ms. Nelson's kindergarten classroom, some of the Chinese American mothers come to school every day at lunch time. They bring hot lunches and hand-feed their 5-year-old children. In another kindergarten classroom, Mexican American mothers walk their children to school. When the bell rings they enter the classrooms with their children. They walk children to their tables and help them take off their jackets. They hang their children's jackets and book bags on the hooks, generally located in the back of the room, before leaving the classroom. When parent-teacher conferences were held in early October, a European American mother proudly told her child's teacher that Elizabeth could tie her own shoes when she was 4 years old.

Issues for Consideration

Note that some families may value interdependence while others may promote independence. How are cultural customs evident in the behaviors of these mothers and children consistent with or in possible conflict with traditional school norms? How might a teacher's cultural perspective influence the ways they judge the behaviors and competencies of the children and parents in each of these incidents?

Vignette 1.2
Excused or Unexcused Absences

In a Texas high school, a 15-year-old girl is allowed by her parents to miss a day of school to get her hair done and prepare for her Quincienera, a cultural rite of passage. In a middle school in the Midwest, a Jewish American tenth grader asks permission to make up a test that falls during a Jewish holiday. Since there is a no makeup test policy, and this student is absent on the day of the test, he loses 20 points. An upper middle-class European American mother explains to the teacher that she will take her fourth-grade child out of school for a two-week family vacation in Europe. The teacher approves of this absence since she believes it is a valuable experience.

Issues for Consideration

What criteria should be used to judge an absence legitimate? Should one absence be considered more valid than another? Who should decide? Should schools have general attendance policies?

In the classroom, some teachers are able to detect differences in home rearing practices displayed in the children's behavior. It is this skillful observation of student behavior that provides teachers with important cultural information. Teachers who succeed with culturally diverse children recognize diverse children's cultural strengths and skills. They use this cultural knowledge to make learning events more meaningful. These teachers encourage children to openly display and apply their cultural knowledge to new learning.

The Power of Culture

Cultural anthropologists describe the enormous power culture exercises over people's behaviors because it determines which norms to apply when organizing thoughts and shaping beliefs (Barrett, 1984; Pai & Adler, 2001). To belong to and receive recognition, approval, and acceptance from their group, individuals learn to make decisions that maintain the group's values and norms. Through repeated social interactions with members from their group, children practice and acquire their group's competencies, skills, values, and attitudes. They learn to control their behavior and to participate in the maintenance of their group norms. Geertz's (1973) definition points out the powerful force of culture:

Culture is best seen not as complexes of concrete behavior patterns—customs, usages, traditions, habits, clusters—as has been the case up to now, but as a set of control mechanisms—plans, recipes, rules, instructions (what computer engineers call "programs")—for governing of behavior. (p. 44)

Given that culture frames people's **habits of the mind** (automatic, internalized thinking routines) and ways of understanding the world, students who are required to engage in unfamiliar habits of mind from another culture in the classroom find themselves having to do things that do not fit with what they know, or forming opinions that do not match the beliefs they hold. Psychologists call this inconsistency **cognitive dissonance**—discord between behavior and belief (Festinger, 1957; Fiske, Kitayma, Markus, & Nisbett, 1998). When faced with these contradictions, an attitude change takes place to accommodate the behavior and individuals' attempt to cognitively justify performing a behavior that violates their beliefs and values.

Festinger (1957) considered the human need to avoid dissonance as basic as the human need for safety and the need to satisfy hunger. Since people require psychological consistency, the tension and discomfort created by dissonance motivates them to (a) reduce the importance of the dissonance beliefs, (b) add more consonant beliefs to outweigh the dissonance beliefs, and (c) make efforts to avoid distressing feelings by either changing the behavior or minimizing the dissonance beliefs. According to Festinger, the intensity of the dissonance depends on the importance of the issue and the degree of discrepancy between the belief and the behavior. Since dissonance theory applies to all situations involving attitude formation and change, it is considered especially relevant to decision making and problem solving. The situations in Vignettes 1.3 and 1.4 show how dissonance in schooling events causes children to expend emotional energy, which may at times interfere with learning.

Vignette 1.3
Status of One

Jason, an African American ninth-grade student, is enrolled in an honors mathematics class. He is the only African American student in the class. He feels uncomfortable and excluded by his classmates. His friends are in other math sections. Dissonance exists between his beliefs that he has signed up for the section that he belongs in and that this class should be comfortable.

Dissonance can be eliminated by deciding that he can handle the discomfort because the class is only 50 minutes long and he has friends in his other classes (reducing the importance of the dissonant belief) or by focusing on the class strengths, such as it is part of his college preparation coursework, he can handle the level of difficulty, and his parents are proud that he is in this class (thereby adding more consonant beliefs). Dropping the class and enrolling in a different math section could also eliminate the dissonance, but this behavior is more difficult to achieve than changing the belief that he should feel comfortable in this class.

Issues for Consideration

In this case, the teacher is not aware of the discomfort experienced by Jason. Jason remained in the class. How are the same classroom conditions different for Jason? Is it the teacher's responsibility to notice, minimize, and eliminate student discomfort? What happens to children when stressful situations accumulate? Why are events of this nature easily ignored? What are some of the signs that the student might exhibit that you, as teacher, would most likely notice?

Vignette 1.4
Sharing a Bread Roll

In the school's lunchroom, Ana, a 5-year-old Mexican American girl, quickly hides her bread roll in her pocket but feels uncomfortable and fears being caught. The lunch monitor often takes the roll away from her and throws it in the trash as she files out to lunch recess. There is a rule that food cannot be removed from the cafeteria. Her parents are proud when she brings something home to share with her 4-year-old brother, and her little brother is delighted with the daily treat.

Dissonance exists between her beliefs that she should share with her brother and that this culturally approved practice should be comfortable. Dissonance could be eliminated by deciding that she can handle the discomfort because some of the time she is not caught (reducing the importance of the dissonant belief) or by focusing on her parents' positive response and her little brother's reactions to the roll she brings home every day (thereby adding more consonant beliefs). Eating the roll and not bringing it home to her brother could also eliminate the dissonance, but this behavior is more difficult to achieve than changing the belief that she should share with her brother.

Issues for Consideration

In this case, the teacher was aware of the situation. She met with the cafeteria cook. Ana was given a baggie for the roll. The roll was put in the teacher's box by a cafeteria student helper. When Ana returned from lunch recess, she put the baggie with the roll in her book bag to take home. Do you think that events taking place outside the classroom affect children's learning in the classroom? How can you as a teacher become aware of what happens in other places, such as the lunchroom or the playground? Do you think it is your responsibility to know what happens to children during the school day when they are not in your classroom?

Cognitive dissonance often takes place in school settings where children have to reconcile and make sense of the customs from another culture that conflict with their own knowledge or opinion about oneself and the world. They may have to resolve conflicting beliefs and values. Changes in beliefs might take place when students have conflicting beliefs because they are required to (a) work independently and competitively, (b) use unfamiliar communication styles, (c) assume conflicting gender roles, (d) maintain a relationship with teachers who they believe dislike them, or (e) interact with the teacher in ways that differ from the ways they interact with significant others from their culture. Repeated demands to function in the unfamiliar habits of mind from another culture places children outside their psychological comfort zone. It is often experienced without the benefit of teacher assistance. The arduous cognitive task and exhausting psychological stress involved is rarely acknowledged. Some students learn to engage in unfamiliar habits of mind and succeed academically; others who do not overcome this barrier are often unsuccessful in school.

The Maintenance of Culture

In societies composed of multiple cultural groups, such as the United States, a dominant cultural group generally surfaces. The dominant cultural group uses available societal institutions, such as universities, public schools, government, and the media, under their control to maintain and sustain its position and to establish acceptable societal norms and values. In the United States, members of the dominant group are part of the **mainstream culture,** and they are identified as the **majority group.** Individuals with membership in the various other groups are identified as part of the **minority cultures.** Since they are perceived as having different characteristics, traits, and abilities, they are considered outside the mainstream and may be viewed as disadvantaged.

To succeed socially, academically, politically, and economically, individuals from groups identified as minority must learn how to function within the dominant, mainstream culture. The dominant group expects minority group members to adapt. For most people, this adaptation involves change through a process of acculturation or one of assimilation. **Acculturation** refers to the changes that occur when individuals from the minority group acquire the dominant cultural group's norms, values, and behaviors. However, these changes are often made under certain conditions, in specific settings, and for particular purposes. Hence, some bilingual (Spanish/English) teachers will choose to speak English in the staff room even when they know that some staff members speak Spanish. They will carefully determine when and to whom to speak Spanish. These individuals are aware of the value of Spanish and will most likely make sure their children learn both Spanish and English. **Assimilation,** on the other hand, is the change that takes place when minority group members accept the dominant cultural group's norms, attitudes, and values and reject or distance themselves from their own cultural group. In this case, native Spanish speakers would cease using Spanish in all public settings. The children of these individuals are likely to experience heritage language loss because their parents might consciously promote an English-only orientation. They might believe that being monolingual English speakers ensures better performance in school, provides access to more economic opportunities, and results in speaking English without an accent. Both acculturation and assimilation for individuals from minority groups requires **decision making** (a judgment and choice) and attitude change. Generally, assuming attitudes and displaying behaviors contrary to one's personal cultural values, norms, and worldviews involve some degree of discomfort.

In the United States the dominant, mainstream cultural group is European American, middle class, and Protestant. The racial group is White. The social and economic status is middle class. Individuals from this group use certain communication styles, speak American English, prefer specific foods, sanction selected holidays, display distinct cognitive and social skills, and hold cultural values that are perceived as normal. Some of this group's cultural values include individualism (self-reliance and autonomy), freedom (personal, intellectual, and political rights), equality (all citizens are entitled to economic, legal, political, and social equality), justice (a sense of fairness, legal and personal), competition (success is based on individual achievement), and diversity (protection of and full participation of diverse groups) (Adams, 1988; Hollins, 1996). While most mainstream U.S. citizens uphold these beliefs, at times, the equitable (fair and impartial) application to all citizens is influenced by factors such as race, ethnicity, gender, social class, economic status, and sexual orientation. Nonetheless, these values are perceived to be part of the national culture, and as such are evident in school practices.

Many European Americans, such as those who have experienced generational poverty and substandard schooling, new immigrants, and individuals with diverse religious affiliations, do not necessarily experience a mainstream socialization process. People from these groups do not automatically acquire the same styles, skills, behaviors, values, and norms of the dominant culture. However, since they inherit racial markers (skin color, facial features, hair texture) the process of acculturation or assimilation, for some, when and if chosen, historically has been less problematic. Additionally, some individuals who share the same race as the dominant culture may choose (or not choose) to identify with the dominate group because they may be excluded or feel excluded by the dominant group or believe that they have not had equal access to opportunities. Thus, some females, people with ability differences, those who come from poverty, gay and lesbian individuals, and White persons who identify with minority groups may not enjoy the same advantages as mainstream European Americans.

One might ask, "Why does a democratic country with a population as diverse as the United States continue to be dominated by a single cultural group?" How is this cultural supremacy maintained and sustained? An important factor contributing to the dominant status of the European American culture in the United States has been the institutionalization of that culture. European American culture is pervasive in the governmental structure, workplace, schools, and media. To illustrate, although there are multiple styles of communication and hundreds of languages spoken in the United States, consider the ways in which a particular style of communication and a specific world language are institutionalized. The mainstream culture determines the appropriate way of social, business, and academic discourse. There is an established code of etiquette that determines the proper volume, tone, and level of intensity, acceptable eye contact, appropriate physical distance, correct grammar, and allowable accent. Depending on the level of annoyance and embarrassment that people who do not follow these communication norms cause, they may be considered rude, uneducated, ignorant, or boorish. Thus, talking too loud, too soft, too fast, being too emotional, standing too close, or speaking with certain types of accents may be considered inappropriate or offensive. This social disapproval is a way people from other cultural and economic backgrounds are discouraged to engage in their own cultural patterns of communication.

English is the *de facto*, and in some cases the *de jure*, language in the United States. American English is commonly referred to as Standard English. Bilingual individuals are discouraged to publicly use their heritage language except when permission is given for economic, entertainment, or political convenience. Speaking in a language other than American English may be suppressed or prohibited in classrooms, faculty rooms, and workplaces. The rise of the English Only movement in the last decade, aimed at eliminating bilingual programs, suggests that language differences may be perceived as a threat to the dominate culture (Gonzalez & Melis, 2001).

The **privatization** (restricted, furtive, and at times, forbidden public use) of the cultural knowledge of people from ethnic groups of color, given the elevated status of the European American culture, has real implications for school practices and student achievement outcomes (Sheets & Hollins, 1999). Vignette 1.5 (Tyson, 1999) exemplifies what happens in classrooms when children's cultural knowledge is excluded or included in the teaching-learning process.

Vignette 1.5
No Little Red
"I asked him why he appeared not to be interested in the stories I read to the class. I will never forget his reply: 'There ain't no Little Red in my hood, and I catch one of 'dem little piggies, I'm gon' have a Bar-B-Que.' . . . [When] contemporary realistic literature and the ways in which the tying of this literature to events in the boys' lives [was used] . . . the boys begin to discover and supplement the fictional information with factual information. They begin to scrutinize and interrupt the information through cause and effect, hypothesizing ideas and predictions, inferring or deciphering character traits bringing personal insight and their own experience to their literary interpretations" (Tyson, 1999, p. 156).

Issues for Consideration
In this classroom event, Tyson (1999) describes issues with the cultural content in the children's literature selections. Initially, why did some African American male children not engage in lessons? What academic changes took place when a more culturally inclusive literature was chosen? What other changes do you think took place?

Along with the curricular content, the quality of teacher-student interpersonal relationships, the types of instructional methods, the emotional tone, and the physical nature of the classroom context generally benefit children who have been socialized in the European American culture. The ability to stand quietly in line, receive directions all day from a single adult, raise hand and wait to be called upon before speaking, work independently and competitively in a classroom with twenty other same-age children, be responsible for only self, and go to the bathroom at a specific time may appear strange for children who come from homes with large extended families, who live in a social context where people freely talk and move about, where they are responsible for the family unit, and where they have access to four or five caring adults as well as older siblings and cousins. Vignette 1.6 describes Benjamin's experience.

Vignette 1.6
First Week of Kindergarten
Benjamin is raised in a traditional Chinese American family with his mother, father, paternal grandmother and grandfather, one uncle, and two older cousins. After a week of kindergarten, he was asked how he liked school. Benjamin remarked, "Well, we just have one teacher. Nobody can talk [ex]cept the teacher." Since he was expecting to learn how to read, he added with disdain, "We don't even read."

Issues for Consideration
Why do you think Benjamin expected school to be different than what he is experiencing? What cultural orientation encourages Benjamin to use *we* instead of *I?* What do you think of his description of unfamiliar restrictive talk and of his observation that there was only one adult in his classroom?

Classroom Applications

The myriad of factors contained within the personality, heritage, intelligence, experiences, and commitment of teachers cannot be minimized in the teaching-learning process. One's personal **cultural knowledge,** shared systems of meaning acquired by observation, imitation, or instruction from members of one's cultural group, guides our behavior. Acquiring knowledge of cultural groups that differ from self is needed to enhance and develop the types of pedagogical tools needed to teach diverse students. Competent teachers acknowledge the connection between culture and learning. They realize that the journey from novice to expert teacher is developmental. This process requires reflection, knowledge, time, hard work, and sustained commitment. The following suggestions may provide a starting point.

Examining Personal Thinking Habits

Critically examine and become attentive to how personal thinking patterns influence your classroom decisions.

1. Acknowledge how you are dependent on your internal and external judgments, as well as influences from the judgments of others, when making decisions regarding your capabilities to teach and your students' ability to learn. Examine your patterns of thinking and make changes when necessary. Develop habits of mind to guide culturally inclusive teaching decisions.
2. Become aware of how you respond to differences in students' appearances, values, and behaviors. View diversity factors, such as ethnicity, language, gender, socioeconomic status, and sexual orientation, as part of the norm and consider them as important as factors such as time, age, grade level, social skills, and academic ability when planning instructional events.

Observing Student Response to Instruction

Consistently interpret how your students respond to the classroom climate, instructional strategies, and curricular content.

1. Adapt instruction in anticipation of the subsequent social and cognitive steps students need to acquire new knowledge.
2. Use cultural knowledge from multiple perspectives to create classroom conditions that uphold the entitlements of more students to a quality education. Competently envision how students may connect curricular content to prior cultural knowledge and experiences.

Assuming Responsibility for Pedagogical Knowledge

Professionally and realistically acknowledge what you do not know and assume responsibility to learn what you need to develop into a culturally responsive teacher.

1. Realize that teaching is a profession not a job and, therefore, requires tenacity, courage, and heart to develop the confidence and skills to teach students equitably. View teaching as a lifelong, honorable profession. Identify the knowledge, skills, and experiences you need to develop from a novice teacher to an expert teacher. Acknowledge the complexity of the teaching-learning process, the intensity of the never-ending work, and the issues of low pay and low status affecting early teacher drop rates without either minimizing or romanticizing these concerns.
2. Identify areas of pedagogical strengths and weaknesses. Develop a plan of action to acquire the knowledge needed to obtain a high level of effectiveness to help you create conditions that enable more students to achieve desired social and academic outcomes. Learn how to teach yourself cultural content knowledge of other groups, from these groups' perspectives, to help you create and evaluate instructional resources and implement effective instructional strategies.

Conclusion

Positive outcomes for some students may depend on the teacher's ability to conceptualize the role of culture and apply it in the teaching-learning process. Teachers who strive to be culturally inclusive realize that students develop and demonstrate high levels of competency without sacrificing any aspect of their identity. They understand that students' out-of-school learning, thinking, and problem-solving skills acquired through participation in ordinary cultural practices and rituals have value. These teachers also realize that cultural differences require instructional accommodation.

The ability to recognize and to respond to students' cultural knowledge, to discern the cultural nuances students disclose, and to know how to adapt instruction appropriately, may possibly be some of the most important factors in the teaching-learning process. Perhaps it is this skill that potentially separates the competent from the well intentioned, the expert from the novice, and the gifted from the ordinary. Although some teachers may develop this skill instinctively, *all teachers* can acquire proficiency through conscious awareness of personal habits of mind and sharp observational skills. Teachers' recognition of the knowledge, competencies, and behaviors children acquire in their upbringing, and their willingness to utilize these characteristics in the classroom, establishes teaching-learning conditions that potentially benefit more students.

RECOMMENDED READINGS

Hollins, E. R. (1996). *Culture in school learning: Revealing the deep meaning.* Mahwah, NJ: Erlbaum.
Pai, Y., & Adler, S. A. (2001). *Cultural foundations of education* (3rd ed.). Upper Saddle River, NJ: Merrill Prentice Hall.

2 Diversity Pedagogy

It has long been recognized that culture is very difficult for humans to think about. Like fish in water, we fail to "see" culture because it is the medium within which we exist. Encounters with other cultures make it easier to grasp our own as an object of thought.

—Cole, 1996, p. 8

Conceptualizing the natural connectedness of culture and cognition is key to linking the teaching-learning process to diversity. Teachers who acknowledge cultural variations in students' cognitive and social development are more likely to recognize the built-in, continuous relationship among culture, human development, teaching, and learning. Competency in the classroom often depends on the teacher's capacity to perceive cultural diversity as the norm and, therefore, view it as fundamental to all aspects of schooling. These teachers realize that organized activities, familiar or unusual routines, and daily rituals reflecting teachers' and students' cultural practices and habits of thinking characterize life experiences, including life in classrooms.

The purpose of this chapter is to introduce **diversity pedagogy.** This ideology views the relationship between culture and cognition as essential to understanding the teaching-learning process. It focuses on the ways teachers' and students' behavior influences the co-construction of new knowledge. This chapter begins with an explanation of the structural components of the ideology, description of its components, and discussion of how diversity pedagogy is conceptualized. The next section focuses on the relationship among culture, cognition, teaching, and learning. This is followed by classroom applications.

Dimensional Elements of Diversity Pedagogy

Diversity pedagogy has eight dimensional elements. Each dimension represents a teacher pedagogical behavior and its complementary student cultural displays. The eight dimensional elements, teacher pedagogical behaviors, and student cultural displays are discussed in this section.

Diversity pedagogy is conceptualized with two paired, tightly interconnected dimensional elements in eight dimensions guiding teacher and student behaviors. In the classroom, these dimensions naturally intersect with each other and rarely occur in isolation. They are not hierarchal in nature. The order and grouping of these dimensions are thematic. The first four are grouped together because they specifically relate to social and cultural development, and the remaining four dimensions address students' learning and knowledge acquisition. Table 2.1 lists the dimensions and briefly describes the dimensional elements. This table is designed as a reference tool. Note that the teacher behaviors, expressed as guidelines, correspond with and encourage the competency and development of student cultural displays. It is theorized that the teacher behavioral principles listed on the left side of the table provide students with more opportunity to display the corresponding cultural behaviors described on the right side of the table. For example, in Dimension 2, if the teacher *Creates classroom conditions through curricular planning, instructional strategies, and interpersonal relationships where students can openly express aspects of their ethnic identity* (teacher pedagogical behavior), then students are more likely to openly display *Signs of developing a psychological, social, and cultural dimension of self, as an individual and group member of a particular ethnic group or groups* (student cultural display). These eight dimensions are expanded and elaborated in Chapters 3–10 of this text. A chapter is devoted to each dimension.

TABLE 2.1   Diversity Pedagogical Dimensions: Definition of Dimensional Elements

No.	Teacher Pedagogical Behaviors	Student Cultural Displays
1	*Diversity:* Diversity refers to dissimilarities in traits, qualities, characteristics, beliefs, values, and mannerisms present in self and others. It is displayed through (a) predetermined factors such as race, ethnicity, gender, age, ability, national origin, and sexual orientation; and (b) changeable features, such as citizenship, worldviews, language, schooling, religious beliefs, marital, parental, and socioeconomic status, and work experience.	*Consciousness of Difference:* Deliberate awareness and thoughtful exploration of diversity in people, ideas, objects, values, and attitudes on a continuum with multiple points of variance. This conceptualization tends to discourage dualistic thinking patterns, minimizes development of prejudicial attitudes, and decreases the frequency of discriminatory actions toward individuals and groups that differ from self.
2	*Identity:* Identity refers to knowledge of who we are and to what groups we belong. A complex developmental process defines self as an individual and as a group member. The explanations and information used to acquire a sense of self and group membership is determined by the biological, cultural, ethnic, social, psychological, and political factors in one's socialization process.	*Ethnic Identity Development:* Ethnic identity is a dimension of self, as an individual and as a group member. It forms, develops, and emerges from membership in a particular ethnic group. It is a consequence of a distinctive socialization process and is influenced by the degree of personal significance individuals attach to membership in an ethnic group.

(continued)

TABLE 2.1   Continued

No.	Teacher Pedagogical Behaviors	Student Cultural Displays
3	*Social Interactions:* Public and shared contact or communication in dyad or group settings that provide participants opportunities to evaluate, exchange, and share resources.	*Interpersonal Relationships:* Familiar social associations among two or more individuals involving reciprocity and variable degrees of trust, support, companionship, duration, and intimacy.
4	*Culturally Safe Classroom Context:* A classroom environment where students feel emotionally secure; psychologically consistent; and culturally, linguistically, academically, socially, and physically comfortable, both as individuals and as members of the groups to which they belong.	*Self-Regulated Learning:* Demonstrations of the self initiated, managed, directed, contained, and restrained conduct required to meet self-determined personal and group goals, to adapt to established classroom standards, and to maintain self-dignity.
5	*Language:* Human language is a cultural tool used to share, convey, and disclose thoughts, ideas, values, and feelings through words, signals, and/or written symbols. It is also one of the most powerful means to preserve and sustain a cultural heritage and history.	*Language Learning:* Linguistic growth evident in listening/speaking and literacy skills (reading, writing, and viewing) acquired in informal home and community settings and/or in the formal language experiences and social interactions in school.
6	*Culturally Inclusive Content:* The culturally influenced substance, meanings, and perspectives present in the instructional resources used in the various fields of study such as literacy, mathematics, science, social studies, art, music, and physical education.	*Knowledge Acquisition:* The process of connecting prior cultural knowledge to new information in ways that promote new understandings and advance the development of knowledge and skills needed to reason, solve problems, and construct new insights.
7	*Instruction:* Teacher actions facilitating the construction of students' new knowledge through teaching strategies connecting students' prior cultural knowledge to new understandings, creation of a classroom context enabling student learning, and selection of culturally inclusive content.	*Reasoning Skills:* Ability to apply knowledge from personal cultural practices, language, and ethnic experiences to gain command of one's thinking through the acquisition and development of the thinking tools needed to gain new knowledge and take control of one's learning.
8	*Assessment:* Organized, structured, ongoing, varied methods used to observe, document, record, evaluate, and appraise the level and quality of individual and group student work and knowledge gained in a given activity or subject, to (a) improve student learning, (b) determine what students know and what they are able to do, and (c) evaluate how student performance matches teacher expectations and standards.	*Self-Evaluation:* Self-appraisal through reflection, review of thoughts and analysis of personal and group behavior to (a) monitor academic and social goals, assess progress, and identify competencies and weaknesses; (b) plan, assume ownership, and take responsibility for one's learning; and (c) evaluate the strategies used to maximize the acquisition, retention, and performance of new understandings.

Teacher Pedagogical Behaviors

Teacher pedagogical behaviors are the classroom actions and attitudes teachers express related to the act of teaching. When demonstrated in classrooms, this results in the (a) nature and quality of interpersonal relationships with students, (b) physical and emotional tone of the classroom environment, (c) selection of teaching strategies, (d) adaptation of instructional resources, and (e) approaches to self and student assessment. Diversity pedagogy identifies eight teacher pedagogical behaviors. These behaviors explicitly and consciously acknowledge the role of culture in the social and cognitive development of students. The eight teacher pedagogical dimensional elements are diversity, identity, social interactions, culturally safe classroom context, language, culturally inclusive content, instruction, and assessment.

Teachers who develop skills and demonstrate dimensional pedagogical behaviors encourage the disclosure and development of complementary student cultural displays, which can be observed and measured. Teachers who consistently recognize, interpret, and respond to student cultural displays have more opportunities to be responsive to students' academic and social needs. These teachers are more likely to consider the diverse characteristics, strengths, and competencies of their students when creating optimal learning conditions. Awareness of student cultural displays increases the probability of teacher potential to support social growth, enhance ethnic identity development, maintain heritage language, and promote self-regulated behavior. This teacher behavior also makes connections between students' prior cultural patterns of knowledge to intended acquisition of new knowledge. Table 2.2 points out potential outcomes of teacher behavior.

TABLE 2.2 Possible Teacher Responses to Student Cultural Displays

Recognition and Response to Student Cultural Display	Indifference or Unawareness in Response to Student Cultural Display
Develop diversity consciousness	Promote dualistic reasoning
Promote ethnic identity development	Support assimilation to mainstream culture
Provide opportunities for social interactions	Control classroom social events
Create a safe classroom context	Maintain a stressful climate
Encourage language learning	Advance heritage language loss and silence
Select culturally inclusive resources	Choose generic instructional content
Adapt specific instructional strategies	Employ universal instructional methods
Use multiple ways to access competency	Adopt limiting assessment criteria

Student Cultural Displays

Student cultural displays are observable manifestations of the norms, values, and competencies children learn in their homes and communities that provide valuable insights into who they are, how they act, and what they know. These culturally mediated, historically developing cultural knowledge, practices, values, and skills that children bring to school emerge during social interactions, daily rituals, and learning situations. They are consequential to their development, achievement, and emotional well-being. In classroom settings, students may choose to reveal or to conceal, or can feel encouraged to display or compelled to suppress culturally influenced behaviors, skills, attitudes, and knowledge. Children's cultural displays can be observed in eight dimensions: consciousness of difference, ethnic identity development, interpersonal relationships, self-regulated behavior, language learning, knowledge acquisition, reasoning skills, and self-evaluation.

Although many teachers can identify student cultural displays, their responses may not always be appropriate. In some cases, teachers might even overlook a cultural display. Consider the possible teacher responses to the event described in Vignette 2.1.

Vignette 2.1
Helping with Seatwork

This incident takes place in an urban sixth-grade classroom. The student population is ethnically and linguistically diverse. The teacher, Ms. Chavez, cannot speak Spanish. She has just completed a whole group math lesson and has assigned seatwork. During seatwork, she walks around the room checking for understanding and helping individual students. She observes Luis asking questions and Greg quietly explaining a math problem to Luis in Spanish.

Issues for Consideration

Consider how each of the possible teacher responses described below affects how children experience the teaching-learning process and how these experiences help children decide whether to reveal or to conceal a cultural display.

1. Hearing and seeing the students' behavior, Ms. Chavez realizes that Luis is asking Greg for help and Greg is explaining the math seatwork to Luis. She does not approve of Spanish being spoken in the classroom. She believes students should do their own work. English language acquisition and developing independent study skills are classroom goals. She goes over to their desks and quietly reminds Greg to speak only in English. She asks Luis to please do his own work.

2. Ms. Chavez observes the interaction between the two students and determines that the conversation is productive and is advancing the goals of the lesson. She approves the student-student, teaching-learning incident. She chooses to acknowledge the benefits of these students' interaction. She walks over and openly praises Luis for seeking help and Greg for helping Luis.

3. Ms. Chavez hears Greg and Luis talking. Since she insists on complete silence during seatwork, students who talk, regardless of the purpose, content, language used, or need for discussion, are asked to stop. She concentrates on fairness and strives to treat everyone the same. Compliance to the "no talking" class rule is important. She is neither aware that Luis

does not always understand lessons and directions nor that Greg serves as a language resource to Luis. Ms. Chavez changes the seating arrangement and separates these two boys.

How are the students' linguistic, academic, and social skills utilized in each teacher approach? Which response do you find has the greatest potential to advance student learning? How does the teacher's stance of treating everybody the same versus treating students fairly affect the learning opportunities of diverse students in these examples, or, depending on the situation, affect diverse students in general?

Conceptualization of Diversity Pedagogy

Diversity pedagogy links culture, cognition, and schooling. It represents a union between classroom practice and theoretical scholarship explicating the role of culture in the social and cognitive development of children (see Bransford, Brown, & Cocking, 1999; Cole, 1996; Greenfield & Cocking, 1994; Hollins, 1996; Lave, 1988; Portes, 1996; Rogoff, 1990, 2003; Zimmerman & Schunk, 2001). Diversity pedagogy views the natural connectedness of culture and cognition as key to linking the teaching-learning process to elements of diversity. As a result, this ideology is centered on the joint role of culture and cognition in human development. Although the classroom teaching base and foundational theoretical structure guiding diversity pedagogy acknowledge the enormous responsibility and pivotal role of teachers in classrooms, they likewise recognize the powerful, active role students play in their own learning. Diversity pedagogy also recognizes that, while teachers may not always be teaching, students are always learning in the classroom. However, students may not always be learning what the teacher intends.

Relationship among Culture, Cognition, Teaching, and Learning

The construction of new knowledge requires a connection between the learners' prior cultural knowledge and the new knowledge being taught and learned. Research on cognition shows that, when faced with new understandings, learners (a) identify the ways they can enter new learning events; (b) select the most appropriate cultural tool for the context and situation from their repertoires of prior knowledge, skills, cultural practices, and life experiences; and (c) use these cultural tools to build upon their prior knowledge and competencies to construct new knowledge (Cole, 1996; Rogoff, 2003). **Cultural tools** can be viewed as culturally mediated devices, such as language, prior experiences, and knowledge, that students use in the process of reshaping a situation so they can enter effectively (Dewey, 1916; Luria, 1928). Students learn to use previously acquired cultural tools to supply them with the knowledge and skills needed to perform a new task. Thus, children use cultural tools from their repertoires of prior learning, knowledge, and skills to gain new understandings.

Competent teachers create optimal learning conditions. They understand how to facilitate the learning process. They know when to provide assistance and how to extend and build on students' cultural practices and experiences. More students have opportunities to learn in classrooms where teachers (a) make linkages between home and school knowledge, (b) provide students with multiple forms of assistance, and (c) actively participate with students in rigorous learning activities to co-construct new understandings. Vignette 2.2 is an example of a classroom environment where children are free to use their cultural tools and to openly display their cultural knowledge (Sheets, 1998b).

Vignette 2.2
Jack-O-Lantern

This event took place in an all-day kindergarten classroom (twenty-eight students) in a low-performing, high-poverty public school. Tanika was the only African American child in the classroom. Seventeen children were Spanish-speaking: twelve had one or more parents from Mexico and five were from other countries in South America. The other children included six Asian American (four Laotian, one Hmong, and one Vietnamese) and four European American. Most of the children were second language learners and all received free or reduced lunch.

Children were asked to complete a single-digit addition math handout (twelve problems); make Jack-O-Lanterns through a drawing, cutting, and pasting art activity; and then select a choice activity. Short verbal directions were given, and the afternoon schedule was posted on the chalkboard. Children were directed to a teacher-made sample and chart posted above the art supplies with written directions. The supplies for the art project were glue, scissors, square orange construction paper ($9\frac{1}{2} \times 9\frac{1}{2}$), and small green and black construction rectangles and squares. Children had access to boxes and baskets with colored paper, fabric scraps, yarn, and buttons.

Multiple thin scraps of white construction paper on Tanika's table showed the degree of determination needed to finally produce the six long, thin, white strips that met her criterion of "braid." She carefully cut and glued five small circles, repeating the pattern, at the end of each strip—two orange, one green, and two red. She drew and cut an orange circle shape. She positioned the strips at the top of the orange circle shape, moving them so three were on one side and three on the other. She cut and glued a green stump, securing the ends of all six strips. More cutting and pasting turned her orange circle shape into a Jack-O-Lantern.

I [teacher] was stapling completed Jack-O-Lanterns on the bulletin board when Tanika handed me her finished product. She said, "You think this is an orange pumpkin, right?" I nodded, warily. She laughed, "It's not orange, it's brown like me." Consciously aware of the beauty in her brown skin, I smiled. "Look at the elaboration on these braids! Wow! Look at the detail on the eyes! They even have eyelashes. It's beautiful, Tanika!" While Tanika explained exactly where on the bulletin board she wanted her artwork placed, a few children gathered to admire the only Jack-O-Lantern with braids. Overhearing the activity over the braids, Lisa and Carmen (Tanika's best friends) insisted that Tanika show them how to make braids. Walking toward the art area, Carmen touched Tanika's arm and said, "Your brown is a pretty color, right?" "Right!" they laughed. In her role as expert, Tanika gave Lisa and Carmen a lesson in making braids (Sheets, 1998b).

Issues for Consideration

An analysis of Tanika's behavior shows that she felt comfortable completing the task and announcing that she and her Jack-O-Lantern were brown. Her friends and teacher acknowledged the beauty of her skin color. Although this cultural display signified an expression of ethnic identity and a declaration of a racial marker (skin color), it was also indicative of Tanika's self-regulated behavior, language, social, and academic competence. Through a deliberate cognitive process, Tanika decided what she was going to do and how she was going to personalize this project to make a statement of self, which she and others publicly acknowledged. Her problem-solving skills, control of fine motor skills, and self-regulated determination to produce this type of elaborated art project are indicators of achievement and intelligence. The designing, cutting, and gluing of thin, long strips, small balls, and tiny clumps of eyelashes to her Jack-O-Lantern are difficult tasks for most 5-year-olds. In addition, her willingness to teach others demonstrated effective and positive interpersonal relationships with peers as well as strong communication skills.

Teacher behavior specific to the Jack-O-Lantern event indicates that awareness of how Tanika's statements and artistic expression may link to her racial and ethnic identity allowed the teacher to respond purposefully. Attentive to her status of one—the only African American child in the class—the teacher was consciously aware that this was an opportunity to promote development of her racial and ethnic identity. "Typically, I read to the children at the end of the day. On that particular day, I chose *Meet Damitra Brown* (Grimes, 1994), a story about an African American girl, who always wore purple—the color of royalty—just in case she was a real princess" (Sheets, 1998b, p. 10). The selection of this story is an example of culturally inclusive content. This shared reading activity was a direct response to the children's knowledge building, which developed through their earlier social and collaborative learning experiences. By capitalizing on Tanika's self-awareness of her color and on the children's interest in examining a Jack-O-Lantern with braids and making braids, this story extended and provided opportunity to examine another African American girl's expressions of self and the cultural role of color. A lively discussion about purple underwear, kings, queens, and favorite colors took place. Brian (Laotian American) commented that he thought kings and queens wore yellow. He intended to ask his grandmother. Larry's (European American) addition of popular cultural knowledge—"Barney (children's cartoon character) is purple!" delighted everybody. Tanika asked to borrow the book overnight, creating a fortuitous home-school connection.

There were conditions in this classroom—instructional and contextual—that encouraged children to express identity factors and prior knowledge during classroom events. During the first two weeks children focused on comparing and enjoying color, rather than identifying and labeling colors. They explored and compared the shades and hues of the colors found in skin, hair, clothing, food, leaves, buildings, flowers, and so forth. As a particular color was studied, the children and teacher brought objects in various shades, which were displayed, labeled, used for art projects, social studies, science, and sometimes eaten. The display for the color green included a small Mexican flag, a sage baby blanket, an emerald dime store ring, an olive Army jacket found at Goodwill, a small jade piece of jewelry, pieces of different shades of green construction paper, tissue paper, samples of wallpaper, and multiple pictures of green things made by the children or cut out of magazines. The children tasted fresh leafy green vegetables and green fruit, which were also labeled. They read *Green Eggs and Ham* (Geisel, 1960) and ate green eggs and ham. They watched tomatoes and chile ripen to a bright red; green bananas turn yellow; hard green avocados soften to a nice brown; and piles of green leaves change to brown, yellow, and red. The children discussed why Granny Smith green apples and tomatillos (green tomatoes) remained green. Maria's mother came to school. She brought green enchiladas and a green cake. She made a mild green chile sauce and guacamole dip.

Baskets of people crayons with various hues of brown skin tones were available for their use. Black and brown, colors rarely used in primary classrooms, were familiar to these children (Sheets, 1997). Children participated in multiple art experiences using only brown and black paper of various shades, textures, and sizes, such as paper towels, plastic, packing paper, fabric, corrugated paper, cardboard, tissue paper, textured paper, construction paper, wood, and big boxes. The playhouse had beautiful long, black taffeta, velvet, and silk gowns and various shades and types of brown fabric pieces, which were used creatively as scarves, skirts, capes, and tablecloths.

Children's home knowledge was valued. It was common for children to teach each other. Most of the children could count from 1 to 10 in at least three languages—English, Laotian, and Spanish. Those who knew colors, alphabet letters, and numbers taught those who did not. In the classroom, children freely used their home languages both socially and academically. Since the children's level of English proficiency varied, some children translated assignments and others worked collaboratively with peers. In the traditional, daily morning circle, children choose to share in their home language or in English. In this classroom, children were liked, treated as scholars, and taught to achieve.

Identify the children's cultural displays and the teacher's pedagogical behaviors in the eight dimensions listed in Table 2.1. Which teaching strategies might you adapt in your teaching or which do you find helpful? Discuss and describe the classroom conditions determining the cultural, academic, and emotional tone of the classroom. What teaching strategies linked the children's prior learning to new knowledge?

Classroom Applications

Kennedy (1999) maintains that teachers' personal K-12 classroom experiences are more influential and powerful than the information gained through teacher preparation courses and field experiences. The knowledge that you internalize during your process of schooling often influences what you believe about teaching and learning. This knowledge shapes what you think the subject matter should be like, how students are supposed to behave, and how they are expected to function in schools. Most teachers teach the same way they were taught. If this is the case for most teachers, the assumption is that it will be different for you. Your preparation and commitment to learn how to teach diverse children will support your efforts to change this trend. One of the ways to you can succeed with diverse students is to understand and internalize a diversity ideology. This theoretical foundation will help guide your practice. To accomplish this task, consider the following suggestions.

Selecting a Diversity Ideology

Select a diversity ideology to help frame your understandings of the relationship among culture, schooling, and your teaching practice.

1. Understand how the application of culture to learning influences the way you make instructional decisions, select curricular content, and design classroom climate. Make linkages among theoretical orientations, your personal philosophical beliefs, and your behavior in the classroom.
2. Reflect how you were shaped by the cultural values promoted in your schooling. Examine whose values should be transmitted in a culturally diverse society. Critically analyze your own cultural position, characteristics, and skills and use this knowledge to identify how these personal skills, characteristics, attitudes, and knowledge help you to develop professionally.

Centering Students in the Teaching-Learning Process

Center children in the schooling process.

1. Acknowledge your responsibility to provide cultural, emotional, and cognitive conditions in classrooms where students from different ethnic, linguistic, and cultural groups feel safe to learn what is intended.
2. Place value on the home knowledge students bring to learning events.
3. Maintain a sense of reality of the complexity involved in connecting and in applying cultural knowledge to teaching-learning events.
4. Focus on changing your behavior without placing blame on your students, their families, or their communities. Acknowledge that experiential differences among children and teachers may produce inequity of outcome. These cultural differ-

ences may simultaneously and unintentionally disadvantage some children while supporting others.

Conclusion

All teachers can begin to, and most do, evolve into culturally competent educators; however, it is important to become conscious that the arduous journey from novice to expert requires hard work, relentless commitment, and a high investment of time and energy. Although acknowledging the role of culture in schooling, developing professional skills, and aligning personal values to address diversity are essential, the complexity of the teaching-learning process cannot be minimized. Knowledge of the ways children learn and the ability to apply and translate a diversity ideology to practice is also required. Teachers, even at a novice level, can develop strong observational skills to help them notice and respond to students' understandings of teaching-learning events. Becoming conscious of one's own thinking patterns can help us respond in ways that enable students to achieve.

RECOMMENDED READINGS

Cole, M. (1996). *Cultural psychology: A once and future discipline.* Cambridge, MA: Belknap Press of Harvard University Press.
Rogoff, B. (2003). *The cultural nature of human development.* New York: Oxford University Press.

PART TWO

Diversity Pedagogy Dimensions

CHAPTER

3

Diversity: Developing Consciousness of Differences

The limits of our understanding are really contingent cognitive biases built into us at this moment of evolutionary history.

—McGinn, quoted in Baker, 2002, p. 4

Schools are complex mini communities that reflect many of the unsolved issues of the larger society—yet culturally diverse teachers and students are required to work together, often, with very little practical services. Teachers are expected to create inclusive, equitable, democratic communities that enable all students to learn. This chapter is designed to help you think about how diversity elements in your classroom affect classroom practices. The assumption is made that acknowledging the naturalness of diversity is a critical first step toward (a) responding competently to differences in students' identity, (b) maintaining culturally inclusive classroom conditions, and (c) providing classroom experiences that benefit more students.

This chapter begins with an introduction to the first diversity pedagogy dimension, diversity/consciousness of differences. It defines the terms diversity and consciousness of differences and describes possible teacher pedagogical behaviors and subsequent student cultural displays. The second section, teacher pedagogical behaviors, examines some of the elements of diversity influenced by family, socioeconomic status, sexual orientation, gender, and ability. Student cultural displays follow with discussion of the ways students develop prejudicial thinking associated with race and ethnicity and the ways they acquire gender information. The chapter concludes with classroom applications.

Diversity Pedagogy Dimension 1: Diversity/Consciousness of Differences

Understanding how one categorizes people and concepts, examining perspectives from the viewpoints of others, and realizing how knowledge is constructed can help us conceptualize how cognitive and social biases influence how we think about diversity.

27

Table 3.1 describes the terms *diversity* and *consciousness of differences*. It introduces the pedagogical strategies (teacher behaviors) needed to apply this dimension in the classroom. Student cultural displays point out how students might demonstrate signs of recognizing and respecting differences in self and others and how they exhibit understandings of the variations in individual and group identities, perspectives, experiences, events, and beliefs.

TABLE 3.1   Diversity Pedagogy Dimension 1: Diversity/Consciousness of Difference

Definition of Dimensional Elements

Diversity: Diversity refers to dissimilarities in traits, qualities, characteristics, beliefs, values, and mannerisms present in self and others. It is displayed through (a) predetermined factors such as race, ethnicity, gender, age, ability, national origin, and sexual orientation; and (b) changeable features, such as citizenship, worldviews, language, schooling, religious beliefs, marital, parental, and socioeconomic status, and work experiences.	*Consciousness of Difference:* Deliberate awareness and thoughtful exploration of diversity in people, ideas, objects, values, and attitudes on a continuum with multiple points of variance. This conceptualization tends to discourage dualistic thinking patterns, minimizes development of prejudicial attitudes, and decreases the frequency of discriminatory actions toward individuals and groups that differ from self.

Teacher Pedagogical Behaviors	**Student Cultural Displays**
Provides continual opportunities for students to develop and master the skills of being witnesses, recipients, and practitioners of honesty, fairness, impartiality, integrity, reasonableness, and justice.	Demonstrations of self-control and skills in balancing their own needs, wishes, and perceived entitlements with those of others, as participant, witness, or recipient of own behavior and that of others.
• Observes and responds to peer and adult interactions involving diversity issues. • Views students' questions and comments as natural openings to explore and expand the social and political knowledge required to evaluate self-actions and behaviors of others. • Encourages responsible and supportive interactions and dialogue with peers. • Takes an active role against hurtful situations in the classroom toward students and groups of students that differ from self.	• Shows behaviors promoting respectful attention to issues of fairness. • Is sensitive and alert to prejudicial and discriminatory events and develops interest and skills in defining difficult abstract concepts such as power, control, abilities, rights, and oppression. • Intervenes with positive support to peers who are excluded because of differences. • Does not use racial epithets, sexist or homophobic comments, or injurious language toward those that differ from self.
Creates a classroom environment that affirms, respects, and acknowledges differences in individuals and groups as a natural and integral part of everyone's humanity.	Expressions of developing awareness of, advocacy for, and knowledge of the complex and diverse sociopolitical issues concerning differences in individuals and groups.
• Challenges students' growth in critical thinking and addresses student comments that reveal conceptual misunderstandings of diversity issues.	• Acquires knowledge of the ways discriminatory biases and actions affect individuals, groups of people, communities, and nations differently.

Teacher Pedagogical Behaviors	Student Cultural Displays
• Encourages inclusive peer relationships and friendships with others that share or do not share the same diversity factors such as race, ethnicity, culture, language, gender, sexual orientation, and socioeconomic status.	• Accepts, initiates, and sustains peer acceptance and close friendships with those who share diversity factors and with those who differ in race, ethnicity, culture, language, gender, sexual orientation, ability, and socioeconomic status.
Assumes accountability for personal practices as a witness, aggressor, or victim that might potentially promote discrimination. • Reflects on what prejudicial issues rooted in race, class, language, gender, age, ability, sexual orientation, and cultural differences affects how one might perceive and respond toward others. • Discusses with staff members any racist, discriminatory, or prejudicial incidents directed at students or other adults. • Seeks professional inservice programs addressing diversity. • Recognizes the power of their words and the impact of their actions.	Signs of understanding their role and responsibility when responding to disturbing incidents as witnesses, aggressors, or victims. • Shows remorse, empathy, and sympathy toward others experiencing hurtful, prejudicial, or discriminatory actions based on differences such as race, class, ethnicity, sexual orientation, or ability. • Thinks critically about what makes a person responsible, heroic, trustworthy, kind, compassionate, and honorable. • Develops the capacity to exert a positive affect on other people's lives. • Recognizes the power of their words and the impact of their actions.

Teacher Pedagogical Behaviors

In a culturally diverse society such as the United States, teachers are trusted to recognize and value differences in self and students. To accomplish these goals, it is helpful for teachers to examine how elements of diversity present in themselves and in students affect behaviors in classrooms. Since the patterns of thinking that we internalize determine our actions, it is important to become aware of how we develop these habits of mind. Unconscious thoughts brought to a conscious level can help us identify what influences our thinking.

Receptiveness to diversity often begins with an evaluation of how we think. We tend to create categories based on differences such as race, ethnicity, language, gender, ability, age, national origin, sexual orientation, socioeconomic status, and so on. Students in your classrooms have memberships in multiple groups. They exhibit knowledge, strengths, and competencies learned through their life experiences. Belonging to and being part of diverse families, different genders, different sexual orientation groups, and multiple ability groups are some of the diversity aspects children own.

Family Diversity

Every child is a member of a family. Regardless of where or with whom children live, they belong to a group of people who share one or more of the following family ties:

kinship, affection, cultural knowledge, and resources. Although the term family diversity is often used to describe ethnic, racial, and cultural variations, other factors such as adoption, foster care, socioeconomic status, religion, and sexual orientation also account for differences among families. These factors in themselves do not determine the amount or the quality of nurturing children receive. All kinds of families can provide the love and support necessary for healthy development.

Family relationships and child-rearing practices exert a fundamental influence on identity development, cognitive strengths, and belief systems. Families create, or fail to create, children's earliest sense of belonging, uniqueness, and competence. Generally speaking, the parents' race, ethnicity, language, and other cultural attributes determine those of the child. However, diverse family structures, adoption, foster care, and extensive child-care services may introduce racial, ethnic, language, and cultural differences among family members. *America's Children 2001* (2001) shows that in 1999, 54 percent of the children (20 million) from birth through third grade received some form of child care on a regular basis from persons other than their parents.

The role children play in their immediate and extended families can differ from the assumptions and expectations made in the dominant society. Vignette 3.1 depicts an incident in an extended, immigrant family. This family places what may appear to be excessive responsibility on the eldest child.

Vignette 3.1
My Brother Luis
This event took place in an urban setting with a majority of Mexican American students. One day Pedro, a Mexican American kindergarten student, brought a $100 bill to school to buy something at the weekly student store. Although Pedro had permission to take a dollar from the family money jar, he accidentally took a $100 bill. He gave the parent at the student store a $100 bill to purchase 5 pencils. Pedro returned to the classroom with 5 pencils and the principal ended up with the $100 bill. When Luis, Pedro's brother who was in third grade, went for the money, the principal informed Luis that only a parent could pick up the money.

As the story unraveled, Pedro mentioned that his parents were still in Mexico because of *la migra* (border patrol). He told the teacher that his parents went to Mexico to attend his grandfather's funeral. They had already been gone for almost a month. When his Mexican American teacher, asked him, "Who's taking care of you?" Pedro smiled, and quickly responded, "My brother Luis." Their uncle left several bills in the money jar, including the $100 bill for an aunt or a teenage cousin who would come by later to check on the boys, buy groceries, and make dinner.

The teacher visited Pedro's home the evening of the $100 bill episode and spoke with the aunt and uncle. She found out that the family decided to let the principal keep the money until the parents returned. They did not want to risk getting *"the welfare people"* involved. They explained the children's home situation. An aunt and teenage cousin lived in the same apartment complex. They came every afternoon to cook, help with homework, and get clothes ready for school.

Their aunt checked on them every evening right before bedtime, and they stopped by her apartment early in the morning before leaving for school. Luis was responsible for making sure they arrived at school on time and returned home safely after school. The aunt and uncle did not want the school informed of this arrangement.

The teacher supported their decision, indicating that she would take care of any school issues that may arise. She applauded Luis for his leadership and responsibility to his little brother. In the classroom, Pedro appeared happy and functioned well, emotionally and academically. As usual, Luis stopped by the classroom to pick up Pedro. Several times a week, the boys stayed after school and helped the teacher. Sometimes she drove them home and visited with the aunt or teenage cousin for a few minutes.

Approximately two months later, after leaving for a five-day trip, the parents returned. They called the teacher on the evening of their arrival and thanked her profusely. When Pedro's mother came to school to pick up the $100 bill, she stopped by with a gift for the teacher—a half-dozen tamales, which she knew the teacher loved (Sheets, 1998b).

Issues for Consideration

This vignette demonstrates the fear and distrust some immigrant families have with schools and with social services. In this case, the teacher demonstrated a high level of trust in the actions of the extended family and took professional risks to honor their request. Why do you think the teacher did not inform the principal of the details surrounding the $100 bill? Do you think the teacher's and family's decisions were appropriate? Why or why not? What might have happened if the teacher or the school had reported this incident to Children Protective Services? What cultural factors are evident in this event?

Socioeconomic Status

Although the United States is considered a prosperous world power, the child poverty rate in the United States is substantially higher, often two to three times higher than that of most other major Western industrialized nations. Research shows that over 12 million children live in poverty in the United States and 35 percent (4.2 million) of the poor children are under the age of 6 (National Center for Children in Poverty, 1999). One in six children live in a family that is below the national poverty level ($13,290 for a family of three). Thirty-nine percent of America's children live in near poverty ($26,580 for a family of three). Many of the concerns of the near poor families are similar to those identified as poor. Seven percent of America's children live in extreme poverty. These children live in families with incomes below 50 percent of the poverty line. In 1999, the extreme poverty line was $6,145 for a family of three. Research conducted by National Center for Children in Poverty (1999) shows that extreme poverty during children's first five years of life has especially harmful effects on their future life chances compared to less extreme poverty experienced later in childhood. The young child poverty rate is highest for African American children (37%) and Latino American children (31%) (Child Poverty Fact Sheet, 2001). Ten percent of European American children live in poverty. This data suggest an association between poverty and race.

Children from economically distressed families often endure conditions such as inadequate shelter, inferior food, unsafe neighborhoods, and substandard schools that affect their emotional and social well-being. Additionally, some children are vulnerable to environmental contaminants in their air, food, and drinking water. In 1998, 23 percent of children lived in areas that did not meet one of the Primary National Ambient Air Quality Standards, and 2 percent (approximately one million) lived in areas with high levels of lead (America's Children: Key National Indicators of Well-Being, 2003).

Often it is not the lack of income, but the presence of stress in the home environment that accounts for the negative adjustment of children (Graham-Bermann, Coupeet, Egler, Mattis, & Banyard, 1996). Women from low-income groups are about twice as likely as those from higher-income groups to suffer from depression, an illness characterized by profound feelings of sadness, low energy, and loss of interest in daily activities (Lennon, Blome, & English, 2001). In mothers, depression compromises their ability to respond to their children. This lack of response potentially places their children at considerable risk because disruptions and traumas in children's lives are often associated with increased social and behavioral problems. For some of these children, teachers and classmates can be a primary source of continuity and emotional support.

Myths and stereotypes about the ideal family can influence teacher expectations and attitudes regarding the ability of students to learn and behave. Some homes may be judged materially unsatisfactory, culturally inferior, or morally unacceptable simply on the basis of socioeconomic status, ethnicity, race, or family structure. By acknowledging and respecting a wide spectrum of families, teachers can discourage prejudgment. They can take an active role in reinforcing the vital link between home and school.

Sexual Orientation

Sexual orientation can be defined as the direction of one's sexual interest toward members of the same, opposite, or both sexes. A dimension of children's identity is expressed through their personal sexual orientation. They also live in families with parents or caregivers with particular sexual orientations. Anyone who provides services to children, especially teachers in classrooms, must value and respect the presence of diverse sexual orientations. Students who display **heterosexual** (have sexual desires or sexual relations between members of the opposite sex) behaviors and students with identifiable heterosexual parents are generally not treated unfairly in school settings because of their sexual orientation.

This section discusses some of the issues students who identify as gay, lesbian, bisexual, or transgender (GLBT), those who are perceived to be GLBT, and those who have GLBT parents, face on a daily basis. A major obstacle to meeting the needs of these students in public schools is the presence of **homophobic** (showing an irrational hatred, disapproval, or fear of gay and lesbian people and their culture) societal attitudes and overtly hostile behaviors, that some teachers and students feel entitled to display, dismiss, or ignore. Vignette 3.2 describes a 16-year-old gay teenager's high school experience.

Vignette 3.2
Tone it Down

"What comes to mind when you hear the words 'high school'? Do you think of a safe and friendly environment where students go to learn? Well, that isn't the way it is for thousands of teenagers across the country. Just try to imagine going to school every day and worrying about your safety so much that you cannot concentrate. Imagine being screamed at, kicked, punched, threatened, and spit upon. How would you feel? You would probably feel the same way that thousands of gay students feel every day—worthless. Now can you understand why so many gay teenagers say that high school was one of the worst experiences of their lives?

"I left high school after six months because of harassment like this and the school's lack of understanding and support. Week after week, I went to the administration, informing them of the names I was called and the many other things my fellow students would do to me and others. I heard that they were doing the best they could—nothing. They blamed me. They told me that I brought it upon myself by the way that I looked, acted, and dressed. I was told that, if I would 'tone it down,' I would be left alone. The irony was that I did not dress, look, or act out of the ordinary. Then, one day I was attacked in the hallway. I was not hurt, but I was badly shaken. The boy who attacked me was suspended for three days! Because the school didn't protect me, I was forced to leave. I was forced to give up a part of my youth, to give up my personal rights to freedom, justice, and the pursuit of happiness as well as to an education. . . .

"School counselors, administrators, and staff can help to end this harassment. I urge you to take a stand against discrimination in your schools, communities, and families. You will be helping more than you can imagine" (Jahr, 2002).

Issues for Consideration

The school experiences of many gay and lesbian youth causes them to feel isolated, face violence, drop out of school, use drugs, experience depression, and attempt suicide (Savin-Williams & Cohen, 1996). Most GLBT students experience harassment in school, many teachers ignore these blatant abuses, and few perpetrators are held accountable for their discriminatory behavior. Do you maintain that some students should expect to experience routine verbal and physical violence in school? Do the students under attack lose their right to learn in a safe environment? What is your role as a teacher? Do you plan to do any of the following and will you encourage others to join you in (a) examining personal assumptions, (b) discussing GLBT student concerns at faculty meetings, (c) confronting homophobic remarks and discriminatory behaviors, (d) integrating gay and lesbian themes into the curriculum, or (e) starting a support group? Will you reason that you teach in a conservative community or there are no gay and lesbian students in your school or there is not an existing school policy addressing this issue? Are you comfortable dealing openly with this topic?

Research suggests that children may be aware of their sexual orientation during childhood and most self-identify as gay or lesbian around age 16 (Ryan & Futterman,

1997). A survey of high school students found that 5.5 percent of the student population self-identified as gay, lesbian, or bisexual or reported some same-gender sexual contact (Massachusetts Department of Education, 1999).

GLBT adolescents from ethnic groups of color often face dual discrimination, (race and sexual orientation) and may not benefit from available resources and support groups (Jackson, 2002). They are at a higher risk for verbal and physical abuse from family, friends, and strangers. Their ethnic and racial communities often reject these young people. Additionally, many of the available support services and programs are based on the needs of middle and upper class European American GLBT youth.

The following are some suggestions made by practitioners in the field who provide training sessions, lead workshops, and focus on creating inclusive programs for GLBT students (Augustine, Jackson, & Norman, 2002):

1. Assess your own values and beliefs regarding sexual orientation and gender identity. Address personal biases; recognize personal limits; identify areas for personal growth; and serve GLBT youth in an open, honest, and respectful manner.
2. Discuss sexual behaviors explicitly rather than assuming that everyone defines sexual intercourse the same way. Avoid terms that make unwarranted assumptions or are disrespectful in nature.
3. Use inclusive language such as *partner* and *civil union*.
4. Make it clear that homophobic sentiments and actions have no place in classrooms. Develop school policies regarding discriminatory words and behaviors directed at GLBT youth.
5. Proactively address stereotypes and misperceptions that may exist.
6. Consider working with students to form a gay/straight alliance group in your school.

Gender

There are four perspectives guiding the discussion on gender differences in this section. First, although the abundant feminist literature has made a significant contribution to understanding the needs of female students, keep in mind that in the classroom teachers must also address the needs of male students. Second, gender is not independent from other dimensions of children's identity, such as race, ethnicity, social class, sexual orientation, and socioeconomic status. These diversity elements influence the **social content of gender** (culturally appropriate ways of behaving), affect the development of **gender identity** (the personal sense of being male or female), and shape **gender roles** (the public expressions of gender identity displayed through choices, actions, and sex roles). Third, the group of students most adversely affected by K-12 schooling practices and policies are males, especially African American and Latino American students. African American and Latino American males have the highest dropout rate, the most disciplinary actions, the lowest grades, and are the least likely to attend college (Natrillo, McDill, & Pallas, 1986; Sheets, 1996). Fourth, although **gender bias** (showing unfairness or discrimination based on gender) is present in teacher actions, instructional resources, and school policies and must be addressed, supporting and valuing girls does not have to be at the expense of devaluing boys. Gender equity in classrooms includes responding to the cultural, social, and academic needs of both boys and girls.

Gender Bias in Schooling. Although research on gender bias in schooling has been studied for over twenty years, it received significant attention in the 1990s (Orenstein, 1994; Sadker & Sadker, 1994). This work found that schools were biased against girls, with Latina American girls affected most adversely (Latina American girls have the highest school dropout rate of female students). Boys were more likely to talk in class than girls, and boys received more teacher attention. Textbooks contained stereotypical images of girls and discounted their accomplishments. They argued that this form of discrimination affected girls' self-esteem and influenced their achievement in mathematics and science. However, other experts point out that on the average girls earn higher grades, experience less disciplinary actions, complete high school, and are more likely to go to college (Woodard, 2003).

A considerable amount of the research on gender in classroom settings focuses on the needs of European American female children, especially in enhancing educational opportunities in mathematics, science, sports, and leadership. Often left out of the gender discourse are females of color and classroom practices that influence low academic achievement, excessive disciplinary actions, and high dropout rates of male children, especially African American and Latino American (Natrillo et al., 1986; Sheets, 1996). In response to what may be perceived as male bashing present in some feminist literature, and the increasing violence displayed by some male children such as school shootings, bullying, and crimes, research is emerging regarding the messages society and schooling sends to boys, which may encourage aggression and violence rather than sensitivity and gentleness (Pollack, 1999). Although it is critical to be sensitive and affirming to girls, this goal does not have to be achieved at the expense of devaluing boys or of crossing gender cultural boundaries. Vignettes 3.3 and 3.4 (p. 36) point out cultural clashes between mainstream gender roles and Mexican American gender cultural roles.

Vignette 3.3
Hombres Don't Color Fingernails
This event took place in a kindergarten classroom in an urban setting with a majority of Mexican American children. During an afternoon play time period, Mirella and her friends set up a beauty shop. Everyone waited in line to have their fingernails painted with water soluble magic markers. When Gustavo's mother picked him up, she warned him, *"Que dirá tu Papá?"* (What will your father say?) The teacher, respecting cultural values, explained that she was not aware that Gustavo's fingernails were painted, would make sure that it did not happen again, and was sure the color would wash out. The next day, during circle time, Gustavo announced, *"Los hombres* don't paint their fingernails." He also warned Mirella not to color any of the boys' nails. Mirella nodded, then added, "Boys can still come to my shop. I'm just cutting hair today." She looked up at the teacher and smiled, "Just pretend cutting" (Sheets, 1998b).

Issues for Consideration

How do the cultural values embedded in the gender roles in this vignette show that a classroom event seemingly insignificant and harmless to the teacher may be considered inappropriate to the child's parents? How would you have handled this situation? What do you think of the teacher's response?

Vignette 3.4
No Way, Jose!

This event took place in a Spanish/English bilingual first-grade classroom. Hearing that their sons would be making tortillas in class, three Mexican American mothers arrived at school early in the morning to explain to the teacher that their sons are not allowed to make tortillas. Ms. Hardin, a bilingual European American teacher, explained politely, "In my classroom everyone participates in group activities. That's the way we build community." Seemingly aware that the mothers were uncomfortable, she added that making tortillas is a culturally relevant learning activity designed to encourage gender equity. The mothers tried to explain that they do not object to how she teaches, but they do not want their boys to make tortillas. They explain that the children's fathers were unable to take time off from work, but that they were concerned that this may confuse their sons' idea on what it means to be male—*un hombre* (Sheets, 1998b).

Issues for Consideration

This vignette demonstrates how gender cultural clashes and differences in the gender socialization process of the Mexican American boys and Ms. Hardin played out in this classroom. Do you think children should display their teacher's idea of appropriate gender roles? Does a reflective analysis of the tortilla incident differ from your initial reaction? Are there gender role stereotypes operating in this teacher's decision?

Ability Differences

Although differences and variations in multiple abilities is a dimension of all students, this section deals specifically with students identified as having special needs. Almost 50 million citizens, nearly one in five, claimed a disability in a 1991–1992 U.S. Census Bureau survey (U.S. Bureau of the Census, 1992). Yet, most people find the subject of special needs easier to avoid than to address. Adult apprehensiveness about the topic thwarts children's natural curiosity and reinforces the confusion and fear they may feel when encountering differences they do not understand. Throughout schooling, students with ability differences often endure painful stereotyping and exclusion resulting from the ignorance and insensitivity of others. The practice of mainstreaming students with diverse abilities is based on the belief that students of all ages have the capacity to interact cooperatively with others of varying abilities. Ideally, mainstreaming does not attempt to minimize or to erase differences; rather, it provides the opportunity to teach students how to respond positively to the full range of differences, including those of ability (Sapon-Shevin, 1983).

Derman-Sparks (1995) describes how children develop awareness about the ability differences of others. By age 2, children begin to express curiosity and concern about unusual attributes such as "funny talking" or the absence of a leg, as well as special equipment and other markers of ability differences, such as crutches, wheelchairs, or eye patches. At ages 3 and 4, they want to know what these people can and cannot do. Preschoolers lack a firm grasp of concepts like permanence and change. They may wonder why a woman with a missing hand doesn't just "grow a new one." It is helpful to explain that ability differences cannot be made to simply "go away," nor is there any need to worry about catching someone's difference in ability.

Teachers can point out that we all have limitations and that we find various ways of overcoming them. Short people use a step stool to reach something on a high shelf. To examine a bug up close, we use a magnifying glass. From these examples, it's easy to proceed to more specialized tools like glasses, Braille, and guide dogs for the sight impaired; sign language and hearing aids for the hearing impaired; and canes, walkers, prostheses, and wheelchairs for those who need help getting around. Learning about these devices as tools makes them seem familiar and normal.

Three strategies can be helpful in fostering empathy and increasing knowledge about ability differences (Edwards, 1986). First, children should be given concrete information about the specific ability difference of their classmate. This will reduce fear as well as the perception of differences as strange. Second, the skills, strengths, and talents of children with special needs should be pointed out so that other children will see them as peers, not objects of pity. The teacher can explain, "Melinda talks to us with sign language. Would you like to learn how to sign?" Third, the feelings of all children, including those with ability differences, should be acknowledged by teachers to make children aware that everyone has similar needs for affection, comfort, and fun. If Liam cannot speak, the teacher can highlight his expressive behavior: "Look at Liam smile. He likes playing with you." or "Do you notice how Liam hugs his bear when he misses his mom?"

The issue of fairness can emerge in classrooms when children with special needs require individual consideration. They may need extra assistance from the teacher or help from their peers, as well as additional time to complete tasks. A child who is functioning at a lower level of cognitive development may need help matching colors, and a child in a wheelchair might have to be first in line more often. In subtle ways, teachers can emphasize that every child, regardless of ability level, has special needs. Careful attention to individual differences helps remove the spotlight from the exceptional child.

Although teachers can employ special techniques to teach students with different abilities, the basic skills such as dressing, sipping from a straw, or reading, only children working together as friends can learn from each other the crucial skills needed to develop socially and academically. If social relationships across ability differences do not develop naturally, teachers can intervene. Students with physical or intellectual challenges might need teacher assistance to enter classroom groups. Likewise, other students might need help learning how to be sensitive to the difficulties and competencies of students with different abilities. Through a variety of social interactions, students come to realize that everyone can participate in their classroom. A classroom in which diverse abilities are represented offers endless possibilities for practicing and modeling empathy and kindness. Students in such settings learn that a truly inclusive community is based not on special accommodation but on mutual adaptation. Vignette 3.5 shows that accommodating the needs of children with different abilities are often screened through the schooling entitlements of other students.

Vignette 3.5
Just Three Hours a Week

Cameron suffered brain damage before he was born and operates at the intellectual level of an infant. He sits in a wheelchair, is legally blind, cannot speak, and occasionally suffers life-threatening seizures. A special education teacher visits him at home, but his parents want him to spend time in a regular classroom. Cameron spends three hours a week in a second-grade classroom at Laurel Elementary. The children in the classroom have embraced him. They invite him to their birthday parties and fight over who can push his wheelchair. His mother says that from this experience he has grown more engaged, makes more eye contact, and listens better.

However, Cameron has been transferred back to his home district due to enrollment growth. Hengel, the superintendent of the school district transferring Cameron, indicated that schools are under pressure to raise test scores, and he is concerned that Cameron will be a greater disruption in a third-grade classroom. "We are not opposed to having Cameron in a regular education classroom but he does make extemporaneous noises due to his condition," said Hengel (Bell, 2000). Although he can attend another school for severely disabled students and will have the option to spend some time with "regular" students in a classroom in his new school, his mother wants him to remain at Laurel so he can move to third grade with the children with whom he has already bonded. Friends and family of 8-year-old Cameron lobby for him to stay at Laurel Elementary with his classmates next year.

Issues for Consideration

Consider whose rights were more important for the superintendent when he made the decision to deny Cameron entry to a third-grade classroom in his district. What role, if any, do you think the third-grade teachers had in this decision? How can Cameron and his parents be supported? What would you do if you were a teacher at Laurel Elementary?

Student Cultural Displays

Thinking, talking, and responding to differences in people, events, concepts, perspectives, and values may make us uncomfortable, in part, because we are culturally, socially, and cognitively conditioned to consider diversity as strange or abnormal. Even young children, due to their socialization in a society that perpetuates racist practices and attitudes, develop racist attitudes and knowingly display racist behaviors (Brown, 1995; Van Ausdale & Feagin, 2001). Socialization in a society that is discriminatory to those who are different from self often promotes negative responses to individuals and groups who possess different or unfamiliar traits. This section includes a description of how prejudicial thinking about race, ethnicity, and gender identity develops. It also examines the influences of culture on these development processes.

Development of Prejudicial Thinking

Prejudice is a preformed opinion or an irrational strong feeling, usually unfavorable, about someone or something. Prejudicial attitudes are formed unfairly and before all the facts are known. **Discrimination** is to act on the basis of prejudice, to show unfairness or to reveal hostility toward an individual or group. **Racism** involves prejudicial attitudes and discriminatory actions against people who belong to another race. Racist orientations also sustain the belief that some races, due to different qualities and abilities, are inherently superior or inferior.

Since psychological research shows that children as young as 3 and 4 years of age display signs of prejudice and discriminatory behavior, scholars examine its development (Brown, 1995; Van Ausdale & Feagin, 2001). Some believe that, developmentally, young children are cognitively incapable of racist attitudes and discriminatory actions (see Aboud, 1988; Holmes, 1995). They think that young children who display prejudicial attitudes, use racist terms, and act in discriminatory ways do not know what their feelings, language, and behavior imply. These scholars argue that children are merely echoing the racist attitudes of adults. Other research contradicts this cognitive developmental trend, pointing out that young children actively reproduce and perpetuate societal racist attitudes and actions in their everyday lives (Van Ausdale & Feagin, 2001). Although some research shows that prejudice in children generally peaks around age 7 and 8, and decreases during adolescence (Aboud, 1988), others find that intergroup bias continues during middle childhood and adolescence (Verkuyten, 2001).

Van Ausdale and Feagin (2001) found that children as young as 3 and 4 years old purposefully and consistently display prejudicial attitudes and knowingly act in discriminatory ways through their use of racist epithets, emotion, and behavior. Young children are capable of negative racial comments in context, and they recognize their full significance. Children are not passive vessels of adult socialization. However, adults have a tendency to dismiss or ignore the seriousness of these racist attitudes and behaviors in young children until they are older.

According to Van Ausdale and Feagin (2001) children take an active part in their own socialization as they interact socially with other children and adults. This process is in their own minds. It is ongoing in their social lives. Vignettes 3.6 and 3.7 (pp. 40–41) exemplify how young children experiment with and learn how to process racial material. These events show that children do not merely imitate what they might hear or see in different settings.

Vignette 3.6
Doll

This event took place in a racially diverse day care center with an antibias curricular focus. The researcher (Debi) spent a year observing children, ages 3 to 6, in a natural setting. In this incident, four girls, Lacey (age 5, White), Sarah (age

4, White), Claire (age 3.5, Black), and Brianna (age 3, White), are playing with dolls. Brianna has a white doll with black hair. Claire has black doll with black hair. There are no adults present, except Debi, who is completely ignored by the girls.

> Brianna says, "You know what?" to Claire, who ignores her. "You know what?" Brianna repeats her question three more times to Claire, who finally looks up and appears annoyed. "My baby doesn't like you," Brianna announces. Claire gazes at her for a moment, then, without a word, returns to ignoring her. Undeterred, Brianna repeats her statement two more times. Claire finally responds, saying, "Well, your baby's white. That's why." Brianna glares at Claire. They play in silence for a while longer. Then Claire leaves. Brianna turns her doll upside down inside a large bottle, announcing to nobody in particular, "She's having her hair washed." She jams the doll down into the bottle hard, scrubbing it up and down and frowning at it. She then turns and frowns deeply at Debi, who says nothing. . . . Lacey and Sarah watch Brianna, then glance at Debi, apparently anticipating that Debi will tell Brianna to "play nice," but Debi maintains her silence. Brianna finally abandons the doll on the ground and seeks other company. Her attempts to engage in interaction with other people have been unsuccessful. Shortly after her departure Claire quietly returns and resumes play (Van Ausdale & Feagin, 2001, p. 106).

Issues for Consideration

Van Ausdale and Feagin (2001) felt that Claire's matter-of-fact statement indicating that because Brianna's doll was white, such dislike might be expected, angered Brianna whose actions demonstrated an expectation that a Black child would be upset by her statement. "Claire, who seems to be a veteran of this type of interaction, merely left the scene, only returning when Brianna departed. The Black child's departure seemed to anger Brianna, who then took out her anger on the hapless doll. That the other two girls waited for adult intervention suggests they, too, were experiencing some tension" (Van Ausdale & Feagin, 2001, p. 106). How did Claire's probable, previous negative experiences with Whites targeting Blacks negatively influence her behavior? What are the negative consequences of prejudice on children's social, emotional, and cognitive well-being? What did the perpetrator, victim, and witnesses learn?

Vignette 3.7
The Wagon

"Debi watches Renee (age 4, White) pull Lingmai (age 3, Asian) and Jocelyn (age 4.5, White) across the playground in a wagon. Renee tugs away enthusiastically, but the task is difficult. Pulling this heavy load across loose dirt is more than Renee can handle. Suddenly, she drops the handle, which falls on the ground, and stands still, breathing heavily. Lingmai, eager to continue this game, jumps from the wagon and picks up the handle. As Lingmai begins to pull, Renee admonishes her, "No, No. You can't pull this wagon. Only white Americans can pull this wagon." Renee has her hands on her hips and frowns at Lingmai. The Asian girl tries again to lift the handle of the wagon, and Renee again insists that only "white Americans" are permitted to do this task. This is the breaking point, and adult intervention is now sought.

Lingmai sobs loudly and runs to a nearby teacher, complaining that "Renee hurt my feelings." Once again, we see the child's discretion at work. She offers no more than hurt feelings to explain her actions to the teacher. Since intervention is in order, the teacher approaches Renee. "Did you hurt Lingmai's feelings?" the teacher asks Renee who glumly nods assent. This is a familiar ritual. "I think you should apologize," the teacher continues, "because we are all friends here, and friends don't hurt each others' feelings." "Sorry," mutters Renee not looking at Lingmai, "I didn't do it on purpose." Lingmai stands silently. The teacher waits for a few moments, then finishes with, "OK, can you guys be good friends now?" Both girls nod without looking at each other and quickly move away. The teacher stands and waits for a moment or two, to assure herself that the conflict does not erupt again, then moves off (Van Ausdale & Feagin, 2001, p. 104).

Issues for Consideration

In this case the White child's actions go beyond "only I can pull the wagon" to more complex racialized thinking. She is applying ideas from the adult world to her own situation. According to Van Ausdale and Feagin (2001), this incident is an example "of an active and very personal ideological construction that adapts to the societal racist ideology. Renee is inventively making use of what she has learned, but she is not acting apart from her history and social milieu. She has embedded the performance of being white as part of her understanding of self. . . . This account shows the ways in which societal hierarchy of racial power is replicated and reproduced over time. Doubtless, the deeper meaning of this action by the white four-year-old was not lost on the Asian child or the other white child in the wagon. Like adults, children teach each other about racial meanings in both overt and subtle ways" (p. 38).

How does adult denial of what children really know and understand and of how they apply the racist societal system around them perpetuate and sustain racist attitudes and actions? How do actions that exclude others reflect children's understandings of individual or group rights? Since negative racial comments and behaviors are hurtful for young peers to endure and disturbing to hear, how can teachers recognize and address the harmful effects of this behavior to the perpetrator, to the recipient, and to all who witness the event? Why is it critical to understand the implications of racial supremacy manifested in children's remarks?

The disturbing results of research documenting how young children develop prejudicial attitudes and discriminatory behaviors, and evidence that this acquired personal social knowledge is internalized and sustained through middle childhood and adolescence, indicates that teachers must develop strategies to minimize prejudice. Teachers can begin by examining their own personal issues. They can take steps to reduce personal prejudicial, discriminatory, and racist attitudes and behaviors toward individuals and groups that are different from self. They can become more aware of classroom incidents reflecting prejudice, discrimination, and racist actions in daily student-student interactions. These observable events should be taken very seriously because they provide valuable opportunities within a social context.

Gender Development and Cultural Gender Information

Knowledge of how young children develop gender identity, stability, and constancy and understanding how they acquire cultural gender information can help teachers foster gender equity in classrooms. This section also provides information about ethnic gender boundaries.

Gender Development.   According to scholars, gender appears to be one of the first dimensions of identity that young children can label in self and others (Katz, 1987; Signorella, 1987). Even before they can say the words, most toddlers, birth to age 3, become adept at pointing out girls and boys, women and men. They can identify boys and girls from pictures around age 2. **Gender identity,** self-identification as boys or girls, typically occurs by age 3. Children draw their earliest conclusions about gender from obvious traits such as clothing, hairstyle, body shape, and the pitch of the voice.

A little later, around age 4 to age 5, they begin to learn about the body parts (biological differences) that make boys and girls different. This fascinating subject leads to serious, and sometimes startling, questions as cognitive and verbal skills develop. Between the ages of 4 and 5, children come to realize the biological conditions that make one male or female. They acquire **gender stability,** which means that they comprehend that their gender is permanent. They realize that little girls grow up to become big girls. They often segregate themselves by gender in playgroups.

Around age 6 and up, they achieve gender constancy, the final step. **Gender constancy** is the recognition that one's gender is not only permanent but is also constant and remains throughout one's lifetime, regardless of outward appearance. Children understand that changing one's clothing, interests, appearance, or activities does not change one's gender. Around this time, children start to expand their ideas about gender to include not just what people are but what they do and how they should act.

Cultural Gender Information.   The development of gender identity, stability, and constancy shows that children during middle childhood and adolescence have a clear sense of their gender identity by the time they reach puberty. However, along with identity, children become aware of the **social content of gender,** culturally appropriate ways of behaving. According to Katz (1987), children acquire the social content of gender awareness in three sequential stages.

1. First, young children learn the culturally appropriate behavior for boys and girls such as the toys, activities, and playmate choices expected of each gender. In this stage, they establish firm boundaries around gender roles, often self-segregating by gender in their playgroups. It does not take them long to assert these patterns verbally: "Girls can't throw" or "Boys don't play with dolls."

2. Next, children learn the expectations associated with adult male and female roles. As they attempt to interpret the adult world, many children make broad assumptions and generalizations, such as "Men can't cook" and "Mommies don't drive tractors."
3. In the third stage, children act out adult gender roles based on these concepts. During pretend play, girls become mothers, nurses, and teachers, and boys are the fathers, workers, and police.

Gender roles develop through a socialization process in the family and community. These roles are screened through specific cultural norms that frame children's ethnic identity. Therefore, gender differs in content and practice, depending on children's ethnic individual and group membership. Other family characteristics such as race, culture, socioeconomic level, class, and religion can also significantly shape children's gender learning. Parents influence emerging gender concepts directly and indirectly through the toys they purchase, by the roles they model in the home, and in the ways they respond to gender situations in children's behavior.

Behaviors that appear to be sexist or stereotypical to the mainstream society may be acceptable gender roles in different ethnic groups. Thus, gender roles can be situational and contextual. Katz (1987) reports that young Latina Americans, as a group, showed a higher degree of gender stereotyping in their occupational aspirations than did European American and African American girls; and girls from single-parent families, regardless of race or ethnicity, showed the least amount of gender stereotyping. However, Katz (1987) used ethnocentric, mainstream, cultural norms to determine what constitutes gender stereotyping. Young children are socialized to follow diverse gender cultural boundaries.

Kohlberg (1966) theorized that gender stereotyping among children ages 5 to 7 often entails a preference for the male role because it is more exciting and powerful. Ethnocentric cultural affirmation of this preference is evident in the differences in status the mainstream culture accords to labels such as tomboy and sissy or Daddy's girl and Mama's boy. In the mainstream culture, being called a Sissy or Mama's boy is often perceived as a negative characteristic. In other cultures such as the Mexican American culture, closeness between male children and mothers is often encouraged and validated.

In addition, gender stereotyping can distort children's perception of nonstereotypical job roles. When 5- to 7-year-olds were shown pictures of adults in nontraditional roles, such as a female physician and a male nurse, most reported that they had seen the reverse. The same study showed that children who displayed less stereotyped notions of gender roles were more flexible and able to accept nontraditional roles for themselves and others (Signorella, 1987). Such evidence suggests that gender stereotyping in children's own thinking may have an adverse effect on the social and cognitive development of both girls and boys. Teachers who model inclusive gender equity for both boys and girls in the classroom and intervene appropriately to counteract gender bias recognize these actions as essential steps in respecting the self-worth, abilities, and potential of all students.

As children move into adolescence, gender role expectations increase due to increased socialization pressures to conform to socially prescribed gender roles. According to Kimmel and Rudolph (1999), there are distinct differences between the experiences of boys and girls during this period (ages 12 to 13). Some of the issues, differences, and gender bias identified by scholarship in the field are summarized below (Debold, 1995; Swanson, Spencer, & Petersen, 1998; Troiden, 1988; Wellesley Center for Research on Women, 1992):

1. Sexuality and intimacy are experienced differently by boys and girls and is often dependent on their sexual orientation or perceived sexual orientation. Most adolescents, including many gay and lesbian youth, become aware of and experience sexuality and intimacy during adolescence. Early maturing girls exhibit low self-esteem and report engaging in more sexual activity.
2. Some heterosexual youth experience sexual issues such as sexual harassment or unintended pregnancies. Four out of five students during grades 8 to 12 claimed some form of sexual harassment, with girls reporting twice as much as boys. Girls often avoid the harasser even when it means giving up activities, friends, or school itself.
3. Only gay and lesbian students, and those who are perceived to be gay and lesbian, face irrational hostility, hatred, and isolation in their homes, classrooms, schools, and community due to their sexual orientation.
4. Girls are generally more sensitive and nurturing. Intimacy with peers and family is important to girls. They seek approval from others in areas such as physical attractiveness, dress, appropriate activities, and popularity with boys.
5. Girls are more likely to report anxiety and depression, attempt suicide, and suffer from eating disorders. Boys, on the other hand, tend to be more assertive, independent, and aggressive. This assertive nature is displayed in discussions where boys tend to speak more and to interrupt more often than girls. However, boys are five times more likely to succeed in killing themselves and more inclined to participate in antisocial behavior such as alcoholism, drug use, and violent crimes.

Classroom Applications

Diversity in all forms play a valuable role in shaping the social and academic environment of classrooms. Teachers who work in classrooms with only European American children are often concerned that their students might develop beliefs, attitudes, and values reflecting a narrow range of differences. Similarly, teachers in classrooms with a majority of children of color are aware of the pervasive, negative messages in schools and society that may affect their students' social and cognitive development. Teachers can use daily learning-teaching interactions in ways that incorporate the multiple dimensions of diversity present in all classrooms to better prepare students for a culturally pluralistic society.

To evaluate the following suggested activities, reflect on changes in your own and your students' perceptions of difference. Does your classroom provide students with experiences to make decisions, ask questions, engage in self-reflection, and work collaboratively toward making their classroom as fair, safe, and democratic as possible?

Recognition and validation for the diversity at hand along with respect and exploration of differences in the greater society can be used to cultivate a commitment to equity and justice in their world.

Examining Student Responses to Differences

Examine how you and your students treat others who differ from self or who are perceived as dissimilar or threatening or who make you uncomfortable.

1. Evaluate and discuss the actions you and your students take when you see discriminatory behaviors against particular students or groups of students in the classroom or hear prejudicial statements made about people who are different or who are members of different groups. Design activities to make new students feel welcome. In the classroom, address when particular classmates are excluded from classroom activities such as cruelty toward or exclusion of immigrant students or students with physical or intellectual ability differences. Openly discuss issues affecting gay and lesbian students, those who are perceived to be gay and lesbian, and those with gay and lesbian parents, and provide the resources needed to take an important role in creating safe and accepting school environments. Examine exclusion of students from lower socioeconomic status.

2. Create a classroom climate that supports children with gay, lesbian, bisexual, or transgender parents and validates children who self-identify as gay, lesbian, bisexual, or transgender. Become aware of and use support organizations, such as COLAGE (Children of Lesbians and Gays Everywhere) and GLSEN (Gay, Lesbian and Straight Educational Network) for parents and students. Utilize books, videos, organizations, and web pages that provide tools to help you create safe, affirming learning environments and provide legal information to combat antigay sentiments and behaviors targeting gay and lesbian students. Serve as a resource for other teachers to help them understand the pervasiveness of antigay bias in schools.

3. Foster gender-role flexibility through activities that encourage students to engage in cross-gender collaborative activities, without infringing on cultural gender roles. Discourage disrespect based on gender. Model attitudes and actions that minimize gender stereotyping. Examine instructional resources for gender bias in message, language, and illustrations. Observe how you handle emotional or disciplinary issues and assignment of classroom duties with boys and girls.

4. Facilitate the entry of students with diverse abilities into your classroom. Create conditions that make all class members feel comfortable. Supply the necessary resources, learning materials, and physical setting to accommodate students with diverse abilities. Incorporate into the curriculum age-appropriate information about students with special needs. Use instructional content to acknowledge how the lifestyles of people with ability differences vary. Help students balance curiosity about ability differences with respect for privacy. Examine how ability differences surface on a continuum; for example, perfect vision on one end and

complete blindness at the other with the rest of us falling on varying points in between.

Respecting Diversity in Self and Others

Help students appreciate the diversity within their own racial, ethnic, gender, ability, and family groups.

1. Develop lessons and use instructional resources to help students realize that even when members of a group (including groups in which they have membership) appear to be the same, there are distinct differences between individuals of any groups. At any given age, girls and boys are not at the same level of intellectual, social, and sexual maturity. People with ability differences enjoy diverse leisure activities. All European American people do not have the same gender, socioeconomic, ability, geographical, and schooling experiences. African American and Latino American people's skin tone can have a wide range of shades of brown. Some children may have two mothers or two fathers, live in a single parent household, or live with grandparents.
2. Structure activities that encourage dualistic thinkers to practice complex, higher level thinking and to consider multiple solutions and perspectives. Teach students how to analyze, evaluate, compare, contrast, and justify ideas on diversity issues. Ask students to use supporting data to explain and defend their points of views.
3. Discuss differences and similarities in students' home traditions, routines, and rituals. Describe how birthday and religious celebrations, food, music, entertainment, sports, and art preferences, and relationships with relatives and significant others differ. Examine how the ways people express joy, sorrow, and loss vary and how they are influenced by cultural practices.
4. Provide multiple opportunities for students to group heterogeneously in organized classroom activities. Encourage peer relationships that differ by gender, popularity, religious orientation, ability, ethnicity, and economic status to provide the broadest cross section of social encounters.

Providing Experiences Valuing Diversity

Provide experiences to help students realize that differences in physical traits, cultural backgrounds, abilities, perceived needs, and preferences are valued in the classroom.

1. Involve children in age-appropriate decision making about classroom activities and rules so they can see themselves and their actions as critical components of their school life.
2. Reinforce the concept that differences contribute to the richness of the classroom community. Discuss how differing opinions help us think about the same idea in new ways. Understand how creative problem solving gives us more options to choose from. Examine how the ways different students find to present knowledge of the same assignment give us more perspectives to examine.

3. Watch for stereotypical images in classroom lessons, resources, and decorations. Acquire the skills needed to create, evaluate, and adapt curricular content and instruction in ways that accommodate and benefit culturally diverse students.

4. Adapt community resources such as local tourism posters and postcards, cultural products, and public library materials so that students make connections from school to home to community. Use Chinese newspapers as bulletin board background, hang Mexican and Chinese restaurant calendars, create displays of African American cultural leaders, and post gay and lesbian informational materials and symbols.

Conclusion

Since children actively appropriate information from their environment (Corsaro, 1979), it is unfortunate that our society often promotes damaging, harmful, and prejudicial attitudes and practices that affect the ways children process and internalize diversity issues. Dominant societal attitudes and behaviors toward individuals and groups who are different influence the ways students respond to diversity concerns.

As teachers, find new ways to advance students' thinking beyond seeing the world through closed mindedness and prejudicial attitudes. Consciously question and challenge your understanding and responsiveness to the multiple aspects of diversity in the classroom. Define reality in ways that promote inclusive, just, safe, and democratic communities. As teachers, facilitate a classroom life where students respect diversity and experience opportunities to grow socially and cognitively.

RECOMMENDED READINGS

Abell, P. K. (1999). Recognizing and valuing differences: Process considerations for preservice teachers. In E. R. Hollins & E. I. Oliver (Eds.), *Finding pathways to success: Teaching culturally diverse populations* (pp. 175–196). Mahwah, NJ: Erlbaum.

Savin-Williams, R. C., & Cohen, K. M. (Eds.). (1996). *The lives of lesbians, gays, and bisexuals: Children to adults.* Orlando, FL: Harcourt Brace.

Van Ausdale, D., & Feagin, J. R. (2001). *The first r: How children learn race and racism.* New York: Rowman & Littlefield.

4 Identity: Understanding Ethnic Identity Development

What bound me to Jewry was (I am ashamed to admit) neither faith nor national pride, for I have always been an unbeliever and was brought up without any religion though not without a respect for what are called the "ethical" standards of human civilization. . . . Plenty of other things remained over to make the attraction of Jewry and Jews irresistible—many obscure emotional forces, which were the more powerful the less they could be expressed in words.

—Sigmund Freud (1926) in Erikson, 1950, p. 20

Ethnicity is a powerful influence in determining individual and group identity. Children identify with their ethnic group or groups. This membership provides them with a sense of belonging. Ethnic group membership influences children's individual personalities, social skills, and cognitive preferences; however, accommodating students' ethnic needs is not something we totally understand or something we do automatically. Some teachers are unaware of how ethnicity influences students' development. Others may be hesitant to take action on the observed variations in the competencies children learn in their ethnic group or groups. Sometimes, teachers tend to ignore or inadvertently suppress these differences. The purpose of this chapter is to examine how ethnicity influences students' behavior in classrooms and to explore how theoretical ideas from research on ethnic identity can help guide teacher decisions.

Usually, we recognize the importance of responding to children's identified needs. Most caregivers make suitable changes when they perceive children are tired, irritated, stressed, or hungry. They understand the need to select age-appropriate toys and to promote activities that correspond with children's age level requirements, interests, and abilities. In classrooms, competent teachers vary the delivery and content of instruction according to age, grade level, and ability. Teachers must also understand how ethnic group membership influences children's social and cognitive development and know how to address these characteristics in the teaching-learning process. This chapter focuses on ethnic identity and its role in teaching and learning. It begins with a description of the second diversity pedagogy dimension, identity and its corresponding cultural display, ethnic identity development. The second section, teacher pedagogical behaviors, includes background information on identity, human development and racial identity. Next, a discussion on student cultural displays describes ethnic identity and considers its effects on schooling. Classroom applications follow.

Diversity Pedagogy Dimension 2: Identity/Ethnic Identity Development

The second diversity pedagogy dimension explains how teachers in classrooms can adapt instruction and create conditions to accommodate students' individual and group ethnic needs. It illustrates how students might display signs of ethnic identity and of affiliation to their respective ethnic group or groups. These definitions, explanations, and observations are based on the work of numerous theorists and researchers (see Aboud, 1984; Bernal & Knight, 1993; Gay, 1999; McAdoo, 1993; Spencer, 1983). Table 4.1 defines *identity* and *ethnic identity development*, recommends teacher pedagogi-

TABLE 4.1   Diversity Pedagogy Dimension 2: Identity/Ethnic Identity Development

Definition of Dimensional Elements	
Identity: Identity refers to knowledge of who we are and to what groups we belong. A complex developmental process defines self as an individual and as a group member. The explanations and information used to acquire a sense of self and group membership is determined by the biological, cultural, ethnic, social, psychological, and political factors in one's socialization process.	*Ethnic Identity Development:* Ethnic identity is a dimension of self, as an individual and as a group member. It forms, develops, and emerges from membership in a particular ethnic group. It is a consequence of a distinctive socialization process and is influenced by the degree of personal significance individuals attach to membership in an ethnic group.
Teacher Pedagogical Behaviors	**Student Cultural Displays**
Creates classroom conditions through curricular planning, instructional strategies, and interpersonal relationships where students can openly express aspects of their ethnic identity. <ul><li>Enables students to process ethnically diverse knowledge through materials, lessons, and discussion.</li><li>Recognizes how ethnically diverse cognitive and social preferences and skills affect the teaching-learning process.</li><li>Accommodates students' entitlement to select friends from same ethnic group and facilitates diverse cross-ethnic social interactions.</li><li>Encourages students to notice and appreciate their own and others' physical traits, cultural practices, and language differences.</li></ul>	Signs of developing a psychological, social, and cultural dimension of self, as an individual and group member of a particular ethnic group or groups. <ul><li>Discusses openly own and other groups' cultural heritage, accomplishments, and language abilities.</li><li>Accommodates to mainstream cultural norms while maintaining cultural values and interests to preserve ethnic identity integrity.</li><li>Interacts comfortably and intimately with members of same ethnic group and is at ease forming friendships with members of other ethnic groups.</li><li>Accepts and demonstrates appreciation of their own and others' personal physical traits, cultural practices, and language differences.</li></ul>

cal behaviors (approaches to creating classroom conditions for the development of
ethnic identity), and provides examples of student cultural displays (signs of ethnic
identity and affiliation to their respective ethnic group or groups).

Teacher Pedagogical Behaviors

In order to understand the pedagogical behaviors associated with the second dimension
of diversity pedagogy, identity, a clear understanding of identity, human development, and racial identity is useful. This section provides brief descriptions and background information on each. The resources cited can provide further explanation and
information.

Identity

Identity, knowledge of who we are and what groups we belong to, is a complex,
multifaceted developmental process that begins at birth and continues throughout the
life span. Identity development, although distinctly personal, does not happen in
isolation. According to Erikson (1950, p. 22) identity is "located in *the core of the
individual* and yet also *in the core of his communal culture.*" Erikson (1950, p. 21) maintains
that this deep sense of communality in its "most central ethnic sense," is known "only
to those who shared in it."

Developmental psychologists who examine identity point out that internal factors (physical appearance, mental abilities, ethnicity, race, gender, sexual orientation)
and external factors (family's and/or caregiver's culture, socioeconomic status, schooling experiences, geographical locations, societal context) impact children's identity
formation (Erikson, 1950; Marcia, 1980; Spencer, 1983). Children develop multiple
dimensions of identity such as ethnic, racial, gender, ability, sexual orientation, and
religion. Since **self-concept** (a cognitive appraisal of one's social, academic, and
physical competence) and **self-esteem** (an emotional response to self) correlate with
identity, it is important to acknowledge how significant others in children's lives, such
as parents, caregivers, teachers, and peers, impact identity development. In the classroom, children need to be physically safe, emotionally nourished, intellectually challenged, and ethnically acknowledged to ensure positive development of self-concept
and self-esteem.

Human Development

Preservice teachers are often exposed to human developmental theories as a way to
understand children's physical, cognitive, and social development. In the United States,
generally, four major human developmental theories—psychoanalytic, behavioral, humanistic, and cognitive—guide and explain human development across the life span.
Table 4.2 provides brief descriptions of each theory and identifies prominent theorists
in each category.

TABLE 4.2 Human Developmental Theories: Psychoanalytic, Behavioral, Humanistic, and Cognitive

Theory	Theorists	Orientation
Psychoanalytic	Freud (1940)	Focuses on unconscious drives and instincts. Attempts to make people more cognizant of things previously repressed through psychoanalysis (a type of therapy).
	Erikson (1950, 1968)	Expanded Freud's theory of stages. States that throughout the life span, individual personality unfolds in eight stages, each involving developmental tasks.
Behavioral	Skinner (1957)	Maintains that learning is observable and learners passively respond to the environment (a stimulus causes a response). Views learning as a result of experience rather than thinking, ideas, or insights. Promotes operant conditioning (behavioral changes occur as a result of expected consequences, that either reinforce desirable behavior or punish undesirable behavior).
Humanistic	Maslow (1968)	Examines how aspects of the total person—physical, emotional, impersonal, and intellectual—respond to situations. Claims that a person's needs and the drive for self-actualization (becoming all that one can be) interact to affect learning, growth, and motivation.
	Rogers (1970)	Assumes that individuals are motivated to seek self-fulfilling experiences.
Cognitive	Piaget (1952)	Emphasizes that mentally active learners construct their own understandings, including complex phenomena such as language learning and problem solving.
	Bandura (1977)	Compares human learning (information processing, input–output) to the ways computers process information. Holds that learning is enhanced by social activity where learners construct (constructivism) new knowledge by connecting new learning to prior understandings.

These theories greatly influence how psychologists and educators view children's development. Missing from these theories of development are the cultural and the psychological influences of ethnicity, ethnic group membership, and personal ethnic identity. Without adaptation to the ethnic diversity present in children in the United States, one can argue that in and of themselves, these theories cannot adequately address the human developmental process of ethnically (and racially) diverse students of color.

Additionally, the **unit of analysis** (how something is examined) in educational psychology has focused on the individual. Thus, research on the teaching-learning process and subsequent student outcomes gives attention to individual differences, but has not included ethnic group dimensions. As a result, we can document the disparity between groups, but we do not fully comprehend group-based inequality. We do not understand why students from ethnic groups of color consistently score lower on standardized achievement tests than their White ethnic group peers. Generations of children are disenfranchised because the relationship between their ethnic background, cultural histories, and knowledge of their human developmental process has not been adequately addressed.

According to Portes (1996), developmental research in the field of educational psychology has not concerned itself with the relationship between culture and cognition. Most has focused primarily on the human developmental process of mainstream White children and on the testing issues in schooling. Ethnicity, as an aspect of culture and as a significant influence in the human developmental process, must be examined to fully understand human growth and development.

Race, Racial Groups, and Racial Identity

Omi and Winant (1994, p. 55) define **race** as "a concept which signifies and symbolizes social conflicts and interests by referring to different types of human bodies." This definition includes the physical (skin color, hair texture, eye shape, facial features) aspects as well as the social, political, and legal characteristics of race involving relationships, opportunities, entitlements, and power. However, Omi and Winant point out that race, unlike gender, is not necessarily biological.

Since 1997, for U.S. government purposes, the categories for race in the U.S. Census include: American Indian or Alaska Native, Asian, Black or African American, Native Hawaiian or Other Pacific Islander, White, and Some Other Race (http://www.census.gov). Mexican Americans and other Hispanic populations (Puerto Ricans, Cubans, and/or other Spanish/Hispanic/Latinos) are recognized only as an ethnic group. They can be of any race. Multiracials, individuals with membership in more than one racial group, can select one or more races.

Although a person's racial classification can change, generally speaking, their social and political statuses remain constant. To illustrate, Mexican Americans have been categorized racially as White and non-White by federal agencies, Census Bureau, and legal decisions; however, this White racial categorization does not necessarily result in status and privilege (Martinez, 1997). Mexican Americans' racial heritage, due to geography, appearance, exploitation, and colonization, is a composite of multiple racial groups—Spaniards (White), enslaved people brought to the Americas (Black), and people from the indigenous tribal groups in the Americas (Indian).

Racial identity refers "to a sense of group or collective identity based on one's perception that he/she shares a common racial heritage with a particular racial group" (Richardson & Silvestri, 1999, p. 49). In the United States, racial identity theorists focus on the stages Black and White adults experience in their racial identity process (Cross, 1991; Helms, 1990). This identity development in Black and White adults is highly associated with racial attitudes, discriminatory experiences, and degrees of assimilation.

Unfortunately, these theories do not use a "developmental framework that extends backward to take into consideration the early developmental experiences" of adults as children and adolescents (Branch, 1999, p. 8). As a result, we do not fully understand the influence of race on the human developmental process. Research on children's racial identity generally asks them to classify themselves in a racial group and to place others in racial groups (Aboud, 1988; Holmes, 1995). Some researchers apply adult racial identity theories to adolescents (Dilg, 1999; Tatum, 1997). In comparison to the research on children, minimal scholarship is available on adolescent racial attitudes and racial identity. There is, however, an extensive body of scholarship showing that parents and teachers are significant contributors to students' development of racial attitudes and behaviors (Aboud, 1988; Branch & Newcomb, 1986). As children get older their attitudes and behaviors resemble that of their parents.

Student Cultural Displays

Some of the signs children might display as members of a particular ethnic group or groups are presented in this section. This section includes information on (a) ethnic identity, (b) ethnic identity in a culturally pluralistic society, and (c) ethnicity and school practices.

Ethnic Identity

Cultural patterns or ethnic profiles can be used as tools to understand and to accommodate variations in communication, play, and learning preferences in the classroom. Teachers must be conscious of these patterns. They must also be cautious that ethnic profiles do not harden into **stereotypes** (oversimplified images or ideas held by a person or by a group toward another person or group).

Sometimes there are misconceptions regarding the terms culture and ethnicity. Ethnicity is narrower than the concept culture, and although they are related there is not a one-to-one relationship (for further explanation of culture see Chapter 1). Ethnicity is one of many dimensions of culture. Knowledge of culture is critical to understanding ethnic identity. Culture plays a primary role in the formation and development of ethnic identity; therefore, ethnic identity is generally examined within a cultural context. The concepts ethnicity, ethnic group and ethnic identity, while appearing similar, have discrete features as illustrated in Table 4.3 (p. 54).

Early in their identity development, children become aware of a wide range of personal, physical, and cultural characteristics in themselves, their families, and others that help shape their individuality and membership in an ethnic group. Young children, those in middle childhood, and adolescents understand how their ethnic heritage (and race) plays a role in their lives. Through a distinctive **ethnic socialization process** (direct and indirect messages children receive from parents, peers, and their ethnic community), children form and develop an ethnic identity. This personal and group dimension of self (a) promotes cognitive strengths and social competencies valued in their homes and communities; (b) determines how they view themselves ethnically; (c) affects how they act, think, and feel about their ethnic group; (d) shapes how they interact with others in society; and (e) influences access to academic and social opportunities.

TABLE 4.3 **Ethnicity, Ethnic Groups, and Ethnic Identity Distinctions**

Ethnicity	Ethnic Group	Ethnic Identity
Ethnicity is part of peoples' personal and cultural history. This category includes all of the cultural, psychological, and social phenomena associated with a particular group. It focuses on the ways social and cultural practices intersect during interactions among diverse groups.	An **ethnic group** is a distinctive social group in a larger society who set themselves apart or who are set apart by others due to distinctive cultural patterns, beliefs, histories, values, attitudes, languages, national origins, and physical traits.	**Ethnic identity** is a personal process, influenced by membership in an ethnic group. It forms within the child and develops throughout the life span. Ethnic identity has individual and group components, is not necessarily limited to one group, and can be internally driven, externally imposed, or both.

Ethnic Identity in a Culturally Pluralistic Society

A person's **national identity** (individual and group membership as a citizen of a nation) is usually highly correlated with ethnic identity. For instance, most citizens of Japan are ethnically Japanese and, for the most part, people born and raised in Italy are ethnically Italian. Since the United States is a culturally pluralistic nation, *American* is not synonymous with the ethnic identity of U.S. citizens. When a person, states, "I am American," he or she is referring to a national identity. Of course, the term *American* is also applicable to individuals from South, Central, and North America. Citizens of the United States are categorized in and identified in multiple ethnic groups (e.g., African American, Italian American, Chinese American, European American, Jewish American, Mexican American, Navajo American).

For many, the words ethnic, ethnicity, and ethnic identity are associated with people from groups of color. When asked to identify their ethnic group membership, many White individuals seem perplexed. Statements that indicate unawareness, such as, "I don't know what my ethnic group is," or those that make one's own cultural group universal and other cultures ethnic, such as "That scarf looks ethnic," are common. This omission might lead some to think that ethnicity refers only to people from ethnic groups of color. Yet, everyone is a member of an ethnic group.

Some White U.S. citizens, whose heritage includes multiple European origin ethnic groups, may assume that a mixture of ethnic groups makes their ethnic heritage nonexistent. They may choose to identify racially as Anglo, Caucasian, or White and may prefer not to classify themselves as European American (an ethnic group designation). White people whose background includes multiple White European ethnic groups might find it more difficult to identify ethnically than White individuals whose ethnic heritage originates from a single group such as Greek American, Italian American, or Norwegian American.

Alba (1990), referring to White ethnics, maintains that children's early home life creates a unique identity informed by ethnicity. This identity exists at deep levels and is present even when individuals openly reject or are unaware of their ethnicity. The skills and knowledge learned through one's upbringing determine how we deal with certain situations and how we define our gender roles. These values, attitudes, and behaviors are ethnically influenced. Consider the role ethnicity plays in how people manage and deal with issues such as joy, anger, family responsibilities, grief, gender, and loss. Or how the ethnic socialization patterns influence children's family and adult relationships, communication styles, play, and cognitive preferences. Although some of the behaviors are similar, others differ in content, purpose, and outcome.

Many of the skills that young children acquire in their socialization process reflect particular values, child-rearing practices, and social structures learned in their homes. Although this process *does not result in identical or even predictable behavior* among children of the same ethnic group, it *does produce cultural patterns or ethnic profiles* that can be used as tools to understand and to accommodate variations in communication, play, and learning preferences in the classroom. Teachers must be both conscious of these patterns and careful not to allow these ethnic profiles to harden into stereotypes.

Observed differences between cultural patterns of children from ethnic groups of color and White ethnic children appear to reflect broader cultural contrasts. Generally speaking, a collective, social, and collaborative style is more prevalent for children from ethnic groups of color, whereas the European American culture has an individualistic, private, and competitive orientation (Greenfield & Cocking, 1994). These respective value systems shape peer interactions, learning preferences, and cognitive development. As they learn in culturally conditioned ways, children prepare for a successful adult life in their particular ethnic group.

As ethnic identity develops, individuals usually make definite movements toward their group. They consciously experience identification, affiliation, and commitment with their group. For White ethnics, these behaviors and attitudes support feelings of solidarity with a particular White ethnic group (Alba, 1990). Due to the Americanization of White ethnics in the early 1900s, many lost their heritage language and much of their culture. This is exemplified in Vignette 4.1, a description of Susan Rektorik Henley's (2001) Czech American experience in Texas.

Vignette 4.1
I Am One of Those Children
Frank and Marie Matous Rektorik immigrated to Texas in 1886 and settled near Moravia, in Fayette County, Texas. Their children spoke Czech. Around 1910, John (Jan) and Louis (Alois), the two eldest sons, moved to Nueces County to establish their own farms. One day they went to Robstown, the nearest town. "They were confronted by a man of Anglo background who was drunk and carrying a rifle. He was with a friend and, to this friend, he said 'These guys are Czech. I've never shot one of them before!' It seemed very likely that it was the strong intervention by the man's friend, which kept John and/or Louis from being shot." Since Czech Texans were treated in a disparate and unkind manner, the Rektoriks and other Czech American families chose to speak English and to adopt the American lifestyle. Therefore, a significant number of children did not learn their heritage language. They also lost a strong connection to their ethnic roots. Henley recalls:

I am one of those children. . . . I am now an adult seeking out my ethnic identity because, in our family, the Czech traditions had faded almost to nothing by the time I was growing up. . . . My Dad recalled many times when he and his friends would be outside playing in the school yard and conversing in Czech when a girl would overhear them and shout out, *"Teacher, teacher, the boys are speaking Bohemian again!"* . . . a common punishment was to have a student stay after school and pull weeds. . . . [Father] spent many an afternoon pulling weeds. . . . As sad as I am because many Texas Czech traditions were not practiced in my home as I grew up, I now fully understand why my parents chose to raise us that way. At the same time, I am glad that I am alive at a point in time where I can still seek out those who know and practice the traditions and incorporate those found traditions into not only my life but the lives of my children and our extended family. (Henley, 2001, pp. 1–4)

Issues for Consideration

Henley expresses a sense of loss of ethnic identity and a realization that adults in her life did not consider ethnic identity important. Although she felt her parents chose to raise her without connections to ethnic roots, she also points out that she intends to reclaim her ethnicity for herself and for her children. Why do you think she is responding this way? Describe the type of psychological damage or loss of skills Henley experienced in her home. Do you think her early school experiences supported her ethnic needs? What types of attitudes, knowledge, and understandings do teachers need to enable children to value their own ethnic heritage and those of others, even if they come from homes where caregivers restrict or suppress natural displays of ethnic behaviors?

Formation and Development of Ethnic Identity

The formation and development of ethnic identity takes place when an individual recognizes, identifies, and affiliates with a particular ethnic group. This important personal and group identification has critical emotional, behavioral, and cognitive significance that affects all aspects of development. The process begins at birth and continues throughout the life span. Ethnic behaviors are interwoven and embedded into the ways individuals process cognitive information, interact socially, communicate verbally or nonverbally, and display cultural elements. These behaviors are consequential to all aspects of social and cognitive growth.

Although the development of ethnic identity may follow similar patterns, variations in the process sometimes produce *within ethnic group differences, which may be greater than the differences among ethnic groups.* Distinctions between members of the same ethnic group are due to multiple factors (e.g., socioeconomic status, degrees of acculturation, multiraciality and biethnicity, gender, adoption, foster home placement, and geographic location), present in the ethnic socialization process. However, this section focuses on the similarities in the formation and development of ethnic identity rather than the differences. Following is a discussion of this process in early childhood, middle childhood, and adolescence.

Early Childhood. In the United States children from ethnic groups of color self-identify ethnically around age 3 and 4, while most White children identify self ethnically around age eight (Aboud, 1984). Whereas self-labeling may require three to eight years, scholars who study ethnic identity development in young children from a socialization perspective believe that the ethnic identity process begins at birth, at the earliest interactions between the child, family, and community (Spencer, 1985). The continual presence of personal, physical, and societal factors such as skin color, language, food choices, values, and membership in a mainstream or ethnic minority group instills in children ethnic roles and behaviors that prepare them for eventual self-labeling.

Because ethnic identity is viewed as a developmental process in constant transformation, Spencer (1985) explains that the ways in which young children display and incorporate ethnic identity content into their personal and group identity differs from the ways these are exhibited and given importance at other life ages. We know that young children (birth to age 3 and 4) acquire ethnic values, customs, language styles, and behavioral codes long before they are able to label and know them as ethnic. Without fully understanding the construct of ethnic identity or ethnicity, a 2-year-old can accurately state, "I Pinopino [Pilipino American]" or a 3-year-old European American girl can display the independent individual strengths valued in her ethnic group.

Around age 4 and 5, children typically use a range of physical characteristics using a mixture of race and color terms, such as black, white, and brown, and ethnic designations, such as Chinese, Mexican, and Japanese, to describe self and others and to include or exclude from ethnic groups. In one study, children aged 3 to 5 from a variety of racial groups categorized people ethnically as Chinese or Japanese on the basis of eye shape and skin color (Ramsey, 1986). In a kindergarten classroom, a five-year-old, Jaime, noticing Andy's eye shape, explained that Andy (native Spanish speaker) should not speak *Mexicano* because he was *Chino* (Sheets, 1998b). When a young 5-year-old Mexican American was asked, "What are you?" She responded, "I'm Mexican, don't you know? I speak Spanish."

Although young children acquire the values, behaviors, and social patterns of their ethnic group before they are able to self-label, the ability to accurately self-label does not mean that the same criteria are used to determine the labeling of others. Sheets (1998b) reports that 5-year-old children from African American, Mexican American, Laotian American, and Black and White biracial groups were able to accurately classify themselves ethnically. These children readily provided distinguishing physical markers (eye shape, skin tone, and hair texture) and cultural elements (native language, food preferences, and ways of eating) as proof to distinguish themselves from others. However, they sometimes used what they perceived to be authoritative or socially accepted reasons to accurately classify others. They would say a peer is "Laos" because "My daddy said so" or someone is "Mexican" because "he was born in the hospital."

The self-labeling at this age may be separate from attitudes of affiliation, commitment, and salience but not from identifiable cultural behaviors associated with group patterns. Some identifiable cultural behaviors include children's ability to speak the languages learned in their homes, display ethnically influenced etiquette codes, and exhibit gender roles influenced by their ethnic values.

Children's expansion of vocabulary, even when it leads to inaccuracy, indicates a growing recognition of racial and ethnic complexities. It also shows that young children can perceive-describe physical differences associated with race and ethnicity and display ethnic behaviors long before they are able to understand that these attributes can categorize them as members of a specific ethnic group.

Children and teachers can see racial, ethnic, cultural, and economic diversity in the larger community. However, superficial and sporadic contact with individuals different from self gives merely rudimentary tools to help classify and label people ethnically (and racially). A deeper understanding of ethnic and racial differences requires continual, personal and social interactions in meaningful contexts. Consider the following kindergarten classroom experience.

Vignette 4.2
Your Eyes Are "Squitched"
Several kindergarten students—Carmen (Mexican American girl), Tanika (African American girl), and Bobby and Lance (Laotian American boys)—were involved in a small group math lesson on the rug. Bobby, excited and engaged, kept blurting out the answers. Carmen, upset at Bobby because he was not taking turns, said loudly, "Stop it! It's my turn! Anyway, your eyes are squitched!" Bobby, surprised at the outburst and perceiving that squitched was an insult, yelled back "No, they're not!" The "Yes, they are" "No, they're not" repartee went back and forth. I [the teacher] remained silent.

While this conflict was taking place, Lance slowly moved behind me and watched the argument. Finally, Bobby looked at me and asked poignantly, "Are my eyes squitched?" I waited a moment. Gently cupping his chin in my hand and looking directly into his eyes, I responded, "Yes, they're oval. They're a soft brown color and actually quite beautiful. Let's get mirrors and look at our eyes." The children quickly got small handheld mirrors from the basket in the housekeeping area and returned to the rug.

Carmen looked at her eyes closely and then stared at Bobby's eyes. She said, "We both have brown eyes." Tanika, searching her eyes, commented, "Mine are mostly round, but they're pretty, too. Right?" Lance stared at his eyes. Then he smiled and announced proudly: "My eyes are squitched, too!" Bobby smiling at Lance concurred, "Yep! That's because we're cousins. We both have the same eyes." Tanika replied, "Yep, both of you have beautiful eyes." Throughout the rest of the day, most of the children in the class freely examined and discussed the differences and sameness of their eyes. (Sheets, 1998b)

Issues for Consideration
Although some teachers might have responded differently to Carmen's discriminatory and hurtful behavior, I believed Bobby's eyes were beautiful and felt that chastising Carmen would send a message to Bobby and to the other children that something was wrong with Bobby's eyes. Although I also believed that Bobby was hurt by the remarks about his eyes, I hoped that he was not hurt by my decision.

This event was perceived as a teachable moment. The purposeful, socializing teacher action protected and affirmed the children's entitlement to differences. I felt that a positive message regarding a physical characteristic, associated with his ethnic identity, would perhaps help Bobby handle future discriminatory remarks toward him as an individual and as a member of a Laotian American ethnic group (Sheets, 1998b).

A myth exists that young children, born prejudice free, only learn discriminatory practices from negative, external sources. In fact, children naturally and consistently display prejudicial attitudes and act in discriminatory ways. Although Carmen's remarks were discriminatory and hurtful, do you agree with the teacher's choice to use this incident as a teachable moment rather than as a disciplinary event? What types of attitudes, knowledge, and understandings do teachers need to enable children to process ethnic differences? What might you have done in this instance, and why would you respond in this way?

Middle Childhood. By early middle childhood most children categorize self and accurately identify others in particular ethnic groups (Aboud, 1984). Schooling, developmental age, maturity, social experiences, and level of cognitive development affect how children recognize the attributes associated with their own group membership. Fourth-grade children who attend integrated schools are more comfortable with their own ethnic identity and those of others than children who attend segregated schools (Dutton, Singer, & Devlin, 1998). During the middle childhood years children (a) are more aware of their own thoughts and feelings and are able to infer those of others; (b) acquire information of their own identity and understand the differences of others, especially if they have direct contact with diverse groups; (c) begin to internalize societal attitudes (positive or negative) regarding their ethnic group that are learned from schooling experiences, peers, and the media; and (d) understand how fairness, racism, prejudice, and discrimination affect them individually and as members of a group (Amir, Sharan, & Ben-Ari, 1984; Sigelman & Welch, 1993). The following vignette illustrates one child's identification with and commitment to more than one ethnic group.

Vignette 4.3
Claiming Both
Jaime, a 9-year-old child with a Pilipina American mother and a Mexican American father, identifies ethnically as Pilipino American. He lives with his mother and stepfather in a traditional Pilipino American home. He hears Tagalo language, celebrates Pilipino holidays, wears traditional clothing during cultural celebrations, eats traditional foods, attends a public school with a majority of Pilipino American students, and has frequent interaction with his maternal grandmother. Although he is close to his father, he only sees him every other weekend and three weeks during the summer.

When his paternal grandmother visited his classroom, the children at his table did not believe him when he told them she spoke Spanish. Since they identified him as Pilipino, they told him that his grandmother speaks Tagalo. When his grandmother spoke Spanish to one of his Spanish-speaking Mexican

American peers, Jaime smiled, nodded, rolled his eyes knowingly, and quietly remarked, "See, I told you so."

One evening, his paternal grandmother took him to visit an African American friend (Gloria), who had traveled to various countries in Africa. Jaime was intrigued by her collection of African artifacts. While examining the masks, statues, small furniture, wall hangings, and collection of giraffes, he inquired, "Do you have anything from the Pilipines?" Gloria replied, "No. I haven't been to the Pilipines." Jaime responded, "I'm Pilipino." Later on during the visit, Gloria pointed out a beautiful, hand-carved three-legged chair, explaining that she purchased it at a local antique shop because she liked the three legs. Jaime approached the chair and examined it more closely.

In the car, on the way home, Jaime, remarked, "She should have something from the Pilipines." Jaime was reminded that Gloria had never visited the Pilipines, and that if she visited she would most likely purchase an artifact. Jaime thought for a while, and then referring to the three-legged chair, concluded, "I think that chair is from the Pilipines. I saw one just like it in an antique store."

Jaime also claims his Mexican American heritage. When studying fractions in third grade he became aware that his 8½ birthday fell on the *Cinco de Mayo*. This realization prompted him to remark that he should have an 8½ birthday party on *Cinco de Mayo* since that day was both his holiday and half-birthday date.

Issues for Consideration

Scholarship indicates that multiracial and multiethnic individuals (a) identify racially or ethnically contextually and situationally, (b) are generally perceived by others of being of a single race or ethnic group, and (c) are entitled to claim any one or all of their ethnic and racial groups (Root, 1992). In this case, Jaime most often chooses to self-identify as Pilipino American; however, he is aware of and accepting of his Mexican American heritage. In school, Jaime's peers (and perhaps his teacher) categorize him as belonging to a single ethnic group. How do you think this affects his identity development? What are some of the things teachers can do to validate his mixed heritage in the classroom? Why do you think Jaime felt the need to claim the three-legged chair as a Pilipino artifact? Do you think it was from the Pilipines? Do you suppose that students might make allegations of this nature in classrooms when they determine that the curricular content either reflects or ignores their ethnic group?

Adolescence. While some adolescents from White ethnic groups may explore their ethnicity, most adolescents from ethnic groups of color begin to question the societal status of their group, fully understanding the implications of this group membership. Ethnic identity and its relationship to self-concept and self-esteem are especially critical during adolescence. They are especially vulnerable to identity concerns in general, and issues of ethnic identity in particular, during this age. Adolescents from ethnic groups of color are aware that mainstream societal values may both differ from and not be beneficial to their group. They notice that their groups' accomplishments may be missing or distorted in the school curriculum. Their self-regulatory acts of resistance to maintain ethnic integrity are often interpreted as misbehavior (Sheets, 1995b).

The following developmental characteristics may directly affect adolescent ethnic identity development (Eccles & Midgley, 1989; Wigfield, Eccles, & Pintrich, 1996):

1. General self-esteem is lower and less stable but their self-consciousness is higher.
2. Self-perception of personal appearance and social acceptance relates strongly to their feelings of self-worth.
3. Attitudes and beliefs about school become more negative, and they have lower intrinsic motivation to achieve.
4. They conform more to gender role stereotypes.
5. Most adolescents from ethnic groups of color have faced multiple experiences perceived as prejudicial, discriminatory, and racist that they attribute to membership in their particular ethnic group.
6. Adolescents have the cognitive ability to process the positive and negative views held by society about their group.

Vignette 4.4 exemplifies how adolescents from ethnic groups of color often face school experiences that they perceive as discriminatory and that they attribute to membership in their particular ethnic group. Since some adolescents are vulnerable to identity issues in general, events of this nature may promote acts of resistance and efforts to maintain ethnic integrity that may be perceived as misbehavior by teachers.

Vignette 4.4
No Tacos Tonight

Arturo, a 16-year-old Mexican American *A* student, lives in a suburban neighborhood. He is one of few students of color in his high school, and the only Mexican American student in his classes. Taco Time, a fast food chain, opened a restaurant in his community. Since Arturo has a new driver's license, his family can count on him to run errands. Yesterday he picked up tacos for the entire family. Today everybody wanted tacos again. Arturo was asked to go get them. He refused. "No! Everyone will think that all I eat is tacos." His older brother laughed and insisted that no one would care. "Ya right," Arturo replied angrily, "Yesterday Mr. Wilson [Arturo's marketing teacher] asked me if I had a green card. Everybody laughed. I just walked out of class. So I'm telling you, I'm not going to Taco Time two days in a row."

Concerned about the classroom incident, Arturo's parents made an appointment with Mr. Wilson. He admitted making the remark in class but explained that he was just joking. He meant no harm. Arturo's walking out of class was not even reported to the principal. According to Mr. Wilson, no other incidents have taken place.

Issues for Consideration

This vignette demonstrates how insensitive teacher actions intended in jest and the possibility of peer teasing or jeering can affect out-of-school experiences.

Consider how Arturo's prior experiences in school settings influenced his cautious stance and how he perceived he could minimize real and perceived harassment targeted at him personally due to ethnic group membership. Why do you think the teacher sees this as a single classroom incident, whereas for Arturo it appears to have a broader impact? How do you think being the only Mexican American student in the class affects the way he experiences the classroom climate? What should teachers do when alerted of issues of this nature? How might you respond?

Ethnicity and School Practices

Ethnic identity may originate, form, and develop in private homes; however, it unfolds and is displayed in the immediate community sector and in institutional settings, such as schools. When one ethnicity dominates the schooling process and other ethnicities provide students, in all likelihood, tension is generated (Portes, 1996). Additionally, psychological dimensions of ethnicity, if compromised, can create conflict for individuals whose social relationships and cultural practices become removed from their sense of identity (Bentley, 1987). In classrooms, teachers may not be aware of the emotional and cognitive stress caused by this psychological dissonance. They may not recognize ethnic signifiers embodied in children's cognitive and motivating structures. Thus, when students compete for the same resources (e.g., teacher time, interpersonal relationships with the teacher, mutuality of expectations), varied degrees of access to and limited numbers of options may be available to some children.

Currently, schools use ethnicity to identify, categorize, and count students. Schools, districts, states, and the federal government report various types of information by ethnic groups. Data are readily available by ethnicity on the number of students in schools, assessment scores, dropout and graduation rates, disciplinary actions, and attendance. However, student ethnicity is rarely taken into consideration when creating the psychological climate of the school, designing instruction, or adopting curricular content. Yet, we know that students' ethnicity affects the degree of inclusion in schooling events and often determines their access to opportunities for participation.

The following set of assumptions, supported by scholarship (Brembeck & Hill, 1973; Gay, 1999; Mintz & Price, 1992; Portes, 1996; Root, 1999; Sheets & Hollins, 1999), can help teachers understand the roles ethnicity, ethnic groups, and ethnic identity play in the teaching-learning process:

1. Students' ethnic characteristics are persistent and continuous. Although the process of acculturation or assimilation influences ethnic identity development, the attitudes, skills, and preferences acquired ethnically are maintained structurally, melt selectively, and may actually elaborate over time. Generally, each ethnic group sustains its own network of friendships, neighborhoods, organizations, and institutions. For the most part, interethnic contacts occur mainly at a secondary group level such as school and employment.
2. Ethnicity as a dimension of culture cannot be separated from other cognitive and social developmental activities. Students' ethnic strengths are available for use in the teaching-learning process. If applied, they will advantage more students to

achieve socially and academically at high levels of competency without the need to sacrifice aspects of their ethnic identity.

3. The difficulties teachers encounter when they lack knowledge of different ethnic groups places them at a disadvantage and may weaken their capacity to develop self-confidence. They may feel trapped by the conflict of values associated with diversity and may experience stress and frustration by what they interpret as apathy, neglect, depravity, instability and cultural poverty of the diverse students in their classrooms.

4. The knowledge, skills, and home experiences of ethnically diverse children from groups of color are usually seen as inferior, when compared and judged through middle class suburban perspectives.

5. Unless instructional content, context, and process are adapted to meet students' strengths, it is almost inevitable that children from certain ethnic backgrounds will have difficulty understanding or following the cognitive style of their teacher.

6. A factor contributing to the social and academic achievement of students from the European American ethnic group has been the institutionalization of their culture in schools and their ability to display their ethnic identity as the norm. Conversely, students from ethnic groups of color have had to construct, maintain, and develop their ethnic identities in schooling contexts that often require them to restrict or suppress the natural display of internal ethnic behaviors.

7. Opportunity to develop a comfortable, multifaceted identity through ethnic affirmation, day-to-day achievement, classroom rituals, and validation of experiential background is at the essence of a culturally inclusive learning-teaching process.

8. Understanding the role of ethnicity in the human developmental process may be key to conceptualizing ways to improve the teaching-learning process to minimize and/or eliminate the growing achievement gap among diverse groups of children.

9. Changing teacher, administrator, counselor, and school psychologists' preparation to include understanding and knowledge of ethnic identity formation and development (of self and others) is central to changing classroom and school practices.

10. Programs that fail to address ethnic identity development will generally produce practitioners who are unable to work effectively with students from diverse ethnic groups. The impact on European American children, although less obvious, is nonetheless harmful because it perpetuates the development of a distorted European American ethnic identity.

Classroom Applications

Through their own perceptions and the messages of others, children construct an understanding of ethnicity and race that significantly shapes their self-knowledge and awareness of the societal status of their ethnic group. By extension, this knowledge influences their behavior and relationships. The following activities can assist in promoting and affirming students' ethnic identity development as individuals and as members of their ethnic group. Measurable improvement of academic achievement and evidence of respect and positive interaction with individuals in their own ethnic group as well as with diverse peers can serve as an evaluation tool.

Recognizing Cultural Positioning

Become aware of your cultural positioning. Recognize how your ethnicity, race, and subsequent socialization process impact your teacher-student relationship and how you view student-student relationships.

1. Reflect on what you consider normal. Expand your concept of normal to include competencies and behaviors from diverse ethnic groups. Identify your own cultural and ethnic heritage and acknowledge inherited beliefs, behaviors, and attitudes that influence your thinking, including subconscious thinking, about your role in the teaching-learning process. Admit discomfort and work on improving any prejudicial attitudes or stereotypes that may hinder student learning.
2. Recognize your skills, knowledge, and teaching competencies. Take ownership for any strengths and limitations and take needed steps to refine skills and obtain knowledge to enhance teaching skills with diverse students.

Examining Classroom Climate and Curricular Content

Evaluate classroom climate and assess curricular content for indirect messages about ethnicity and race and implicit judgments regarding ethnic and racial markers.

1. Encourage students to notice and appreciate their own physical traits and respect those of others. With young children, provide handheld mirrors for them to inspect their own faces and a large mirror at child level so they can see themselves full size with their friends. Engage children in self-portrait activities using a variety of media such as people colors paint or crayons, collage, and clay and give careful attention to skin color, hair texture, and facial features. Make alternative individual and class portraits by using snapshots of children's hands or the backs of their heads. Have a guessing game for identifying the photos and then display them as a group portrait. For older children and adolescents, discuss how beauty, power, conflict, family, and music are affected by diverse worldviews, media stereotypes, and the dominant culture. Develop awareness and knowledge about own and other ethnic groups. Discuss why some ethnic groups are associated with negative or positive stereotypes. Debate benefits and disadvantages of issues such as assimilation/acculturation, heritage language maintenance/language loss, same-ethnic/cross-ethnic friendships, same-race/cross-racial relationships, cross-racial adoptions and foster care placement.
2. Create opportunities where students can process ethnically and racially related information. Affirm children's curiosity about their own or others' ethnicity. If six-year-old Gustavo says "I'm Mexican American," point out appropriate, special facts, such as the ability to speak two languages, beautiful skin color, unique

cultural traditions; if possible, point out other individuals in the class or school who are also Mexican American or add other examples. Use curricular materials and lessons that honor the accomplishments, values, and heritages of diverse groups. Explain how and why people identify ethnically.

3. Allow students of all ethnic groups to use same-race, same-ethnic, and same-language interactions as a personal resource and to build group cohesion as well as encourage cross-ethnic interactions. Permit children to self-select work groups. Avoid individualistic orientations and overemphasis on independence by balancing these strengths with development of strong interpersonal group skills and effective collaborative work habits.

4. Lead discussions and activities that openly value ethnic diversity and racial diversity in the classroom. Compare and contrast skin colors and affirm the beauty of all of them. Explain that people usually, but not always, inherit physical traits similar to those of their family members. Include a variety of materials in black and shades of brown in art projects and room decorations. Watch for patterns of association between light- or dark-colored characters and traits in books and posters perceived to be positive or negative. Use actual classroom events involving ethnic conflict or joy as teachable moments to enhance understandings.

Conclusion

The ethnic diversity in the U.S. student and teacher population implies that diversity in values (and a possibility of conflict among these diverse values) may be present. Since schools are social institutions, sometimes schooling is viewed as a place to socialize and "Americanize" children. Some educators may think that children are on their way to being assimilated as Americans; therefore, their ethnic differences may be viewed as transitory. In other words, these differences do not have to be taken seriously; and it is not the responsibility of the schools to deal with these differences. However, this is not the case. History shows that cultural and ethnic differences may be intensifying rather than diminishing. And, although we all share commonalities, complete assimilation is an ideal, not a reality.

Since ethnic groups operate in a social, political, and psychological context, attention to the distinctive worldviews found in various cultural groups and knowledge of their cultural history are important. Members of ethnic groups develop behavioral patterns to maintain their ethnic identity in welcoming settings and to help them survive in hostile environments. Children who are members of an ethnic group of color are affected psychologically (their self-esteem is threatened) when they perceive that the mainstream culture holds their ethnic group in low regard. Likewise, children from White ethnic groups come to understand the valued status of their group and are at risk of developing identities based on the devaluation of others.

Evidence that teachers bring highly ethnically influenced orientations to the classroom is documented in the literature on how teachers learn to teach (Sugrue, 1996; Wideen, Mayer-Smith, & Moon, 1998). Teachers' behavior is guided by a complex set of rules, norms, and principles learned in their socialization process where ethnic identity forms and develops. Similar to other aspects of identity, such as gender, ability, and sexual orientation, ethnicity influences teachers' decisions in classrooms. Further research is needed to help us understand how children's ethnic distinctions affect their developmental process. Whereas such issues may be sensitive for adults, children speak candidly about their observations and feelings about differences.

RECOMMENDED READINGS

Alba, R. D. (1990). *Ethnic identity: The transformation of White America.* New Haven, CT: Yale University Press.

Greenfield, P. A., & Cocking, R. R. (Eds.). (1994). *Cross-cultural roots of minority child development.* Hillsdale, NJ: Erlbaum.

Sheets, R. H., & Hollins, E. R. (Eds.). (1999). *Racial, ethnic, and cultural identity and human development: Implications for schooling.* Mahwah, NJ: Erlbaum.

CHAPTER

5

Social Interactions: Improving Interpersonal Relationships

It is sometimes easier for schools to target social behaviors or teach social rules than to commit to efforts to foster friendships. This is unfortunate, given a wealth of evidence that suggests the availability of even one friend changes the social experience of a child.

—Doll, 1996, p. 5

Generally, the first thing teachers do at the beginning of the school year is to organize the classroom's physical space, which includes a seating arrangement for students. For most teachers, this task, linked to classroom management, remains obvious and paramount throughout the year. However, deliberate attention to the classroom's emotional tone is not always the case. Yet, both the physical and emotional aspects of classroom life serve as valuable tools to support and nurture students' social strengths. The purpose of this chapter is to help teachers view the classroom as a place to learn and as a living space where students experience a rich cultural, linguistic, social, recreational, and academic life.

Students who experience multiple opportunities to practice interpersonal skills develop peer acceptance and experience a sense of community. They use the classroom context as a resource to initiate and sustain friendships. This chapter examines the third diversity pedagogical dimension. It begins with a description of the third diversity pedagogy dimension (social interactions) and its corresponding cultural display (interpersonal relationships). The second section, teacher pedagogical behaviors, includes background information on the role of friendship, peer friendship development, and factors influencing students' friendship selections. Next is a discussion on student cultural displays, which examines students' gender preferences, race and friendship choices, and issues of social isolation. Classroom applications follow.

Diversity Pedagogy Dimension 3:
Social Interactions/Interpersonal Relationships

The third diversity pedagogy dimension introduces pedagogical strategies (teacher behaviors) needed to apply this dimension in the classroom and points out how students might display signs of cultural competency and evidence of social skills. Definitions, explanations, and observations are based on the work of numerous theorists and researchers (see Crosnoe, 2000; Hartup, 1989; Rizzo, 1988). Table 5.1 defines the dimensional elements (*social interactions* and *interpersonal relationships*), recommends teacher pedagogical behaviors (approaches to creating classroom conditions for the development of social skills), and provides examples of student cultural displays (demonstrations of social and cultural competence in diverse social settings).

TABLE 5.1 Diversity Pedagogy Dimension 3: Social Interactions/Interpersonal Relationships

Definition of Dimensional Elements

Social Interactions: Public and shared contact or communication in dyad or group settings that provide participants opportunities to evaluate, exchange, and share resources.	*Interpersonal Relationships:* Familiar social associations among two or more individuals involving reciprocity and variable degrees of trust, support, companionship, duration, and intimacy.

Teacher Pedagogical Behaviors	**Student Cultural Displays**
Creates multiple opportunities for students to experience different social interactions. • Honors students' entitlement to select friends. • Provides classroom events to help students develop peer relationships, friendships, and a sense of social belonging and group affiliation with individuals and groups sharing common attributes and with other diverse individuals and groups. • Encourages, facilitates, and provides opportunities for students to interact socially with others in multiple diverse settings.	Demonstrations of social and cultural competence in diverse school settings. • Initiates, maintains, and sustains friendships. • Shows behaviors promoting respectful, responsible participation in multiple cultural, academic, and recreational classroom events with individuals and groups sharing common attributes and with other diverse individuals and groups. • Accepts, initiates, and sustains same-race, same-gender, as well as cross-race and cross-gender peer acceptance.
Promotes the skills students need to function as contributing members of own and other social groups, ethnic communities, and as citizens of a pluralistic national and world society. • Understands the difference between cooperative and collaborative group skills and teaches related skills. • Provides opportunities for students to develop leadership skills and responsible group participation.	Expressions of developing social skills needed as a contributing member of own and other social groups and ethnic communities and as a citizen of a pluralistic national and world society. • Interacts comfortably and responsibly in dyad, small group, and whole group classroom and school settings. • Exhibits growth in leadership and group negotiation skills.

Teacher Pedagogical Behaviors

This section provides a brief review of the scholarship examining (a) the role friendship plays in the cognitive and social development of children, (b) the development of peer relationships during childhood and adolescence, and (c) factors influencing friendship selections among young people. This background knowledge may be helpful when applying the third pedagogical dimension in the teaching-learning process.

The Role of Friendship

During childhood, children require peer acceptance to develop a sense of emotional adequacy (Dodge, 1989). To have, to be, and to keep a friend is more than a wishful expectation—it is a basic need. Doll (1996) explains the difference between peer acceptance and friendship. She defines **peer acceptance** as "the degree to which members of a group like a child and want to spend time with him or her" while **friendship** "represents a mutual selection in which a child chooses and is simultaneously chosen by another as a preferred friend" (p. 1). As such, friendship offers children both recreational prospects and the emotional comfort previously provided by their families. According to scholars, it is the special dyadic friendships (between two individuals), rather than overall group acceptance, that offer the vital social support children need (Doll, 1996; Hartup, 1991; Ladd & Oden, 1979). Considerable evidence suggests that intimate friendship connections support students' cognitive and emotional development by

1. Providing coping assistance to stressful events. Friends often serve as an emotional resource by facilitating solutions to problems. They are trusted to listen emphatically.
2. Functioning as a resource for academic tasks. Friends naturally provide assistance with academic tasks by explaining concepts, homework, rules, and translating from English to the friend's heritage language.
3. Creating opportunities to acquire and develop social skills. Friends can ease inclusion into social and academic work groups. They can foster a sense of group belonging and often serve as a basis of social comparison and self-processing. Friends also provide opportunities to negotiate concerns, practice leadership, and learn cooperation. They can minimize peer conflict through resolution.
4. Facilitating comparisons necessary for identity development. Friendships often are the means youngsters use to process the delicate balance between the cultural demands of home and school. Being with friends provides children with group membership and often changes the way they are treated by their peers.

Additionally, students who relate to others in socially acceptable ways are usually well liked and included in work projects and in recreational activities. They are generally more cooperative, emphatic, self-confident, and less lonely. Factors that hinder or disrupt the emerging bonds of friendship can have lasting negative effects on children's lives. Ladd (1990) found that children with friends like school and show academic performance gains. Conversely, students who experience early peer rejection have less favorable perceptions of school, display higher levels of school avoidance, and have lower academic performance.

Peer Friendship Development

Children's peer connections develop sequentially. The following description of friendship development is based on the scholarship on social growth during childhood (see Crosnoe, 2000; Hartup, 1989; Rizzo, 1988; Sherman, de Vries, & Lansford, 2000; Tesch, 1983). Although some friendship studies assume that different ethnic groups and social classes characterize friendship in similar ways, most of the current knowledge is based primarily on the social interactions of middle-class European American children (Krappmann, 1996; Sheets, 1999). Descriptions of social development in specific age groups follow.

Infant to Age 2. Infants as young as 6 months crawl toward and investigate other babies for information or signals that might involve them in a social interchange. Toddlers often display a preference for certain partners in parallel play. Intermittently, they may interact with each other and even create imitation games. One child picks up a block and a few seconds later a peer copies, or one says *"Da"* and another mimics the sound. The word *friend* enters many children's vocabulary in the early months of speech and is reinforced by frequent adult references. Pets, playmates, and toy creatures may all receive the label friend. A 2-year-old may point to someone with whom he shares playground space or who plays with him at school and exclaim, "That's my friend!" The designation reflects the pleasure and comfort of emerging social routines. Children at this age are concerned with whom to call a friend and what playmates are liked or not liked at the moment.

Ages 3 to 5. For 3-, 4-, and 5-year-olds, friendship takes on a more intentional aspect. Preschoolers and kindergartners confer and withdraw the status of friend at will according to a number of criteria, including proximity, general compatibility, variable moods, and the nature of the present activity. At this stage, comments such as "Will you be my friend?" "You're not my friend!" or even "I hate you!" are not literal expressions of emotion but rather perceptions of the momentary prospects for play. Although children may experience disappointment and even anger at a rebuff during playtime, such feelings of momentary rejection generally reverse at the next positive encounter. At this age, children use friendship as a convenience to facilitate bonding and to promote access to play.

Ages 6 to 12. Around ages 6 through 12, children's friendships acquire a more sophisticated and lasting content. At this age, children have a need to be successful socially. They understand the reciprocity of friendship, experience increased peer influence, and detect their own and others' social status. Friends are nice. They exchange resources and services, share activities, and maintain a relationship over time. Children at this stage share secrets, things, and promises with their friends. They may also choose to terminate friendships if they perceive that a partner refuses to help, ignores their needs, or destroys feelings of trust. It is common to see primary school age children visibly upset (e.g., crying, distraught, isolated) in the classroom and on the playground when friendships are momentarily suspended or severed. These feelings and experiences provide the groundwork for the mutual respect, responsibility, and long-term relationships that characterize more mature friendships.

Age 12 and Older.   Adolescents 12 years old and older show many precursors of adult behaviors and attitudes in terms of understanding friendship relationships. At this age, they recognize that friends have rights and that their friends might engage in other relationships that may not include them. Adolescents begin to comprehend the need to be satisfied by friendships and to value the importance of sustained relationships. Mutual aid, intimate self-disclosure, trust, commitment, and loyalty become important functions of friendship in adolescence. A major difference between adolescent and adult friendships is that adolescents have not acquired the autonomous interdependence characterizing adult friendships. As a result adolescents may often fulfill the needs of their friends, to their own detriment.

Factors Influencing Friendship Selections

Multiple factors influence friendship selection among young people. They are most often attracted to peers of the same gender, race, and social class. Children also form friendships with those who share similar recreational activities and with peers who are in their classrooms and neighborhoods (Clark & Ayers, 1988; Hartup, 1996). Friendships are largely voluntary and reciprocal. They show commitment between individuals who more or less perceive each other as equals (Hartup, 1996). This section discusses how the teacher and classroom environment, gender, and race play critical roles in childrens' selection of friends.

Classroom Environment.   Although family, church, and community are important sources for developing friendships, for most students school is a primary place to acquire a sense of social group belonging and to practice the skills necessary for making and keeping friends. A teacher's understanding of the developmental aspect of friendships, acknowledgement of children's social expectations and perceptions of friendship, along with kindness, affection, and respect toward all students, can provide a nurturing environment and a positive model for the development of interpersonal relationships. Thoughtful planning and skillful observations of classroom social interactions can affect students' social and cognitive development.

At all developmental levels, children exhibit varying degrees of success at making and keeping friends. The skills required for positive social experiences that come naturally to some may prove more challenging for others. When children have difficulty establishing friendships, it is important for teachers to understand the situation at hand

and to identify other possible sources for the problem. *There is a distinction between students who do not have friends because they lack social skills and those who are targets of bias, prejudice, and discrimination.* In the case of the former, guided activities and instructional interventions help students overcome shyness, control aggressive tendencies, or meet other challenges. When students are excluded because of differences in skin color, language, appearance, social class, clothing, religion, gender, sexual orientation, ability level, or other factors, it is the teacher's responsibility to intercede with reassurances to the victim and corrective guidance to peers and witnesses involved, as well as appropriate instructional interventions to understand the causes and to minimize reoccurrences. Research shows that teachers often overrate the social competence of well-behaved and compliant students and underrate the social skills of disruptive students (French & Tyne, 1982).

Peer relationships and friendship connections allow students to develop social competence. Curricular content incorporating friendship as a basic component provides students with multiple experiences to enjoy and benefit from their friendship choices. If the classroom is racially diverse, these social opportunities can also prepare them to function competently with cross-race peers.

The powerful resources resulting from the self-selection of friends from the same racial, ethnic, language, and gender groups can be promoted in the classroom. Disruption of friendship connections in the name of diversity may be harmful to some students. The challenge becomes how to purposefully balance students' advantageous friendship choices with multiple social and academic experiences involving peers from different races, ethnicities, genders, abilities, interests, and social classes with the unique benefits experienced with members of their same group.

The ways teachers design the classroom environment and plan instructional events play an important role in friendship selection, formation, and development. Epstein (1989) found that the design of the classroom context (physical, instructional, and social) affects patterns of interaction and friendship selection. When teachers assign students to particular tables or rows, place them in ability instructional groups, and select certain children for leadership roles, they are limiting or expanding opportunities for children to form and develop friendships. Teachers' behavior toward particular students, the ways they form instructional groups, and the decisions they make regarding classroom seating assignments can restrict or expand students' choices of friends (Epstein, 1989; Sheets, 1999).

Epstein (1989) further noted that physical proximity places students in a specific social context and defines the boundaries from which friends are chosen. Thus, the formations of friendship cliques, including opportunity for cross-racial friendships, are closely related to classroom characteristics and teaching practices. Additionally, variables such as class size, racial proportions, presence of different races in the same-ability instructional groups, integration of youngsters with diverse characteristics (e.g., race, ethnicity, language, gender, ability, socioeconomic status) at the same tables or seating areas, and participation in afterschool sport and recreational activities may affect the likelihood that students will form friendships among a diverse group of peers. Teacher decisions regarding physical proximity in the classroom are exemplified in Vignettes 5.1 and 5.2 describing classroom seating arrangements.

Vignette 5.1
Attention to Gender

Mr. Williams is a second-year third-grade teacher. His classroom has eighteen African American (eleven girls, seven boys) and two Mexican American children (boys). Student records indicated that David and Gustavo both spoke Spanish; however, Mr. Williams was unable to determine their levels of proficiency as English language learners. Knowing that children prefer same-race friendships and boys prefer boys as friends, he organized his classroom in a U-shape. David and Gustavo were assigned to the middle table in the back row (Table 3) with Jason and Tyree. The rest of the boys and girls were assigned to tables where there were at least two children of the same gender next to each other. He deliberately assigned Table 3 the responsibility for the outdoor play equipment the first week of school.

Vignette 5.2
Self-Selection

Ms. Stuart, a fourth-year teacher, works in an ethnically diverse urban high school with a majority of students from groups of color. She allows students to choose where to sit in her eleventh-grade U.S. History classes. Although most students sit in the same seats, they can change or move the individual desks to form groups. She determines the number of groups and often selects the concepts or topics under discussion for group work. Students self-select for group assignments, and there are no limitations to the number of students per group. Students receive two grades for group projects, an individual grade and a group grade. They are encouraged to work collaboratively.

Issues for Consideration

Teachers who use diversity as a factor when forming academic groups may inadvertently limit rather than advance cross-racial and cross-gender friendships. Friendship connections, by nature, are mutually selected constructions. Failure to provide an authentic social and academic context with explicit freedom to choose friends may ultimately deny students opportunity to form emotionally binding relationships. Rejected students may be ignored or forced into uncomfortable interactions rather than given opportunities to self-select groups during collaborative work and social activities.

Consider the teacher decisions in these vignettes. Mr. Williams' physical arrangement and classroom job assignments were purposeful. He wanted David and Gustavo to have each other as resources; however, he also wanted to give them multiple opportunities to interact with the other boys in the classroom. By placing them next to each other and in the center of the room, potential friends surrounded David and Gustavo. Ms. Stuart, on the other hand, did not assign seats. She allowed students to self-select working groups. Students received an individual and group grade for their group work. How did these teacher decisions increase students' social opportunities? What are the advantages and disadvantages of teacher assigned groups versus student self-selection to working groups?

Why does the location of a student's seat make a difference in the development of social skills?

District Policies. District and school policies, frequently beyond the control of classroom teachers, can also affect opportunities for social interactions in school classrooms, gyms, playgrounds, and lunchrooms. Consistent student separations may discourage the selection of certain individuals as friends. School districts may segregate students by socioeconomic status, ethnic groups, language skills, gender, or ability. Assignments to neighborhood schools, special education, gifted programs, honors classes, and second language learning classrooms isolate particular students. In many school districts neighborhood schools can range from high income to abject poverty. Sometimes students who are identified as having special needs are isolated in portables. Second language learners, advance placement students, and gifted students may be located in particular wings of the school or may be segregated in particular classrooms within schools. Multiple lunch and recess schedules, as well as the availability of bussing for after school activities, can also affect the availability of friendship choices for some students.

Student Cultural Displays

This section provides a brief review of the scholarship examining (a) gender preferences, (b) race and friendship choices, and (c) social isolation. This information may be helpful when applying the third pedagogical dimension in the teaching-learning process.

Gender Preferences

Gender appears to be one of the first dimensions of identity that young children label in self and others. As young children develop they establish rigid lines around gender roles, which include gender sorting in their selection of playmates and self-segregation on playgrounds. This same-gender social preference continues through middle childhood and into adolescence.

Research has shown that gender, regardless of race, plays a powerful role in the selection of dyadic peer friendships (Graham & Cohen, 1997; Hallinan & Teixeira, 1987a; Kistner, Metzler, Gatlin, & Risi, 1994). Graham, Cohen, and Zbikowski (1998) point out that (a) preferences for same-sex friends emerge in preschool, continue, and increase through childhood for African American and European American children; (b) nearly 90 percent of school-age children's friendships are of the same gender; (c) the small number of cross-gender friendships are less stable than same-race friendship selections; (d) girls' friendships are more intimate and exclusive (smaller friendship networks), and the same-race biases tend to be greater among girls than boys; (e) the play style of boys (e.g., large group play activities) tends to promote cross-race interactions; and (f) when children have opportunity for cross-race and cross-gender friendships, gender is generally a more important variable of mutual friendships than race.

Race and Friendship Choices

Numerous studies show that children express preferences toward same-race friends, with racial agreement stronger in adolescence than during early and middle childhood (Graham & Cohen, 1997; Kistner et al., 1994). In spite of racial preferences in friend choices, children can develop positive attitudes toward those who differ racially from themselves. Generally these relationships remain at the level of peer acceptance rather than friendships. Studies on the friendship selections of Native American Indian, Asian American, and Latino American children are limited. Research on cross-racial friendships often examines Black and White relationships. This section examines same-race friendship selection and maintenance.

Preschool and Early Elementary. Aboud's (1988) work shows that most 3- to 6-year-old African American children do not reject playmates who differ from them racially. However, around age 7 African American children form attachments to their own group and become pro-Black. They develop neutral attitudes rather than rejecting attitudes toward European American children but acquire negative attitudes toward Native American Indians, Asian Americans, and Latino Americans. Between the ages of 3 and 6, Native American Indian, Asian American, and Latino American children appear to exhibit the same early sequence of attitudes and behaviors as African American children. However, around age 7 they too prefer their own group, are neutral to European Americans, and are negative toward African Americans.

In research settings two-thirds of European American children between five and seven selected pictures of Asian American, African American, or Native American children as both bad and disliked and identified pictures of African American children as their least preferred playmates (Aboud, 1988). Some psychologists point out that studies of this nature are faulty because they do not take into account the children's interpretation of the word bad, nor do they prove that these preferences are transferable from the photo to individuals or to real play situations (Branch, 1999). However, in real-life play settings, most European American children at age 7 to 8 exhibit preference for other European American children as friends over children from other racial groups (Aboud, 1988).

Middle Elementary. Graham, Cohen, and Zbikowski (1998, p. 12) report that "Boys and girls of both races had more mutual friends of their same sex and race when they were older [age 10 to 12] than when they were younger [age 7 to 9]." As children grow older, they are likely to maintain same-race friendships. Same-race, rather than cross-race, friendships are more frequent at the elementary level. Both African American children and European American children are likely to select same-race peers as best friends (Hallinan & Smith, 1987). Although African American children (ages 10 to 14) do not select European American peers for best friends, they do show greater overall friendliness towards cross-race peers than do European Americans.

Junior High and High School. Students generally choose to self-segregate racially during adolescence. Branch (1999) points out that attendance in racially integrated public secondary schools has not necessarily increased adolescents' cross-racial friend-ships. He cautions that "the superficial mixing of adolescents in extracurricular school activities such as athletic teams and clubs should not be construed as a statement that there is racial harmony or . . . an openness to interracial friendships" (Branch, 1999, p. 333). Atwater (1996) adds, "merely attending an integrated school does not neces-sarily foster interracial friendships. A lot depends on the climate of learning in the classroom. When minority students are competing with Caucasian students, especially when many of the latter have more advanced skills and higher socioeconomic status, racial prejudice is increased on both sides" (p. 219). Vignette 5.3 illustrates the role of race in the selection of friendships and the importance of being aware of students' friendship needs (Sheets, 2004).

Vignette 5.3
Multiracial Friendships
The following study took place in an urban high school (approximately 1,200 students) with a majority student population of color (60.6%). A total of forty-two first generation (ninth to twelfth grade) multiracial students participated. Twenty-five had one parent from a racial group of color (Black or Asian) and one White parent. The parents of the other seventeen students had one Black parent and one from another racial group of color (Native American Indian, Asian American, or Latino American).

Students in this study felt that rejection was spread and transmitted from one small social clique to another as they tried to "fit in" various groups (Sheets, 2004). They described rude, judgmental, and intrusive attitudes and behaviors of peers from groups of color as well as the insensitive and racist actions of White peers. The frustration of constantly having to prove allegiance to a specific racial group and the inability of their close friends to shield them from incessant, racialized pressure often resulted in painful, inconsistent, short-lived friendships. Lecia (Black mother/White father) explains:

> Middle school was the worse. They came right out and asked you "What are you?" For a time I hung out with White friends because Black people were judgmental. But then after a while I went back to my Black friends because the White kids dumped me whenever they did things where I wasn't welcome. Black kids didn't want me to talk to White kids. They would say, "Do you think you're a White girl?" They'd pick on me constantly and make me feel self-conscious. Whites didn't want me either. Blacks were more accepting, but you had to be blacker than Black.

Melissa (Pilipina American mother/White father) adds:

> I was only in a White group for a short while. I tried so hard to belong. I had a right to belong; I'm part White. But it was happening right before my eyes. They would leave and not ask me to come. They would move and sit at a different table at lunch. I finally just went back to my Pilipino clique.

Issues for Consideration

This vignette describes how multiracial adolescents experienced making and keeping friends in middle school. Although these students indicated that they always knew they were of mixed heritage, they also reported that by age three or four they sensed that relatives, teachers, and peers perceived them as having a single racial and ethnic heritage of color. Their multiracial identity did not necessarily limit cross-racial relationships in the early grades; however, around fourth through twelfth grade, race became a factor in their friendship patterns. Multiracial children stated that they had to prove racial loyalty and project a single ethnic or racial heritage to make and keep friends. Attempts by multiracial students with a White heritage to forge intimate friendships with White peers occurred mostly during junior high; however, these relationships were intermittent, short lived, and characterized by rejection.

Students in this study felt that they had to resolve issues about self, teachers, and friendship expectations without assistance from the significant adults in their lives. One student stated, "teachers don't care if you're biracial, they just assume you're just Asian or Black" and "my parents don't know what I go through, they're not mixed." Why do you think most of these students repeatedly reported that teachers and parents were unaware of the social pressures and emotional stress they encountered in school on a daily basis? How can you make your classroom emotionally safe for multiracial children?

Social Isolation

Excessive peer rejection in childhood predicts later behavioral and emotional disturbances (Berndt, 1984; Dodge, 1989). Isolated, aggressive, or extremely passive children are "at risk as adults to be unemployed or underemployed, lack independence, be overly aggressive, or experience serious mental health problems" (Doll, 1996, p. 1). Along with issues in later life, other researchers point out that repeated problems with peers are major factors when decisions are made to place students in special educational programs for behaviorally and emotionally challenged children (Hollinger, 1987; Schonert-Reichl, 1993).

Some students may want to interact with their peers but choose to deliberately exclude themselves. They may find it difficult to tolerate large group social settings, may have limited social skills, or may have experienced repeated peer rejection. Often self-isolating students mask their discomfort and anxiety by appearing uninterested and aloof (Engfer, 1993). Researchers who study self-isolating children maintain that these children's solitary behavior may appear to be developmentally normal in early childhood but becomes increasingly atypical as they grow older (Asher & Renshaw, 1981; Coie, Belding, & Underwood, 1988).

Although teachers are able to identify students with extreme social issues, "it is differentiating the less strikingly rejected but still isolated child that challenges teachers" (Doll, 1996, p. 8). Another challenge teachers face is evaluating the source and responding appropriately to students' antisocial behavior because we know that this behavior is closely associated with peer rejection and the absence of quality friendships (Coie et al., 1988). Students who consistently isolate themselves or who display excessive aggression may require referral to a specialist.

Sometimes teachers inadvertently ignore the needs of isolated children and minimize the stress caused by constant peer harassment and rejection. Teachers who believe in forcing friendship patterns and peer acceptance, might say, "In this class we are all friends" to justify making instructional and social grouping decisions. Vignette 5.4 exemplifies the issue of isolation in the classroom and points out the value to students when friendship connections are supported.

Vignette 5.4
Merchant Teller
This event took place in an all-day kindergarten classroom (twenty-eight children) in a low-performing, high-poverty urban public school (Sheets, 1998b). Keith was one of four European American children (two males, two females). Seventeen children were Spanish speaking (eight males, nine females) and six were male Asian Americans (four Laotian, one Hmong, and one Vietnamese). Most of the children were second language learners and all received free or reduced lunch.

Every Friday, a 60-minute free-play period was scheduled to minimize the disruption caused by the school's pullout programs. (During this period, two groups [eight or nine children per group] of English language learners were pulled out back to back by the ESL specialist for 25-minute blocks each, one child went to the speech therapist for 25 minutes, and one attended a conflict prevention counseling session every other Friday for 30 minutes). The teacher used this weekly period to focus on specific social or academic goals for individual children or small groups. The incident took place during this time frame.

Keith, a 5-year-old European American male, had eleven older brothers and sisters between the ages of 14 and 27. Raised by his deaf grandfather, he generally played alone in silence. In the classroom he rarely initiated play and found it difficult to join existing playgroups. Keith's extreme shyness appeared to prevent him from interacting with children even when they joined him in his selected activity.

I believed that providing him with consistent and varied opportunities to choose to interact socially in nonthreatening ways would enhance Keith's social competency. A solution could include creating situations where children would naturally seek Keith out. I began by making Keith a desirable playmate by giving him things and jobs to attract his peers. Children would join him if they wanted to use the classroom's basket of new magic markers, a new puzzle, a new batch of homemade play dough, a pile of specially cut small pieces of multicolored construction paper, a page of stickers, or a box of Fruit Loops. He could choose a partner to take messages to the office, to the librarian, or to the lunchroom cook. He chose peers to help him pass out worksheets and to organize the science table.

Since all independent work and play groups were self-selected, I watched for optimal conditions that could potentially provide opportunity to ease his entry into group play or work experiences. One day a large mixed-gender group spontaneously created a game they called "Mall." Some children owned stores, some delivered goods, and others shopped. Blocks became loaves of bread at the bakery, green beads were peas at the grocery store, and play clothes were sold at the "Sears" store. Keith watched wistfully from his desk. He seemed to want to join. I quickly cut small stacks of white, red, green, and blue rectangles to represent money and joined Keith who was coloring alone at his desk. I explained the role of a merchant teller at a bank while we made a cardboard sign that read—M E R C H A N T   T E L L E R. I told him my friend was a merchant teller in a real bank. When we finished the sign, I said, "Keith, go tell them, *'I'm a merchant teller. If you need money, come to my bank.'*" I moved away from his table. He hesitated, then picked up the stacks of paper money and slowly walked to the "Mall." I was not able to hear the negotiations; however, within minutes, a beaming Keith had a spot in the "Mall" (Sheets, 1998b).

Issues for Consideration

Keith was progressing academically, and his art projects were detailed, creative, and colorful. His work was accurate and neat; however, since he spent a lot of time watching other children, he usually had difficulty completing his assignments. Although children did not appear to purposefully reject Keith, he was ignored. Rarely was he invited to join small work or play groups. He did not seem to possess the social ability to freely initiate or join small groups on his own. He worked and played alone. He was a silent member of the group when other children joined him at his table or at his selected activity. Children were beginning to perceive him as different, and he was beginning to develop a reputation as a loner. Miguel, his deskmate, once asked me if Keith could talk. Although he was one of four European American children, the two girls played together or joined other cross-ethnic groups and the other European American male was part of the most popular small group of boys who were so involved in their own social events they rarely noticed Keith's solitude.

Concerned about Keith's social reticence, apparent withdrawal, and potential for becoming the subject of peer rejection, the teacher contacted his mother the second week of school. She carefully explained that he was doing well academically but seemed to avoid playing with others and rarely talked. Keith's mother described his family background explaining that she worked full time and was involved in the various extracurricular activities of the other children. She did not seem to be overly concerned about Keith's social development. His mother felt his "quiet nature" was part of his personality and was probably influenced by his strong attachment to his deaf grandfather and placement in the family. She explained that he did not have neighbors to play with and that his siblings' interests did not generally include Keith.

Throughout the year, Keith was consistently provided nonthreatening social experiences, designed instructional activities, classroom discussions with friend-ship themes, and encouragement for his efforts to set and achieve small step interpersonal objectives. Since Miguel expressed concern about Keith, pairings of these two children were arranged as often as possible. As the school year evolved,

Keith's personality remained intact. He continued to be quiet and shy; however, his tendency to withdraw socially decreased. He occasionally joined small social playgroups, joined Miguel in play activities, interacted and chatted in small workgroups, and showed pleasure when others joined him.

Consider the following. In what ways did teacher intervention encourage (or discourage) peer acceptance and friendship connections? How might Keith's pattern of isolation express itself in middle grades, junior high, or high school, if the social concerns are not addressed in elementary school? What can teachers do to minimize students' social isolation?

Classroom Applications

Teachers can play a significant role in helping children develop the social skills necessary to achieve peer acceptance and to initiate and sustain friendships. Well-designed, appropriate interventions can help students adapt to social interactions in the classroom and in other school settings. The following suggestions are designed to promote positive social encounters. A way to assess students' social competence is to observe their interactions with others. The degree to which they are liked or disliked and their ability to make and keep friends can also serve as a barometer of social adjustment. Changes or lack of change in students' behavior can assist you in planning and modifying particular intervention strategies.

Acknowledging the Importance of Friendship

Use curriculum to acknowledge the importance of friendship to the social and cognitive development of students.

1. Discuss the role of friends and what friendship means. Make a list of what friends do for each other. Share stories, read books, listen to music, and view videos with friendship themes. Have children draw themselves playing with friends or have them write essays and stories of incidents where friends' intervention and support helped them. Explore the continuum of enemy/bully to friend and discuss the intensity of the role, purpose, and characteristics of these concepts in terms of personal label and behavior toward different individuals and groups.
2. Explore feelings associated with lack of friendship or with friendship loss. Discuss how it feels when personal friendship advances are rejected or when issues such as death, family moves, foster home changes, parental instructions, or disagreements, remove friends' proximity. Discuss how it feels not to have a close friend. Create going-away friendship books with pictures and autograph books with messages to give to students who are moving.
3. Examine friendship as an emotional and cognitive resource. Describe ways friends provide comfort and share resources. Prepare and present skits and role-plays in which friends offer hugs, have fun together, translate from one language to

another, help with seatwork or homework, explain school norms, and involve others in school activities or functions.

Recognizing Harmful Behavior and Intervening

Recognize when discriminatory or exclusionary behavior is harmful and intervene by providing positive models for forging friendships.

1. Observe how the diverse skills (motor, artistic, academic, musical) and attributes (ethnicity, language, race, socioeconomic status, class, and gender) that students possess influence their ability to select, make, and maintain friendships. Become aware of your students' social behavior, identify students without friends, and plan inclusive projects and activities. Balance racial, ethnic, socioeconomic and gender segregation by providing opportunities for diverse friendships to develop while supporting students' self selection of friends.
2. Intervene and stop harassing or bullying attitudes and behaviors. Openly discuss how actions of this nature, that are especially damaging to the victim, also hurt the perpetuator and witnesses as well. Encourage and expect all students to take an active role in stopping verbal insults and harmful actions toward others.
3. Give students multiple opportunities to practice choosing and maintaining friendships. Allow students to choose where to sit. Provide numerous classroom cooperative and collaborative group activities and allow students to self-select friends for these learning events.
4. Model inclusive social behaviors and develop social interventions. Adopt a classroom policy that provides all students with unlimited social access. Use puppets, stuffed animals, skits, videos, and interviews to model appropriate actions students might take to include others. Discourage expulsion from a group as a solution to group conflict by teaching and encouraging negotiation skills. Discuss ways for students to learn how to expect responsible group participation and how to stand up for themselves. Purchase games, books, and materials that encourage sharing, empathy, cooperation, and collaboration.

Conclusion

Parish (1996), in examining the basic principles of friendship, reminds us that "friends are the ultimate form of social security" and "a friend is someone who helps you to like yourself." Most schools implicitly promote positive peer relationships and expect cross-racial and cross-gender relationships to develop; however, often they do not strongly emphasize friendship development. Yet the fundamental role of friendship in the cultural, social, and academic lives of students suggests that teachers should acknowledge the benefits of friendship and consider adopting an up-front, proactive curricular approach to foster its development.

RECOMMENDED READINGS

Bukowski, W. M., Newcomb, A. F., & Hartup, W. W. (1996). Friendship and its significance in childhood and adolescence: Introduction and comment. In W. M. Bukowski, A. F. Newcomb, & W. W. Hartup (Eds.), *The company they keep: Friendship in childhood and adolescence* (pp. 1–15). New York: Cambridge University Press.

Hartup, W. W. (1996). The company they keep: Friendships and their developmental significance. *Child Development, 67,* 1–13.

Sheets, R. H. (2004). Multiracial adolescent perception: The role of friendship in identification and identity formation. In K. Wallace (Ed.), *Working with mixed heritage students: Perspectives on research and practice* (pp. 139–154). Greenwich, CT: Information Age Publishing.

CHAPTER

6

Culturally Safe Classroom Context: Advancing Self-Regulated Learning

When people experience what is called "culture shock" on going from one society to another, it is probably not the obvious differences which cause the greatest sense of personal disorganization. In other words, it is probably not the differences in physical landscape, climate, religion, dress, or even food which brings about the strongest sense of confusion. Most often it is the assumptions underlying everyday life, shared by members of a society by virtue of constant interaction from birth, assumptions which are so much a part of the culture that they are not even consciously held.

—Watson, 1974, p. 29

Anthropologists point out that everyday life has culturally determined patterns of behavior, which for the most part are outside one's conscious awareness, called the **invisible culture** (Gumperz, 1977; Hall, 1959; Watson, 1974). Because schooling is part of children's everyday life, it is important to understand how children with culturally diverse socialization experiences interpret and respond to the invisible culture present in their classrooms. Teachers need to be aware of what they can do to create classroom environments that minimize cultural disorganization for diverse students. The purpose of this chapter is to help teachers use the classroom context—the unnoticed norms, the specialized language codes, the written and unwritten rules, and the daily, face-to-face happenings experienced through the social interactions between teachers and students and among students—as an essential aspect of the school curriculum to support learning. This discussion focuses on how the classroom context is influenced by the socialization process of teachers and students and on how the classroom climate is dependent on their ability to control their behaviors.

These issues are examined through the fourth diversity pedagogical dimension, culturally safe classroom context, and its corresponding student cultural display, self regulated behavior. The first part introduces the fourth diversity pedagogical dimension, defines the terms (culturally safe classroom context and self-regulated behavior), and describes teacher pedagogical behaviors and student cultural displays. The second and third parts provide background information needed to apply this dimension's teacher pedagogical behaviors (classroom management and discipline and creating culturally comfortable classrooms) and student cultural displays (self-regulated learning and culture and self-regulation) in the classroom. The chapter concludes with suggestions for practice.

Diversity Pedagogy Dimension 4: Culturally Safe Classroom Context/Self-Regulated Learning

This dimension focuses on the role the classroom context plays in both the formal and informal curriculum and acknowledges that students, as well as teachers, are active participants in the teaching-learning process. It addresses how social relationships in classrooms are culturally organized and often controlled by teachers. Table 6.1 describes the terms *culturally safe classroom context* and *self-regulated learning*, identifies some of the pedagogical strategies (teaching behaviors) needed to apply this dimension in classrooms, and describes how students might display signs of cultural fidelity, social competency, and evidence of self-control.

TABLE 6.1 Diversity Pedagogy Dimension 4: Culturally Safe Classroom Context/ Self-Regulated Learning

Definition of Dimensional Elements	
Culturally Safe Classroom Context: A classroom environment where students feel emotionally secure; psychologically consistent; and culturally, linguistically, academically, socially, and physically comfortable, both as individuals and as members of the groups to which they belong.	*Self-Regulated Learning:* Demonstrations of the self initiated, managed, directed, contained, and restrained conduct required to meet self-determined personal and group goals, to adapt to established classroom standards, and to maintain self-dignity.
Teacher Pedagogical Behaviors	**Student Cultural Displays**
Creates culturally inclusive, emotionally secure, academically rich, and comfortable spaces where students develop ownership and responsibility for their cultural, academic, and social behavior. • Identifies the cultural nuances present in student behavior and adapts contextual elements accordingly. • Observes how the physical and emotional classroom context is experienced by diverse students and makes necessary changes.	Signs of acquiring knowledge and developing skills to self-monitor, direct, guide, and control cultural, social, and academic behavior in the classroom where space and resources are shared. • Sets and meets personal conduct standards and classroom norms while maintaining ethnic integrity. • Adapts individual and group behavior to situational and contextual classroom events and conditions and sustains cultural norms.

Teacher Pedagogical Behaviors	Student Cultural Displays
• Promotes self-control in classroom management decisions and disciplinary actions. • Is aware of personal style of authority. • Views self equally responsible for classroom disruptions and order. • Establishes culturally balanced participation structures.	• Takes responsibility for personal and group actions and respects teacher behavioral expectations. • Monitors behavior and sets goals. • Takes responsibility for own actions and responds responsibly with classroom rules. • Understands and cooperates with teacher academic expectations.
Recognizes, acknowledges, and responds to students' culturally diverse displays of knowledge, initiative, perseverance, and competence as individuals and as members of particular groups. • Observes and identifies diverse patterns of competency and acknowledges cultural factors when judging behavior as appropriate or inappropriate. • Allows students to make and to learn from mistakes. • Is aware of the students' social, cultural, and academic classroom interactions. • Recognizes and evaluates group achievement as well as individual efforts. • Acquires classroom management skills and instructional strategies that help students practice self-control. • Understands the reciprocal teacher-student interpersonal process involved when making disciplinary decisions.	Manifestations of behaviors indicating ability to internalize and self-monitor personal, cultural, social, and academic decisions to advance cultural, academic, and social growth. • Uses particular strategies and resources to compare individual and group performance with expected social and academic outcomes. • Is able to take risks and learn from mistakes. • Negotiates effectively and handles obstacles in diverse cultural situations. • Anticipates competence and monitors social and academic choices. • Directs motivational elements, examines why one acts in certain ways, and engages in self-evaluation. • Controls feelings generated by behavioral choices, balances conflicting goals, and evaluates consequences to choices.

Teacher Pedagogical Behaviors

The choices teachers make to guide and control their actions in classrooms are influenced by their socialization process and are, in part, based on their perceptions of the anticipated actions of others. One can reason that differences in student-teacher socialization processes inevitably generate misunderstandings, misperceptions, misjudgments, and misbehaviors (actions judged inappropriate) for both teachers and students. Aspects of these cultural mismatches in classrooms might even produce discomfort, anxiety, or conflict for both teachers and students. In spite of these phenomena, two assumptions can be made: (a) All teachers can learn to create safe, culturally comfortable classroom contexts that support learning and provide opportunity for students to evaluate, direct, and control their behavior; and (b) high achievement outcomes and acceptable social standards are not sacrificed when creating culturally inclusive environments. This section discusses classroom management and discipline and creating culturally comfortable classrooms.

Classroom Management and Discipline

As they approach student teaching field experiences, some teacher candidates express anxiety about their ability to manage a classroom, especially when faced with the prospect of teaching students who differ from them racially, ethnically, and economically. Sometimes teacher candidates and newly credentialed teachers are apprehensive about the types of disciplinary problems they might encounter in public schools and are uncertain about appropriate responses to these issues. Although the former requires classroom management expertise, the latter involves discipline. These are two distinct constructs, each requiring different knowledge, abilities, and skills.

The capacity of teachers to conceptualize classroom management and discipline as two distinct areas of pedagogical knowledge and skill can influence teachers' potential to create culturally comfortable, safe classroom contexts that support learning, decrease resistance, and promote the development of committed compliance. Blurring these two constructs tends to (a) minimize the role of culture in schooling; (b) disregard the power, vulnerability, and status of students as active, resistant, or compliant participants in the teaching-learning process; (c) reduce the issues of control in classrooms to the procedural, technical skills of teachers; and (d) ignore how teacher-student interpersonal interactions influence classroom behavior. Briefly, **classroom management** involves the personal technical skills and management proficiencies teachers acquire to advance the teaching-learning process. **Discipline** (or **disciplinary action**) is located in the interpersonal interactions between students and teachers and involves self-regulatory decisions of either or both to ignore, comply, or acquiesce to specific behavioral demands.

Classroom Management Skills. Classroom management techniques help teachers organize, direct, and sustain a classroom environment that advances the teaching-learning process. Doyle (1986), views classroom management as the "actions and strategies teachers use to solve the problem of order in classrooms" (p. 397). Thus, organizational skills and knowledge of what happens or what can happen in classrooms (with children present) help teachers manage their time, distribute available resources, arrange classroom space, design instructional activities, and anticipate potential misbehavior. Understanding classroom management, as a concept, involves both **declarative** (i.e., goals, rules) and **procedural** (i.e., strategies, techniques) knowledge. Teachers acquire classroom management knowledge in settings without children, such as teacher preparation courses, professional development sessions, and faculty rooms, as well as through observation and experiences in actual classrooms. Teachers often identify explicit goals and develop organizational techniques in the area of classroom management that they believe will prevent or minimize possible classroom disruptions. As they identify and establish their management styles, teachers also become conscious of their personal goals, behaviors, and skills. Two examples of teacher goals and attendant organizational techniques are presented in Table 6.2.

Students do not have to be present when teachers make conscious decisions to establish a goal or activate a particular classroom management skill. Teachers can use declarative and procedural knowledge without interacting with students. At the end of

TABLE 6.2   Teacher Classroom Management Goals and Organizational Techniques

Teacher Goals	Organizational Techniques
To acknowledge students' cultural, linguistic, academic, social, and developmental needs when facilitating learning events.	• Adapt lesson plans, instructional strategies, and instructional resources to meet the needs of linguistically and culturally diverse students. • Anticipate and develop ways to connect lesson content with students' prior knowledge. • Provide a balance of instructional strategies to meet students' cognitive preferences. • Schedule the sequence of classroom events and time given to particular activities to meet students' developmental needs.
To use physical resources to accommodate student's individual and group needs, ability differences, linguistic skills and friendship choices.	• Organize the classroom physically in ways that provide multiple opportunities for students to select to work and communicate with others of the same race, ethnic, linguistic, and gender groups, as well as diverse groups. • Provide small group collaborative work and resource areas. • Create large group community building spaces. • Anticipate how the room's physical arrangement affects movement patterns, access to shared materials, and opportunities to develop interpersonal relationships.

the day teachers can change the classroom's seating arrangement, duplicate materials, prepare for an art project, or decide what rule changes need to be made to improve order. This teacher behavior, although deliberate, is anticipatory and preventive in nature, not interpersonal.

Although classroom life is extremely complex, teachers develop an understanding of how to minimize potential classroom distractions. They become aware of how their decisions meet personal needs and of how their choices affect individual students, groups of students, and the classroom as a whole. The ways teachers (a) exercise their authority; (b) respond to student misbehavior; (c) organize interpersonal relationships between themselves and students and among students; and (d) determine the emotional, social, and academic climate of the classroom contributes significantly to the ways students experience classroom life and accept responsibility for their behavior. The development and implementation of classroom rules is a common strategy used by teachers.

Establishing Classroom Rules.   A basic objective of classroom management is to create a setting that sustains a culturally safe, friendly, fair, and consistent classroom environment. Classroom rules promote this goal by encouraging certain behaviors and preventing others. Three factors contribute significantly to the classroom tone set by rules: (a) the process by which rules are developed, (b) the manner in which they are expressed, and (c) the method used to enforce or reinforce them.

Fixed, imposed rules presented to students often support an authoritarian role for the teacher. Involvement in the rule-making process, even if only to the extent of discussing and adopting teacher-derived rules, gives students a vested interest in their classroom community. It also provides a starting point for building a collaborative social environment.

In most classrooms, rules addressing issues of safety, both physical and emotional, are generally non-negotiable. Rules concerning hitting, inappropriate touching, or name calling must be addressed. Yet even safety rules contain ideas that can be expressed either positively or negatively, depending upon the desired classroom tone. "In our room we respect each other's bodies" and "no hitting allowed," or "don't touch inappropriately" are versions of the same rule, expressed in the first instance as a goal and in the other two as boundaries. In either case, it remains the teacher's responsibility to stop unsafe, unwanted behavior when it does occur. Rules that promote social harmony and care of materials vary more in content, expression, and implementation. This includes rules that involve student-student conflict and those that define sharing space or materials, turn taking, or room cleanup.

Students' developmental and cultural need to preserve a sense of personal welfare is also important to consider when establishing and enforcing classroom rules. Sharing is not useful to 5-year-olds when there is only one basket of magic markers and everyone wants to use them; listening and waiting for a turn may seem irrelevant to most 12-year-olds who have something important to say; for 16 year-olds, being needed by a best friend may require being late for class. Familiarity with rules does not guarantee that students understand and agree with their function or that they are able to generalize from one application of the rule to another. "You know we don't run in the classroom" has no meaning the moment a student decides to chase a peer or "We don't speak Spanish in our classroom" is irrelevant to students who might distinguish between academic, social, and cultural responses to this directive. Likewise, high school students who choose to be in the hall without permission easily disregard the hall pass requirement.

The ability to recite a rule does not guarantee compliance in all possible situations, and enforcement of rules may not generate the desired result. Knowing that one can be suspended if caught "cutting" class in junior high and high school makes little difference when the choice is made to go with friends to a nearby fast food restaurant during fifth period. Likewise, time-out, widely perceived to be an effective disciplinary action for routine misbehavior, might not be the solution for repeated infractions. This short-term solution does not model, coach, or reinforce positive social skills. Further, it fails to address possible cultural, racial, or economic factors in both the teacher's expectations and the students' resistance. Additionally, sometimes teachers forget and the student is punished for longer periods of time than originally intended.

Successful teachers understand that punitive actions such as public chastisement, exclusion from the group, and removal from the classroom accentuate the imbalance of power between teacher and student and may be in opposition to cultural disciplinary norms. The more equitable goal is to help students develop the self-discipline necessary for being respectful, responsible, and considerate individuals. All teachers face situations in which students are uncooperative, angry, moody, or manipulative. *It does not benefit students when teachers make excuses for disruptive students or attribute misbehavior to cultural differences, upbringing styles, or poverty issues.* Defining and creating classroom environments needed to minimize disruptive and uncooperative behavior is more challenging. Reductions in the occurrence of conflict in culturally receptive classrooms requires teachers to consciously practice the following:

1. Establish positive interpersonal relationships with students. Understand how personal value orientations, communication styles, and motivational systems influence the way one thinks and responds. Acknowledge how cultural knowledge affects one's ability to relate to diverse students. Identify personal behaviors that provoke recurring patterns of student resistance.
2. Acknowledge the teacher role in conflict. Sometimes teachers regard a continuing student-teacher conflict as the child's problem, rather than the product of the student-teacher interaction. Understand why conflict occurs and what conditions exacerbate it. Be cognizant of the criteria used to judge behavior as inappropriate.
3. Understand the reciprocal nature of disciplinary decisions. Expect appropriate behavior from all students and believe that you possess skills, knowledge, and ability to sustain a safe, culturally inclusive classroom context. Realize that the way you treat students may influence how they respond to you.
4. Acquire knowledge of different cultural groups to recognize the ways in which diverse students display their interpretation of rules and why they choose to comply, adapt, ignore, or resist. Distinguish between misbehavior and variations present in diverse cultural codes of etiquette, communication styles, and responses to conflict. Use incentives and accountabilities that are congruent with what individual students and groups of students expect and value. Learn how different ethnic groups sanction conduct and reward accomplishments.
5. Avoid overpersonalizing students' noncompliance.
6. Treat all students equitably, fairly, and honestly rather than equally, the same, or underhandedly. Tell students why you handle Mia's outbursts differently, why Samuel can choose to sit at his table and listen rather than join the group, or why their cooperation is appreciated when the principal visits.

The acquisition of classroom management skills helps teachers identify their management styles. It may also increase their understandings of the behavioral issues in the classroom. Potentially, this information raises consciousness of how teacher thinking and personal behavior affects learning events. Therefore, processing knowledge on the ways to organize and manage one's behavior, learning the elements needed to create a culturally safe classroom environment, and exploring ways to establish productive social relationships with students is significant.

Discipline. Classroom disciplinary solutions are located in the interpersonal interactions among students and teachers and in the expectation that everyone involved controls his or her behavior. When teachers decide to enforce a classroom management technique, such as requiring students to follow a classroom rule, they initiate an interpersonal interaction requiring discipline (self-initiated or other imposed) for both the teacher and the student. These disciplinary actions take place when teachers judge students' behavior inappropriate. Teachers may demand immediate submission, expect conformity, or anticipate obedience. Students' willingness or unwillingness to comply with teacher requests or commands to obey may require teachers to reward student compliance, punish misbehavior, or overlook students' refusal to obey. Conflict can occur when students refuse to comply with a request or command that they perceive (a) does not meet their immediate needs, (b) clashes with their immediate interests, beliefs, or goals, and (c) cannot be achieved simultaneously with their own personal goals within the given situation.

Diversity elements such as ethnicity, culture, language, gender, religion, socioeconomic status, sexual orientation, or individuality generally contribute to the multiple causes of conflict. To minimize conflict in classrooms where teachers and students have dissimilar goals, behavioral patterns, and background experiences requires that teachers be consciously aware of why and how they choose to make disciplinary decisions.

Sometimes teachers make disciplinary choices to meet their own needs and fulfill institutional requirements rather than to accommodate students. Judgments made to advance, continue, or accelerate the pace of the lesson might at times be a disservice to some students. Singling out students and calling attention to them in a public way, such as disciplining them from across the room rather than privately at their work area, might be problematic for some students. Since it is generally quicker and seemingly successful, teachers may decide to train students to conform by using rewards and punishments rather than taking the necessary time to teach them strategies for self-control. They may comply with administrative expectations and directives to maintain silent, oppressive classrooms, where learning may or may not take place. Novice teachers might respond to the expectations of senior teachers.

Although teachers determine when, how, and who to discipline, it is the students' decisions to act or not to act in accordance with the teachers' commands or requests. Both are meeting their personal goals. Student noncompliance may be influenced by their (a) perception of what they think is fair, (b) judgment of teacher competence and consistency, and (c) feelings toward the teacher.

Some teachers possess extensive classroom management knowledge and understand the importance of establishing interpersonal relationships with students, yet they may not be able to **conditionalize** (application in a specific situation and context) or successfully demonstrate this knowledge in classrooms with students present. Teacher candidates who earn *A*s in classroom management courses may have difficulties controlling a classroom full of students, or a scholar in classroom management may not succeed in managing a fourth-grade classroom in an inner city setting. Novice teachers may have the desire but not know how to relate effectively with students who are different ethnically. The interpersonal processes among teachers and students can neither be managed nor controlled. Developed interpersonal skills, rather than classroom management techniques, often determine how teachers and students relate responsibly to each other in actual classroom settings.

Creating Culturally Comfortable Classrooms

Teachers serve as significant caregivers and classrooms are places where students experience a specific cultural, linguistic, social, and academic life. The classroom context is a resource for students to develop self-regulation (self-control) in ways that support school learning. The teacher's ability to create a **culturally safe classroom context** (a classroom environment where students feel secure and comfortable culturally, linguistically, academically, emotionally, and physically) provides more students with greater opportunities to learn. In these classrooms, students are more likely to maintain ethnic integrity while developing ownership and responsibility for their cultural, social, and academic behavior.

Although teachers cannot always influence the overall cultural, social, physical, academic, and psychological conditions of the entire school environment, they can determine the academic conditions, emotional tone, social nature, cultural inclusiveness, and physical appeal in the classrooms they share with children. Teachers can provide students with multiple opportunities to practice self-regulated learning. They can create the optimal conditions for learning for all students including those from ethnic groups of color.

Several factors present in the classroom context improve instruction and learning. Some of these are discussed in other chapters in this text (see discussion on the role of peer relationships in Chapter 5, language development in Chapter 7, culturally inclusive instructional resources in Chapter 8, and teaching strategies in Chapter 9). This section of the chapter examines how teachers exercise authority over students through the control of the social relationships or classroom interaction patterns that Philips (1972) calls participation structures. The basic assumptions guiding this section include the following:

1. The degrees to which students gain new knowledge depend on the nature of the social relationships between teacher and student and between student and student.
2. Communication in the classroom, including tone, volume, rhythm, style, who decides who speaks when and the ways of speaking to each other is (a) culturally influenced; (b) controlled by a specialized, often invisible code; and (c) generally responsible for many of the academic and social problems linguistically and culturally diverse students face in schools.
3. Language (spoken and silent) is an important part of the cultural history and ethnic identity of the speaker.

Participation Structures. In classrooms, teachers have the power to organize classroom events. One of the ways they exercise this authority is by controlling classroom interactions. This includes the ways (a) teachers use language to teach, (b) students demonstrate what they know, (c) students interact with teachers, and (d) students are allowed to interact with each other. Since classroom interactions involve some form of communication, language is fundamental to all interactions—social and academic.

Sociolinguistic studies show that "the language of the classroom is a specialized code that students need to master" (Mehan, 1987, p. 124). The culturally determined ways in which this code is constructed, enforced, and performed by teachers is influenced by the way students interpret and respond to these context-specific, often invisible codes. The ways teachers control students (negatively and positively) and the ways students resolve this domination vary cross-culturally. Teachers' and students' willingness to adapt and to accommodate diverse classroom communication codes often minimizes conflict.

Cazden (1988) points out that the classroom is the only social context where a single individual—the teacher—is in control of everyone's speaking rights. Along with controlling speaking rights in the classroom, teachers determine (a) the function of the language by deciding how it is to be used in academic, personal, and social situations; (b) the linguistic competency of the child by approving or disapproving language usage, grammar, pronunciation, variations, and status; and (c) the cultural communication norms that generally involve incorporating the mainstream language norms from the European American ethnic group.

Researchers identify differences in home and school interactions that create conditions in classrooms that are unfamiliar and threatening to some students from diverse ethnic groups of color (Cazden, 1988; Philips, 1972; Taylor, 1990). For example, differences in communication are expressed in a variety of ways, including gestures, silence, pronunciation, vocabulary, bilingualism, style, tone, and volume of voice. Taylor (1990) maintains that most classroom talk rules are based on mainstream cultural communication norms. He states that teacher-established participation and communication structures in the classroom, such as rules of when and how to speak, listen, and take turns, often increase the type of talk behavior that teachers consider unacceptable. Some of the ways students' communication may be considered unacceptable include

1. Seeking help at a time considered inappropriate by the teacher.
2. Speaking when not acknowledged by the teacher or when expected to be quiet.
3. Responding in a voice that is too soft or too loud.
4. Showing emotion during teacher-student or student-student disagreements.
5. Challenging the teacher's perception of a disciplinary event.
6. Interrupting the teacher or other students.
7. Refusing to participate orally.
8. Choosing to socialize in class without permission.
9. Speaking in a teacher restricted language.

Students also respond to teachers' communication styles. Consider how students may react when teachers choose to yell. Some students may be able to ignore it, others might personalize this behavior even when it is not directed at them, and still others might find it extremely offensive. In a study examining the causes of disciplinary actions on the high school level, African American, European American, and Mexican American high school students easily dismissed and ignored teacher yelling, especially when it was not directed at them (Sheets, 1995b). European American students depersonalized this behavior and saw it as a teacher characteristic, such as being a control freak or, as a temporary problem, such as having a bad day. However, Pilipino American adolescents personalized this behavior and found it offensive, even when it was not directed at them. They commented, "Our parents don't yell; when we're in trouble we get the silent treatment," and "You yell at dogs, not people." In one instance, a teacher appeared perplexed when a Pilipino American male student abruptly walked out of class while she was yelling at an African American male student.

Differences between the communication patterns of African American students and those commonly used in schools are sometimes problematic. Gay (1981) explains that the communication habits of African American children reflect socialization in an oral tradition where emphasis is placed on verbal dexterity and the use of words as power devices. A communication behavior, call-response, used by African American students may create teacher-student disagreements. The call-response involves an active and spontaneous verbal and nonverbal interchange between the speaker and listener. African American students might inadvertently or purposefully use the call-response, rather than raise their hand and wait for teachers to acknowledge them before speaking. Students' inability or unwillingness to **privatize** (not use in public) this cultural form of communication may be perceived by teachers as rude and disrespectful because they violate their classroom participation protocols.

Kochman (1981) adds that African Americans and European Americans use different types of arguments. African Americans use one type of argument to state their point of view, to explain a difference of opinion, or to explain their position. They use a second type of argument to express hostility and anger. Although both appear to be animated, emotional, and passionate, the latter type is more forceful and used only when African American students are actually angry. By comparison, European American children use argument (an emotional and passionate voice) only when angry. Their communication with teachers, preceding argument, is characterized by speaking in a calm, low-key conciliatory style. They use what students refer to as a kissing-up approach to plead their case and to explain the situation. These differences in expressive communication modes might lead teachers to view African Americans as negative, confrontational, and intransigent when, in fact, they are presenting their position and attempting to persuade. Sheets (1995b) also found that African American students used silence to keep anger from escalating. This communication style took place after the argumentative stage indicating anger and hostility. Some teachers may erroneously interpret this form of student behavior (silence) as a type of compliance.

Ideally, teachers provide a secure classroom context that supports learning, safety, enjoyment, harmony, fairness, ownership, and responsibility for each student, various groups of students, and all students collectively. The teacher creates a sense of community in classrooms that are culturally comfortable for everyone. Unfortunately, for some students, the classroom is neither pleasant nor comfortable. Although children enter school with adequate resources—language abilities, knowledge in progress, emerging self-regulation, established concepts of reality, ideals of conduct, and cultural competencies learned in their homes and practiced in their communities—some teachers may not be able to provide some students with a learning environment that responds to their ethnic identity, linguistic skills, and cultural backgrounds. The result is a cultural mismatch or **cultural discontinuity** (differences in language, experiences, values, lifestyles, and practices between the school culture and the home culture that often produce stress, conflict, and cognitive dissonance) between teacher and students.

Although some may believe that students should conform to existing school standards, others contend that some students might not benefit from schooling designed to indoctrinate them with the skills and behaviors valued by the dominate culture, such as competition, individualism, monolingualism, and assimilation (Boykin, 1986; Hurn, 1993). Teachers must be aware that although some students accept and comply to mainstream cultural patterns present in classrooms, others may chose to reject or challenge teachers' efforts. This type of self-regulation may interfere with teachers' potential to form nurturing, interpersonal relationships with some students. These student behaviors are likely to disenfranchise students and put them academically and socially at risk.

Successful teachers acquire knowledge of the cultural heritage of the students in their classrooms. They exhibit the observational skills needed to adapt the learning context to accommodate students' cultural preferences. These teachers understand that (a) children have learned skills, behaviors, and norms to function effectively in their home and community environment; (b) students enter school with a perception of self as special, knowledgeable, skilled, and competent; and (c) as teachers, they are significant others in the lives of the students they teach. Therefore, when students in their classrooms choose to withdraw, resist, or act in ways that limit their engagement in the teaching-learning process, they first examine their role in the conflict and then analyze environmental factors that may promote stress. Most importantly, they are conscious of classroom behaviors that may place students at risk.

Student Cultural Displays

Children are constantly required to make decisions to adapt to classroom life while simultaneously attempting to maintain cultural and psychological consistency. Erikson and Mohott (1982, p. 139) explain, "what one has to know in order to act appropriately as a member of a given group includes not only knowing what to do oneself, but also how to anticipate and judge the actions of others." Children use their cultural knowledge to determine which behavior and communication styles to use in classrooms. Children use their cultural knowledge cognitively to help them (a) adapt behavior to the school's cultural norms; (b) appraise the cultural appropriateness of their behavior in classroom settings; (c) evaluate and respond to peer's behaviors; and (d) judge teacher's attitudes and expectations against their cultural standards, values, and attitudes. The decisions students make to guide and control their actions are influenced by their socialization process and are, in part, based on their perceptions of the anticipated teacher and peer actions. To help recognize and respond to student cultural displays associated with the fourth diversity pedagogy dimension (self-regulated behavior), this section provides brief descriptions and background information on self-regulation and the cultural influences affecting self-control.

Self-Regulated Learning

Drawing from well-known psychological theories such as operant conditioning, social cognition, and constructivism, scholarship on self-regulated learning emerged in the late 1970s and early 1980s. Table 6.3 provides brief descriptions and identifies well-known theorists in the field.

Advocates of self-regulated learning maintain that children's perception of self and their capacity to apply self-regulatory strategies to themselves, such as the ability to control, adapt, and adjust their behavior to meet situational and contextual demands, are critical factors in understanding their subsequent social and academic success in school (Zimmerman, 1995; Zimmerman & Schunk, 2001). In this section, scholarship describing how self-regulation develops in early childhood, middle childhood, and adolescence is followed by the role culture and socialization play in this developmental process.

TABLE 6.3 Operant Conditioning, Social Cognition, and Constructivism

Theory	Prominent Theorists	Description
Operant Conditioning	Thorndike (1910) Watson (1913) Skinner (1979)	Operant conditioning (also known as behavior modification) is a type of associative learning used in clinical and school settings. In classrooms, it is used to train students through rewards and punishments or to teach them in programmed, repetitive, scripted programs. Undesired behaviors are controlled by discomfort or chastisement whereas acceptable behaviors are reinforced through satisfaction and incentives.
Social Cognition	Bandura (1986)	Social cognition or social learning theory emphasizes the importance of observing the behavior, attitudes, and emotional reactions of others in order to organize, rehearse, and practice the modeled behavior. Broadly speaking, social cognition studies the mental processes that shape social perception, social judgment, and social influence.
Constructivism	Bruner (1986) Lave (1988) Rogoff (1990) Vygotsky (1978)	Psychologists aligned with constructivism maintain that learning is an active process where learners construct new meanings based on their current and past knowledge. They use these new understandings to make decisions. Instruction is structured, from easy to difficult, so new learning can be easily gained.

Early Childhood. Children as young as 12 and 18 months develop self-control (self-regulation) to initiate, maintain, and cease behaviors to comply (or not comply) with adult requests and commands. A 1-year-old uses self-regulatory behaviors to sit willingly in a stroller during mall excursions with her Auntie and also to refuse to do so with her parents. By age 2 children are able to delay on request and at age 3 can self-regulate to meet changing situational demands. Four-year-olds can express **committed compliance,** a willingness to embrace the mother's, father's, or caregivers' agenda, accepting it as one's own (Kochanska, Coy, & Murray, 2001). This scholarship indicates that children enter school with emerging self-regulatory skills.

Research with children during the first four years found that it was more challenging for them to sustain an unpleasant task request than it was to avoid a prohibited command (Kochanska et al., 2001). It was more difficult for young children to continue picking up toys (an unpleasant task) than it was to avoid touching a brightly colored toy (a forbidden object). The effortful control required in sustaining what they perceive to be an unpleasant task involves more focused attention, while suppressing the desire to do something that is forbidden could be easily accomplished with effective distractions and/or through enforcement generating approval or fear. Committed compliance, although reflecting a child's submission to a parental directive, is considered to be a first step to internalizing (carried out without surveillance) self-directed behavior. Consider 4-year-old Renee's internalized compliance. She is overheard telling her 2-year-old sister, "I can't hit you. Momma said not to hurt you. So just give it to me."

Since committed compliance is unique to the particular parent-child relationship it does not necessarily transfer to other adults in authority, such as teachers. This means that children may willingly comply with their parents' or caregivers' directives but may employ a self-regulatory behavior to meet personal needs and thus choose to disobey teachers' commands. This noncompliant behavior, or form of **resistance** (self-regulatory behavior to meet personal goals), can be observed when children have not established a strong interpersonal relationship with their teachers or when they have established negative interpersonal connections with their teachers.

Middle Childhood. According to Bandura (1993), children between ages 7 and 12 develop a sense of **self-efficacy,** a belief about their ability to control their behavior when setting goals and making decisions to meet and reach these goals. Children become more aware that they choose to maintain and sustain self-control. However, how they regulate from external (direction from others) to internal (self-initiated) behaviors may be influenced by their individual, peer, and family standards. Thus, decisions at this age level may be dependent on the characteristics of their development, the influences from peers, as well as the need to maintain consistency with the norms, attitudes, and values experienced in their socialization process.

Students use both **motivation** (why people think and act as they do) and **emotional control** (feelings affecting the choice of behavior) to decide which actions to take (Carver & Scheier, 1990; Corno, 1993). Consider the motivational factors involved when a 10-year-old Cantonese-speaking student decides to discuss a math problem in Cantonese with a peer, knowing that speaking Cantonese is not allowed in the classroom. How long did it take him to initiate the activity, how hard it is to break the no-

Cantonese-speaking rule, how long is he willing to remain at the activity, and what is he thinking and feeling while engaged in the activity? Making decisions under these conditions affects children's motivational control and commitment to conform. Complicate this choice by a cognitive awareness that he may (a) not fully understand the rationale generating the rule, (b) be developing a sense that the language of his family and community is devalued, and (c) realize that his peers may also be unwilling to internalize the teachers' values as their own, and may also refuse to follow teachers' rule disallowing Cantonese in the classroom.

Adolescence. Developmentally, adolescents also have the capacity to self-regulate. They have an increasing ability to think abstractly, consider multiple aspects of a problem, reflect on the consequences of their actions, and have a greater variety of opportunities to practice self-control. Nevertheless, they may not be motivated to select school-imposed behavioral standards (Wigfield et al., 1996). Adolescents have more freedom, choices, and options than younger children. The value they assign to a particular activity such as socializing, studying, listening, working on a classroom task, or attending class, can have a substantial effect on their behavior. Personal goals such as obtaining their friends' approval are generally more dominant than academic goals (Nicholls, 1979).

Additionally, students "who have felt excluded from the culture of academic achievement in school" or who "learn from an early age that there are doubts concerning their capability to develop intellectually" may not necessarily be motivated to control their behavior to meet teacher imposed social norms and academic goals (Moses, Kammi, Swap, & Howard, 1989, p. 436, 437). This lack of motivation may result in actions judged as misbehavior (noncompliant and inappropriate) by the teacher. Behaviors of this nature are also self-regulatory actions directed toward meeting their own goals or are focused on preserving feelings of psychological safety.

Often for students from ethnic groups of color, a sense of fairness and loyalty to their referent ethnic group may take priority over a teacher command (Sheets, 1995b). European Americans often believe that each individual is responsible for their own actions. The following events were observed in two different high school language arts classrooms.

Vignette 6.1
Please Mind Your Own Business

The teacher (European American male) was verbally chastising a group of ninth grade African American boys for "playfully" throwing wadded papers toward a group of European American girls sitting across the room. Amidst the ignored "They started it!" comments from the boys, Latoya (African American) interrupted the scene. She told the teacher the boys did not start the paper throwing. Despite a teacher warning to stay out of the discussion, she continued presenting the case, even after the teacher told her, "Please mind your own business." The teacher punished Latoya, along with the boys, with a 30-minute afterschool detention.

Vignette 6.2
Privately in the Hall
Ms. Torrez (high school Mexican American teacher) reprimanded Matt (European American) for talking instead of concentrating on his work. Most of the European American students sitting at his table had been talking; however, they all focused on their work while the scolding took place. A few minutes later, Ms. Torrez walked over to Bertha (Mexican American) and asked her to stop rummaging through her purse and get to work. Keeping her purse open, Bertha looked at the teacher. Lynette and Veronica quickly told the teacher that Bertha was just looking for a pen. Ms. Torrez ignored the two girls and repeated her command. "Bertha, I'm asking you to please put your purse away and get started on your work." The two girls, joined by two other Mexican American girls, explained that Bertha was just trying to get a pen. One girl offered Bertha a pen. Ms. Torrez asked to speak to Bertha privately in the hall.

Issues for Consideration
For both vignettes, consider the students' perspective of the event, their peer relationships, and the type of self-regulatory behavior (compliance or resistance) engaged in. What significance did the students give to possible teacher chastisement? How was the teachers' behavior similar? How did it differ? Can you identify specific student cultural displays in each situation?

Culture and Self-Regulation

More research is needed to examine how culturally diverse students move from externally (teacher imposed) to internally regulated self-control behaviors reflecting compliance rather than resistance to classroom norms. We need to understand how they transition from a parent-child to a teacher-student relationship and what conditions motivate students to achieve academically and socially. Insights into the factors culturally diverse students use when making decisions to ignore, comply, or resist teacher requests and directives are also critical. Nonetheless, current scholarship in this area suggests that the following points be considered (Carver & Scheier, 1990; Corno, 1993; Kochanska et al., 2001; MacLeod, 1995; Sheets, 1995b; Zimmerman & Schunk, 2001):

1. Children enter school with emerging self-regulated learning skills allowing them to initiate, maintain, and cease behavior to comply with teacher commands to do something (request) or not to do something (prohibition). Consider what social conditions in the classroom context affect students' behavioral decisions.
2. School-age children are developmentally capable of using self-restraint to comply with disciplinary actions taken by teachers that prohibit them from engaging in a particular activity in a given situation. That is, students are able to understand the teacher's judgment that their conduct is hindering the teaching-learning process, is inappropriate at the moment, or cannot be allowed to

continue in the specific context. What influences their decisions to comply or resist?

3. Students who stop a prohibited activity may not necessarily comply with the teachers' request or command to engage in an academic task. Hence, students who stop talking when asked may not read, write, or compute, and quiet, compliant students are not necessarily learning what is intended. Does social conduct judged acceptable by the teacher always translate to academic achievement?

4. Students' early self-regulation skills learned in the home lay the foundation for social competence in other settings with other adults in authority. Examine cultural inconsistencies in the student-teacher interpersonal relationship to understand why or how student resistance is maintained. Consider why students choose to ignore, sabotage, and resist teachers' academic requests and social prohibitions. Why does students' self-control remain situational (dependent on teacher control) rather than committed, which developmentally encourages internalization? How does the match or mismatch in the teacher-student home culture, language, ethnicity, and socioeconomic status affect self-regulated learning?

Student resistance (a type of self-regulatory behavior used to meet personal goals) develops early in the schooling process (D'Amato, 1988; MacLeod, 1995; Tyson, 1999). Teachers who respond by personalizing this behavior often exacerbate these actions. Attitudes and behaviors such as, "You will not disrespect me," or "I saw you pass that note after I specifically said no note passing," all indicate that the teacher views the student action as a deliberate personal offense, which may differ from the student perspective. Hollins (1996) points out that sometimes conflicting teacher-student reciprocal behavior of this nature results in students' (a) refusing to conform to expected classroom behaviors, (b) deliberately displaying different values, (c) openly defying teacher authority, (d) exhibiting ethnic pride, and (e) establishing ethnic group boundaries for its members. To minimize this resistance, teachers must recognize the pattern of resistance; understand its causes; and acknowledge their role in initiating, exacerbating, and perpetuating the conflict.

The problems teachers encounter in the classroom dealing with management and discipline issues may be due to experience, to competency, or to their ability to develop interpersonal relationships with diverse students. Expert teachers (a) have well-established routines to govern classroom procedures and transitions, (b) are flexible in the ways they respond to classroom events, (c) can depart from lesson plans to meet student needs, and (d) are more organized in the way they present lessons. Novice teachers possess less knowledge and experience in most pedagogical areas than expert teachers. However, some research confirms that novice teachers working in U.S. public schools with a high percentage of students from ethnic groups of color report difficulties in establishing meaningful relationships with students (Freeman, Brookhart, & Loadman, 1999). Vignettes 6.3 and 6.4 (Sheets, 2002b), illustrate diverse views of disciplinary events. The first provides insights from students' perspectives, and the second describes a teacher's response to a student-student conflict.

Vignette 6.3
Pieces of the Puzzle

A teacher (European American female) calls the office. She reports that three students are in the hall disturbing her classroom. The vice principal (European American female) arrives and finds Jaime and Miguel in the hall. She listens to the teacher's version of the story in the hallway. The teacher identifies Jaime and Miguel as the culprits. On the spot, the boys are suspended for three days. They are told to get their things and go home. Jaime and Miguel become argumentative with the vice principal. Security is called and the boys are escorted to their lockers.

Feeling mistreated, Jaime and Miguel decide not to leave campus. Instead, they call district headquarters, file an appeal, ask for a hearing, and demand that their parents be contacted. The appeal is granted due to the nature of the offense and to their allegation that the vice principal did not follow district policies. For example, their parents were not notified, the suspension was not written or documented on school records, the students did not write down their side of the story, and witnesses were not interviewed.

The principal (African American male) is called by the district office and told that the three-day suspension cannot take place until a district hearing determines whether the misconduct merits suspension. This student action and subsequent district decision prompts the principal to use the emergency expulsion policy. He asks security to find the boys and has them immediately escorted off campus (across the street). He calls and informs the school district of his decision. They withdraw the appeal. The students lose their right to remain in school until a hearing is conducted.

Jaime and Miguel receive a formal written emergency expulsion for being in the hall, talking to girls, and disturbing a class. Their parents are never contacted. This disciplinary action happened in an urban school where emergency expulsions are only used as safety measures to remove students who fight, threaten teachers, or have weapons or drugs in their possession. The Chicano American students interpreted this administrative action as discriminatory.

Although Jaime and Miguel believe that what they did was unacceptable, they view their action as a "stupid prank." Jaime remarks, "What's so serious about being caught in the hall? I wasn't judged right. I was punished for something petty, something everyone does every day." Carmen (another student in the study) also concludes that Jaime and Miguel were punished for their past reputations, for being Chicano, and because the principal thought their parents would not intervene. Carmen, incensed, but not surprised, explains:

> Once you're known as being suspended, they suspend you again. She [vice principal] doesn't like the way Jaime and Miguel look. They judge you by the way you talk and the way you dress. Look at Jaime! He doesn't look White. So to her he doesn't look respectful. White people see him as a Mexican (she laughs). It makes me mad. Because of the way he looks they think he's a menace to society just for

knocking on the door and talking to some stupid girl. They never call our parents. They say, "They don't talk English." It's not right!

Jaime and Miguel felt that the pieces of the event were overlooked because teachers and administrators see misbehavior as a whole case. According to them, teachers conclude that students misbehave and deserve to be punished. They then deliberately construct a complete, believable case to determine and justify the type and amount of punishment. By doing so, teachers disregard specific circumstances, multiple explanations, and important details. Thus, in the students' view, teachers essentially lie. They do not think this teacher behavior is necessarily intentional, but rather it is "the teachers' way of seeing things." Students believe they need to be heard. Students see the inconsistencies in the teachers' case and as a result question the type and severity of the punishment. Jaime's version describes the teacher's and administrator's behavior:

> The teacher felt we were wrong and all the little pieces where she lied didn't matter. She thought we shouldn't be in the hall in the first place so she said she saw everything and the principal believed her. It didn't matter that it didn't fit. She just had her puzzle together and me and Miguel had all the pieces, which were the truth. The teacher was so caught up in that we were wrong that she wouldn't listen. Nobody would listen. We could have worked something out.

In this case Jaime and Miguel felt that important details—the door was already open, they did not open it; Jaime stuck his tongue out to make the girls laugh not to disrespect the teacher; they disturbed the class yesterday not today (today they were just hanging around in the hall trying to contact the girls not meaning to disturb the classroom); and the teacher said there were three students involved but there were only two—should influence the type and severity of the punishment. They felt the support staff was discriminatory: "If security [staff] liked us, they would just walk us to class along with the other clowns in the hall. We were punished for something everybody does everyday" (Jaime).

Students also believed that the administrators' role was to keep teachers satisfied. Therefore, although angered, they knew that administrators generally focused on teachers' needs at students' expense. Carmen stated, "The principal always believes teachers over students even when teachers are racists." Jaime pointed out:

> The teacher gave a different impression. The principal didn't take into consideration what we said. She just said, "You're suspended." She (vice principal) brought out my past (prior suspensions) so she could have a stronger reason to suspend me, because what I did wasn't enough.

Issues for Consideration

This vignette provides explanatory information of a disciplinary action as perceived by Chicano American high school students. These students judged this disciplinary action as discriminatory. Do you agree? Why do you think the administrators disregarded district policies when suspending these students? The administrator did not conference with them in the privacy of an office, parents were not notified, written statements from all parties involved were not obtained, and the students were not given a written notice of the initial three-day suspension. Why might the differences between how students view disciplinary events (pieces) and the ways students believe teachers and administrators (whole case) view disciplinary events be critical to minimizing student-teacher conflict? What role, if any, did ethnicity play? What differences in attitudes and values in student, teacher, and administrator socialization processes generate misunderstandings, misperceptions, misjudgments, and misbehaviors (actions judged inappropriate) for the teacher, administrators, and students?

Vignette 6.4
He Kicked Me

This event took place in a third-grade class of a public elementary school located in a high-poverty neighborhood. Sixteen of the twenty children were African American (ten males, six females), and four were Mexican American males. Although Ms. Tillman (African American) was working on her state teaching credential, this was her fourth year in this school. In general, the children were relaxed, well-behaved, and involved in their lessons. The infraction took place in the afternoon during a whole group math lesson.

Ms. Tillman's math lesson focused on multiplication. She asked the students what objects had four items. Students eagerly responded—tables, chairs, and four tires on a car, four buttons on my shirt. She drew four cars and asked children to write the equation and solution in their math booklet. "Who has the equation and solution?" "It's $4 \times 4 = 16$," said LaTosha. As she wrote 6×3 on the board, Francisco rubbed his leg, and raised his hand. "Yes?" asked Ms. Tillman. "Manuel kicked me." Ms. Tillman asked the children to draw an illustration and to find the solution to the problem on the board. While students worked in their math booklets, she went to Francisco's table, listened to his side of the story, and inspected his leg. A slight bruise was visible. "Are you OK? Do you want to go to the office and get an ice pack?" Francisco shook his head indicating that he did not want to go to the office. Ms. Tillman looked at Manuel, walked over to him, and calmly and softly told him to stay after school. She explained that she would talk to him at the end of the day (in about 30 minutes). She went back to the chalkboard and continued the math lesson. This entire interruption, although not rushed, took less than two minutes. When the math lesson ended, Ms. Tillman again checked on Francisco.

When the children were dismissed at 3:00 P.M., Manuel was visibly uncomfortable. He watched while Ms. Tillman made phone calls to his and Francisco's home. He fidgeted in his seat, looked for a pencil in his desk, worked on his math homework, and waited (about 5 minutes) while Ms. Tillman organized her desk. When Ms. Tillman approached Manuel, she repeated Francisco's side of the story (according to Francisco, he did nothing to provoke Manuel and getting kicked was unexpected). Manuel concurred. She asked, "Why did you kick Francisco?" Manuel replied, "I don't know." "Do you think you should be punished?" He nodded. "What do you think should be your punishment?" He thought for few seconds, and then answered, "Go to the office tomorrow during the Valentine party."

After the children were dismissed, Ms. Tillman made two telephone calls. She cleared her desk and made notations in her planning book. She later explained that she purposefully wanted to give Manuel time to think. When Manuel replied, "I don't know," she accepted his response. She talked to him softly explaining that it hurts when somebody kicks you. She told him that the kick was hard enough to leave a bruise, so it was not an accident. Manuel nodded when she asked him, "Do you wish you had shown more self-control and not kicked Francisco?" At the end of the conference, Ms. Tillman made her point. "What do you think would be the best for everyone? For you not to go to the Valentine party tomorrow or for you not to ever kick Francisco or anyone else again?" Manuel agreed not to kick anyone. "OK, Manuel, watch the clock. You can leave at 3:30." At 3:30, Manuel gathered his things, said goodbye, and left the classroom.

Issues for Consideration

Why do you think Ms. Tillman's class time focused on the hurt child? What types of self-regulating behaviors were expected from the two boys and the rest of the students? Why was the child's "I don't know" response accepted? What would you have done in this case?

Classroom Applications

The classroom climate conveys strong messages to students about how they are regarded and how they should behave toward each other. What teachers omit is just as important as what they include in the cultural, emotional, and physical elements of a classroom. Exemplary classroom management programs and disciplinary decisions take into account diverse cultural norms and developmental needs of students. They provide coaching, model desired behavior, and emphasize ways to practice self-control.

The following suggestions might help you construct a nurturing, culturally inclusive classroom environment. As you explore these options, remember to promote self-discipline in students. Adapt these activities to your personal management style and grade level. Evaluate success by monitoring changes in interpersonal conflict. Periodic evaluations of your classroom climate will allow you to make changes.

Establishing an Emotional Climate

Involve students in establishing an emotional climate that includes mutually acceptable rules and guidelines.

1. Examine how the beliefs, values, and social conventions of diverse cultures are reflected in your classroom rules, procedures, and policies. Keep a tally on how frequently and severely you discipline certain students or various groups to identify patterns in how and why you determine their behavior unacceptable.
2. Create classroom standards that encourage responsibility and acceptance from students and teachers. Develop class rules through consensus and discussion. Use Peace Tables or peer mediation teams where students work out their own conflicts. Role-play possible solutions to actual conflict situations and include a variety of ways to solve problems.

Enabling Self-Discipline

Assume that students have the capability and the desire to demonstrate self-disciplined behaviors.

1. Focus on teaching students to internalize self-discipline. Avoid behavior modification techniques to manipulate and control students such as giving stars, stickers, points, or free time. Teach students to share space, materials, and skills. Help students understand and monitor anger and joy. Develop activities that build trust and respect, and encourage responsibility.
2. Give students opportunity to practice self-regulation by providing concrete symbols with a shared meaning, such as teaching students to not interrupt a lesson when the teacher puts on a red hat. Choose a catchy signal to determine a series of behaviors to transition from one activity to another.
3. Provide curricular experiences that promote student reflection and inspection of their ability to self-regulate behavior. Use literature, film, and discussion focusing on the benefits of self-reliance, persistence, resiliency, and commitment. Allow students to self-code their performance in a given action in terms of emotion control. Discuss how to balance conflicting goals. Promote self-monitoring.

Involving Students in the Physical Context

Model acceptance and collaboration in the physical aspects of the classroom space.

1. Promote ownership and responsibility for classroom physical space by involving students in the decision-making process. Ask students to help identify types of activity zones and displays, select locations, choose personal work, and determine the duration of specific displays. Discuss with students how furniture arrangements can create quiet and active spaces, and enhance small or large group activities. Provide areas that are accessible to students who are physically challenged.
2. Create a text-rich, culturally inclusive classroom context. Label pictures, objects, and artifacts in a variety of world languages. Display posters, bulletin boards, and decorations to reflect a wide variety of interests, abilities, and cultures. Decorate

with fresh flowers and other natural materials and care for live plants or animals to foster respect and responsibility toward the shared natural environment.

Developing Strategies for "At-Risk" Students

Incorporate comprehensive, coordinated strategies for students who are "at risk" behaviorally.

1. Work together with school, family, church, and community services to create a multidisciplinary team to achieve long-term goals.
2. Design and implement family support programs for students whose parents find traditional services intimidating or confusing. Arrange for reading classes for parents with low-literacy skills, English classes for native speakers of languages other than English, transportation options for parents who have transportation problems, or evening conferences for parents with conflicting work schedules.

Conclusion

Students develop a **school identity** (how they perceive themselves and how others view them as student and peer), thus school experiences are consequential to their sense of efficacy and achievement attitude. If students perceive themselves judged unsatisfactory, angry, or inferior, they may respond by demanding attention, seeking revenge, or reacting defensively or aggressively. This student behavior may cause teachers to become annoyed or threatened, which can generate punitive actions.

All teachers have the potential to design culturally safe environments. They can improve observation skills, develop purposeful reflection habits, and acquire the cultural knowledge needed to create a classroom context that does not advantage a specific group, economic class, or child-rearing practice. By acknowledging the unique experiences students bring to school, teachers can consciously develop classroom rituals and promote inclusive procedures where all students are free to display cultural, linguistic, social, and academic competence.

RECOMMENDED READINGS

Kiang, P. N., Lan, N. N., & Sheehan, R. L. (1995). Don't ignore it: Documenting racial harassment in a fourth-grade Vietnamese bilingual classroom. *Equity & Excellence in Education, 28*(1), 31–35.

Kohn, A. (1993). *Punished by rewards: The trouble with gold stars, incentive plans, A's, praise, and other bribes.* New York: Houghton Mifflin.

7 Language: Creating Conditions for Language Learning

Language determines not only how we are judged by others but how we judge ourselves and define a critical aspect of our identity: who we are, is partly shaped by what language we speak.

—Bialystok & Hakuta, 1994, p. 134

Since language is a tool for thought, language development is central to students' cognitive development (Vygotsky, 1986). Interpersonal relationships and active student participation in classroom events are at the heart of the language developmental process. Students must have multiple opportunities to interact with others and to participate in planned activities promoting language growth. These social attachments, connections, and learning events create optimal language learning conditions. The purpose of this chapter is to (a) examine how language learning develops, (b) explore the conditions for language learning, and (c) discuss ways to meet the needs of linguistically diverse students.

Many students attending public schools are linguistically diverse. Therefore, teachers must value and respect children's diverse linguistic skills. Although the linguistic transition from home to school may be easier for most native English speakers, **English language learners** (ELL), students whose first language is not English, need appropriate English language learning support. Meaningful classroom experiences for ELL students require knowledge of second language pedagogy. The fifth diversity pedagogical dimension addresses language concerns in schooling. The chapter begins with an introduction to the fifth diversity pedagogy dimension. The second section, teacher pedagogical behaviors, examines language and culture, language diversity, and language instruction in U.S. schools. The next part, student cultural displays, discusses first and second language acquisition and explores the issues surrounding heritage language loss. Classroom applications follow.

Diversity Pedagogy Dimension 5: Language/Language Learning

Language is not a neutral concept. It is often associated with value-laden diversity issues such as the English-only political movement, immigration, language loss, bilingualism, legal entitlements of students who speak a home language other than English, illegal aliens, and poverty. Teacher beliefs and assumptions about language and the subsequent social, cultural, political, and economic value given to language in a culturally diverse society often shape classroom practices and language policies in schools. The fifth diversity pedagogy dimension describes *language* and *language learning* and points out possible pedagogical strategies (teacher behaviors) needed to apply this dimension in the classroom. Cultural displays show how students might demonstrate language development and develop respect for differences in diverse languages and communication styles. See Table 7.1.

Teacher Pedagogical Behaviors

Language is an essential part of everyday communication. Children learn to talk and listen through informal, social, cultural interactions in their homes and communities.

TABLE 7.1 Diversity Pedagogy Dimension 5: Language/Language Learning

Definition of Dimensional Elements

Language: Human language is a cultural tool used to share, convey, and disclose thoughts, ideas, values, and feelings through words, signals, and/or written symbols. It is also one of the most powerful means to preserve and sustain a cultural heritage and history.	*Language Learning:* Linguistic growth evident in listening/speaking and literacy skills (reading, writing, and viewing) acquired in informal home and community settings and/or in the formal language experiences and social interactions in school.

Teacher Pedagogical Behaviors	**Student Cultural Displays**
Extends the development of English language learning through instructional strategies and culturally inclusive content.	Signs of developing and expanding English language speaking, listening, understanding, reading, comprehension, and writing skills.
• Uses varied styles of classroom discourse to provide multiple, active, repeated encounters in conveying and receiving oral communication.	• Expresses feelings, exchanges opinions, and presents information to others and listens, respects, and responds to other perspectives.
• Develops strategies to think critically of issues, texts, and mass media expressed through language.	• Recognizes the distinct viewpoints and values of a culture expressed through its language.
• Extends prior knowledge to improve reading and writing skills and to increase vocabulary learning in a word-rich environment.	• Understands the relationship between home language, second language, culture, and identity to enhance the acquisition of literacy skills.
• Provides a classroom context where students can practice oral, written, and visual linguistic skills.	• Comprehends, interprets, and analyzes spoken, written, nonverbal, and visual symbols of language.

(continued)

TABLE 7.1   Continued

Teacher Pedagogical Behaviors	Student Cultural Displays
Encourages and fosters heritage language learning and heritage language literacy, as well as English second language learning with the goal of developing speaking, reading, and writing proficiency in more than one language. • Adapts instruction for English language learners. • Plans activities and lessons to support students' adjustment to different linguistic contexts. • Encourages respect for linguistic diversity. • Understands the cultural, social, and economic value of bilingualism and advises parents to maintain heritage language learning at home.	Indications of preserving heritage language, developing heritage language literacy, and maintaining cultural communication styles, while simultaneously attending to second language speaking, reading, and writing proficiency. • Shows measurable growth in language skills. • Acquires and develops literacy skills in the heritage language and English language. • Respects own language skills and the diverse languages of others. • Is motivated to develop heritage language skills and understands the cultural, social, and economic value of bilingualism.

Their linguistic competence in particular languages and their preferred communication styles are influenced by their ethnic heritage and cultural history. This section discusses language and culture, language diversity, and language instruction in schools.

Language and Culture

There is a strong relationship between language and culture. Language functions beyond direct exchange of information. Language is a powerful cultural tool. In classrooms, speakers and writers use it to express thoughts; and listeners and readers use it to make inferences about perceptions, ideas, and intentions of others. As such, language contributes significantly to students' cognitive performance and social adjustment in the classroom. Language is also an aspect of identity. The language or languages students speak categorizes them as members of distinctive linguistic, social, cultural, and ethnic groups. Every language embodies both the historical experience of a particular cultural group and the group's conscious effort to transmit its collective values (Vygotsky, 1962). Native speakers of a given language utilize not only its grammar and vocabulary, but also its distinctive verbal customs, patterns of thought, and styles of communication.

According to Fishman (1991), languages are related or linked to a particular culture in three ways: indexically, symbolically, and in a part/whole fashion. **Indexically** refers to the role language plays in preserving the terms and expressions appropriate to the groups' artifacts, realities, concerns, needs, and interests. Only the language historically and intimately associated with a given culture is able to transmit their interests or to name the things of that culture. Japanese, for example, has pronouns indicating status differences. Eskimos have several words for snow (wet, dry, thick, thin). American

English has unique sports and technological expressions. **Symbolically** indicates that, outsiders and insiders make associations among the person, language, and culture. During World War II, many German Americans chose not to speak German in public. The United States was not at war with the German language but the language symbolized the German nation. Another example is the shame or fear of discrimination that some Mexican Americans associate with whether or not they speak Spanish. For these individuals, the Spanish language is a negative symbol of membership of a particular group, such as Mexican nationals, immigrants, migrant farm workers, and minorities. **Part/whole fashion** addresses the cultural specificity of language and the two-way relationship between the part/whole of a particular language and its culture. Since some expressions, sayings, and figures of speech are difficult to translate, their meaning evolves from a cultural context. In this sense culture is expressed through language. For example, to take *a seventh inning stretch* is an American cultural expression originating in baseball that means *take a break.*

Language Diversity

We often think of languages other than English as foreign; however, in 1995 the National Association for the Education of Young Children's (NAEYC) position paper on language and cultural diversity made two important points. First, linguistic diversity is most common with young children under the age of six; and contrary to popular belief, these children are neither foreign born nor immigrants. Second, language issues also affect students who understand and speak English but come from different linguistic backgrounds. This includes bilingual African American children who speak American Black English; children from Appalachia or other regions with distinct speech patterns; and students who live in homes where some English is spoken, but a heritage language other than English is dominant.

Approximately 45 million school-age children—more than one in five—live in households where languages other than English are spoken (NAEYC, 1995). According to the National Center for Educational Statistics (NCES), over 2.1 million public school students in the United States receive services as Limited English Proficiency (LEP) students (NCES, 2001). Often LEP and ELL (English Language Learners) are used interchangeably to refer to the same students; however, ELL is generally the preferred term. ELL students account for 5 percent of all public school students and 31 percent of all Native American, Asian American, and Latino American students enrolled in public schools. These students are concentrated in urban areas, western states, schools with a 20 percent (or more) student of color population, and in schools where 20 percent of the students receive free or reduced-price lunches.

Language Instruction in Schools

Some form of language learning takes place throughout the school years. Formal language learning can be in the same or in a different language from the one students speak in the home. In the United States most language learning instruction can be placed in one of four categories: English language learning, world language courses, English as a second language, and bilingual programs. During the K-12 schooling experience, most students participate in more than one program. Each is discussed.

English Language Learning.   If students in the classroom all speak English, they do not necessarily come from the same speech community. Diverse cultural backgrounds, socioeconomic statuses, and life experiences determine differences in language usage, grammatical rules, notions of competence, and participation styles used by students. Beyond sharing a common language, awareness of differences in English language usage and understanding of how students apply their linguistic competencies within the classroom's social, academic, and cultural context are also necessary.

The purposes of English instruction in K-12 schools are to teach students American English (commonly referred to as Standard English) and to develop oral, listening, written, and reading skills. Course content in the areas of language arts and reading begin immediately once children enter school and continue throughout the elementary grades. When students enter junior high and high school, English language instruction continues in courses such as Language Arts, English, Composition, and Literature. English language growth also continues in all subject areas, since the medium of instruction is English.

World Language Course Work.   World language teachers, usually called foreign language teachers, work with students to acquire a second non-English language. Although multiple world languages are sometimes taught on the elementary level, these programs generally begin in junior high and high school. Some states require two years of a world language to meet graduation requirements.

English as a Second Language.   Students who speak a heritage language other than English or students who are identified as English language learners (ELLs) sometimes receive special instruction to advance English language acquisition. Identified students are placed in English as a Second Language (ESL) classrooms or participate in special pullout services for part of the day while assigned to classrooms in the regular program.

Sheltered English is one of the instructional approaches used to teach ESL students. ESL teachers or trained classroom teachers who use this strategy segregate (shelter) English language learners from the English-speaking students and provide content area instruction in English with a focus on developing English language skills. Although the content in the instructional resources is challenging, it is presented at a very low reading level. Abstract concepts are simplified, controlled vocabulary is used, and the simple language used is slowed down and supported with visuals. This approach attempts to bridge the academic content in the ESL classroom to the content found in the mainstream classes, with a goal of making the transition from ESL classrooms to the regular classroom more successful. Sheltered English is common on the middle and high school level with students who have some knowledge of English language and who have mastered some of the knowledge and skills in another language.

A ninth-grade Spanish-speaking student with minimal English skills, schooled in his native country, may have reading, math, and science skills. This student needs a program that helps him transfer the skills from one language to another. An English as a Second Language program can be one of the best possible ways to meet the needs of second language learners who come from many language groups.

Bilingual Programs. Scholars in bilingual education, for purposes of pedagogical research, define heritage language as a non-English language spoken in the home (Valdés, 2000). Thus, students who are heritage language speakers live in a home where a language other than English is spoken. To some extent, they speak or understand the heritage language, or both. Along with heritage language competency, they have acquired variable degrees of proficiency in the English language. Therefore, unless there is language loss while acquiring English, heritage language students become bilingual. According to Haugen (1953) "bilingualism . . . may be of all degrees of accomplishment, but it is understood here to begin at the point where the speaker of one language can produce complete, meaningful utterances in the other language. From here it may proceed through all its possible gradations up to the kind of skill that enables a person to pass as a native in more than one linguistic environment" (Haugen, 1953, p. 7).

Bilingual programs are characterized by instruction in dual languages, with English being one of the languages. The purpose of the program and the ways in which time is allotted to each language varies. In the United States there are three widely used types of programs—transitional, maintenance, and two-way bilingual.

Transitional Bilingual Program. The purpose of the transitional program is to provide students with English language skills to literally transition them from their heritage language to English as quickly as possible. A goal is to replace the heritage language with English within two or three years and transfer these students to the regular program. Transitional bilingual programs often encourage assimilation. Sometimes students are moved to a mainstream program before they have reached the English proficiency needed to succeed academically.

Maintenance Bilingual Program. Students in this program, which usually takes five to seven years, become literate in their heritage language and in English. The students' home languages and cultural practices are valued, and students are encouraged to appreciate both languages. This model is rare.

Two-Way Bilingual Program. In this type of program, native English speakers are immersed in a second language at the kindergarten level. Each year more and more time is allotted to English, and by sixth grade most of the instruction is in English with one or two hours in the second language. Canada has many French-English successful two-way bilingual programs. This type of program in the United States is voluntary, generally highly successful, and often has long waiting lists. Parents who choose to place their native English-speaking children in these programs see the social, cultural, and economic advantages of having their children speak, read, and write in two languages.

Student Cultural Displays

This section provides information on the ways linguistically diverse children display language development in their first or second language, or both. It also discusses some of the issues associated with language loss.

First-Language Acquisition

Infants and young children learn their first language or heritage language in the home. Since multiple languages are spoken in the United States, most classrooms will have students who speak different home languages. Language acquisition is one of the most complex achievements in a child's cognitive development (Crystal, 1987). Infants and young children learn language through social, cultural interactions and experiences in their environment. Some linguists view language as part of the brain's mental equipment, and, although cultures may vary in the linguistic socialization process of infants and toddlers, the result is always cultural identification and complete fluency (Bialystok & Hakuta, 1994; Brown, 1973; Chomsky, 1957).

Although children learn at different rates, the process is gradual and steady; and, it usually takes place during the first five years. Regardless of socioeconomic status, when children come to school at age 5 or 6, they have mastered a fully formed, rule-governed grammatical system (Gumperz & Hernandez-Chavez, 1972). Thus, children come to school ready to use their language to communicate their needs, make social contacts, construct learning, influence others, and assert their identity.

Research on English language acquisition shows that normal language acquisition develops in stages with different linguistic skills emerging at various developmental levels (Brown, 1973; Chomsky, 1972). These stages and their corresponding skills are described below.

Birth to Age 1.   Language learning begins at birth. During this stage infants learn to watch, listen, and understand language. They cry and laugh—noises signifying pain and pleasure. They respond differently to various sounds. They are startled at loud noises, and they may find the parents' voices soothing. They cry, coo, gurgle, and babble. They smile at familiar voices, respond to facial expressions, and indicate wants with gestures. Between 4 and 6 months they understand the word *no* and are responsive to changes in voice tone. Their babbling increases. Between 7 and 12 months they play simple games (peek-a-boo), respond to simple requests such as "Give it to Daddy" or push bottle or cup toward the caregiver when asked "More juice?" At this age they can also recognize their own name. They say their first words, which are recognizable to the immediate family, but sometimes not spoken clearly (*Dada, mo*[re]*, no, up*).

Age 1 to Age 2.   From age 1 to age 2, children's comprehension increases rapidly. They enjoy stories, rhymes, and music and often want these repeated. They make connections between the spoken word, illustrations in books, and things in their environment. They respond to simple questions and requests. During this stage they meaningfully string two and three words together, which can be interpreted as sentences or questions. A child might say *mo juice*, which shows the communication intent, "I want more juice" or *Sam puter*, which translates to "Sam is working on the computer." During this stage, young children acquire around fifty to sixty words, and their pronunciation is clearer.

Age 2 to Age 3. At age 2 to 3 children follow complex instructions: "Bring your toy and put it in the box." They use sentences to talk about and ask for things. As vocabulary increases, children begin to use grammatical markers. They use present progressive verbs *(it falling, I going)*, plurals *(my cars, two trees)*, and some prepositions *(in box, on head)*. Dualistic thinking begins to emerge in their understandings. They learn and use words with opposing meaning such as no/yes, hot/cold, nice/yucky, boy/girl, big/little, stop/go, in/out, and good/bad. Language clarity increases, and most family members can understand what the child is saying.

Age 3 to Age 4. At age 3 to 4 children understand questions involving who, what, and where. Their vocabulary is increasing at a fast rate. Their ability to use more grammatical structures is also accelerating. They can use irregular past tense *(Me fell down)*, possessives *(Daddy's car)*, and forms of the verb *to be (Are we there?)*. Children add articles *(a* book, *the* cow) and begin to use regular past tense verbs (she jump*ed*, he laugh*ed*) and third person regular present tense *(he runs)*. Their sentences become longer, words clearer, and other people can understand what they are saying most of the time.

Age 4 to Age 5. At age 4 to 5, children understand most everything they hear at home or at preschool. They speak clearly and fluently. Most have a vocabulary of 1,500 words or more. They construct long, descriptive sentences and can tell short stories. They can use the third person irregular verbs *(she does)* and full forms of the verb *to be*, including contractions *(Are they coming? He's here. They coming)*. By age 4 and 5 their grammar is indistinguishable from their parents, and most people will understand everything the child says.

First-language English acquisition progress continues throughout childhood and adolescence through day-to-day social interactions in the home and community, school language social experiences, and planned language instruction. Vocabulary, attention skills, and interpretations of situations continually increase. Different elements of language such as expression, pronunciation, understanding abstract concepts, and listening become refined over time. Pronunciation takes a lot of practice and is generally not fully mastered until age 7 or 8.

Second-Language Acquisition

Most people acknowledge the societal and economic value given to second-language acquisition. Likewise, most understand how difficult it is to achieve fluency and literacy in a second language. Parents who want their children to speak, read, and write in more than one language extend considerable time and effort. Some people pay for special language instruction. In 1991 alone, Berlitz offered five million world language lessons in twenty-nine countries (Berlitz, 1991). Many countries introduce second-language learning during the elementary years. In some countries it is not unusual for individuals to acquire fluency in two or three languages. Some non-English countries import native English speakers to teach English to their students.

In the United States, most junior high and high school students can choose to take courses in a second language from the world language departments in their schools. Sometimes, these students have opportunities to participate in immersion programs abroad. American high school students who take French in high school may spend a year in Paris or those taking Spanish spend a semester in Madrid or Mexico City. Of course, students who speak a language other than English are offered second-language instruction in English.

Second-language learning, unlike first-language learning, takes place for different social, economic, political, and educational reasons and under different conditions. It involves individuals of different ages and cultural backgrounds and results in various degrees of fluency. This complexity makes it difficult to understand how second-language learning develops. However, the following principles, gleaned from scholarship, apply to English second-language learning in the United States (McLaughlin, 1995; Valdéz, 2001).

Bilingualism as a Cultural Asset.   Bilingual individuals have cognitive, cultural, and economic advantages. Language is a significant cultural resource, and bilingualism is encouraged for children whose parents do not speak English. Maintaining the heritage language supports critical parent-child communication, bonding, and nurturing. It also strengthens the family structure and frames the child's identity.

Fluctuating Bilingualism.   Children's bilingualism fluctuates. Rarely are both languages perfectly balanced. One language is usually dominant because it is spoken more often and literacy skills are learned in that language. Sometimes it may appear that children do not have age-level proficiency in either language while learning a second language. This is temporary. Children eventually reach proficiency in the dominant language. Some achieve full bilingualism, others obtain variable degrees of bilingualism, and in some cases the first language is lost.

Classroom Accommodation.   Cultural patterns in language use require classroom accommodation. Students who speak a language other than English may experience culture conflict and psychological stress due to linguistic differences in the home and school. When the language of their natural competency is not being used, students need support to adapt to the diverse styles of communication, to interpret different linguistic codes, and to respond to unfamiliar classroom routines.

Code-Switching. Code-switching, for most bilinguals, is a normal language phenomenon. Although it may appear that students are confusing two languages, code-switching (inserting a word or phrase from one language when speaking the second language) is characteristic of second-language acquisition. It is often used purposefully to clarify and convey social and cultural meanings. Code-switching also indicates sensitivity between language and context and between the degrees of bilingualism of the participants.

Heritage Language Development. Heritage language develops when spoken and practiced in the home. When English becomes the dominant language in the home, children are at risk of losing their heritage language. Bilingual students come from homes where conscious and consistent efforts are made to speak in the heritage language. Various family members speak to the children in the heritage language, or they adopt a one-parent approach. In the one-parent approach, one parent or caregiver always speaks to the child in the heritage language (Dopke, 1992). Some children maintain the heritage language through daily contact with relatives or live-in caregivers. Full bilinguals also learn literacy skills in the heritage language.

Communication and Meaning. Language is used to communicate meaning. When the medium of instruction is English, teachers who work with ELLs must be aware of their level of English proficiency and the skills required for them to engage in planned instructional activities. Likewise, when correcting grammatical errors in student's speech, teachers must also attend to the child's ability to construct meaning to the correction.

Language-Rich Environment. Language flourishes best in a language-rich environment. Optimal classroom conditions encourage children to practice speaking, listening, reading, and writing in the heritage language and in English. They must be exposed to meaningful, contextual verbal activities and text-rich, visual literacy experiences. Vignette 7.1 illustrates a language situation involving both cultural communication styles and aspects of a child's English language proficiency.

> *Vignette 7.1*
> *You Have to Speak Up!*
> This event took place in a first-grade summer school classroom in an urban setting. The twenty children in this six-week program with a focus on improving literacy and language skills included eight African Americans, six Chinese Americans, four Mexican Americans, and two European Americans. The majority of the children attended other neighborhood schools during the school year. The incident took place during a calendar activity, a daily morning ritual. Individual children were asked to classify the weather as sunny, cloudy, or rainy and to announce the date and day of the week. When the correct answer was given, the teacher placed a sun, cloud, or raindrop symbol and new date (number) in the appropriate placeholder on the calendar chart.

The twenty children sat on the rug. The teacher drew a name from a cup full of Popsicle sticks with each child's name written on a stick. Winnie, a Chinese American girl, was chosen. The teacher pointed to the calendar, "What is today?" Winnie smiled, stood up, and responded correctly, but softly. "Speak up," prompted the teacher. Winnie repeated her answer in the same volume. The teacher reminded, "You have to speak up," then, added in a loud voice, "Winnie, if you refuse to speak up, we will have to call on someone else." The teacher waited a short time and then called on someone else. Winnie sat down quietly, dropping her head (Austin-Carter, Brown, Deligiorgis, Dixon-Eberhardt, & Sheets, 2000).

Issues for Consideration

It cannot be discerned if Winnie's behavior may be attributed to (a) personality factors; (b) a culturally responsive mode of discourse based on the norms, values, and competencies learned in her home and community; or (c) to a combination of the two. However, her behavior provided valuable insights to her needs. Winnie's actions immediately following the dismissal of her correct response showed signs of discomfort, indicating awareness that her correct response did not meet teacher expectations and classroom discourse requirements. The degree of harm, if any, resulting from this experience to her development as a second-language learner cannot be determined. Winnie's response may also suggest that the teacher's directive to "speak up" was not understood in terms of language (instruction given in English) or concept (meaning of the abstract objective).

The teacher did not appear to notice Winnie's actions immediately following the dismissal of her correct response. She seemed oblivious to the possibility that Winnie's cultural patterns, modes, and styles of social discourse may differ from her own or from what was expected in the classroom. What is problematic about this child-teacher exchange is the teacher's unawareness of the potential and real harm her actions may cause Winnie's linguistic, cognitive, and social development. When this lack of consciousness occurs, an assumption can be made that this type of teacher behavior may be a common occurrence rather than an isolated incident.

Do you think Winnie's linguistic needs as an emergent English language learner were considered or addressed? Lack of mutual expectations and frustration over the child's response seemed to direct teacher behavior. If teachers expect children to articulate words clearly and speak in a volume loud enough to be heard by everyone in the classroom, should these skills be explicitly taught? How do you think language development is enhanced or hindered when most of the sanctioned dialogue involves teacher questioning, followed by short individual student response until the correct answer is given? How might you have responded?

Language Loss

Language loss of immigrant groups and indigenous groups in the United States has taken place throughout our history. This linguistic loss may even be perceived as an expected aspect of the "Americanization" process. However, for many, the restrictive use of heritage language can be painful, damaging, and demoralizing. This viewpoint in Vignette 7.2 is one example.

Vignette 7.2
Navajo Language Loss

"I just feel that the United States government tried to take it [the Navajo language] away from us. They almost succeeded; you see people who are ashamed of who they are and I'd like to say that it's part of the United States' fault, that because of them we're this way, that we're in this situation today. . . . They made older people not want to talk Navajo. . . . I feel mad at them because they took away from us—any Native American—they took our, a lot of people's languages. Some people don't even know their language. . . . They wish they knew, but they can't find it. They don't know it. That's what they did to us. Sometimes I feel mad about that" (House, 2002, p. 64).

Issues for Consideration

When the learning of English results in native language loss in childhood, this cognitive and cultural disadvantage may produce feelings of anger and guilt in adolescents and adults. It is also the starting point for alienation from the family, distancing from cultural practices, and deterioration of cultural values. In the case of Native Americans (see Adams, 1988), many were removed from their homes as young children and placed in federal boarding schools. They were punished for speaking their home language.

The Navajo, one of the largest Indian tribal groups in the United States, has experienced significant language loss. How did early government boarding school experiences and subsequent public schooling play major roles in the attempt to destroy a language and a culture? What are the advantages and disadvantages of language loss?

In the past, language shift among immigrant groups was slow and cumulative, generally taking three generations (Fishman, 1966). The following pattern was typical: (a) Individuals in the first generation learned as much English as possible, but the heritage language was spoken in the home; (b) those born in the second generation continued speaking their heritage language at home, but spoke fluent English in school and in the workplace; and (c) those born in the third generation only spoke English. The shift from the heritage language to English is complete when English becomes the dominant language in the home. Vignette 7.3 is an example of this process.

Vignette 7.3
Third-Generation Language Shift

Tomas, a first-generation Italian American, was 18 years old when he came to the Chicago area in the 1920s. Tomas's daughter, Mia, a second-generation Italian American, grew up speaking Italian in the home. She learned to speak English at school. Although she continued speaking Italian at home, she used English exclusively in most settings outside the home and in the immediate neighborhood. Mia marries. Mia and her husband are bilingual, speaking both Italian and English. Their children, Matthew and Sophia, third generation, speak only English. Although Mia and her husband may occasionally speak Italian to each other and to their parents, they only speak English to their children. The home language is English. Italian language loss is complete for their children.

Issues for Consideration

Many European Americans have living ancestors who speak both English and a second language. If you are not bilingual, in what generation was your heritage language lost? Have any efforts been made in your immediate family to reclaim this language?

Today, language loss takes place at an accelerated rate, usually in the second generation and sometimes in the first. The personal costs and cultural conflict of this language shift by young immigrant children is alarming. At a very young age, they are required to negotiate difficult transitions between home and school. Although it is challenging for any child to enter a new environment, this experience can be terrifying for young children whose home language differs from that of the classroom. For some children, the resulting psychological trauma may be a more debilitating consequence than the original different language issue. Vignette 7.4 describes a situation involving first-generation language loss.

Vignette 7.4
Kai-fong, aka Ken

Kai-fong was 5 years old in 1989 when he arrived in the San Francisco Bay Area from Hong Kong with his mother, father, 4-year-old sister, paternal uncle, and paternal grandmother. His grandmother took care of the children while his parents and uncle worked in a Chinese restaurant where English was not necessary. Since the school had no services for English language learners, Kai-fong (called Ken) and his sister were placed in a regular kindergarten class with an English-only speaking teacher. When she had time, the teacher tried to help the children who did not speak English. Although his sister made friends and learned enough English to learn to read in the first grade, Ken's situation was different. He was not as outgoing as his sister and had difficulties making friends. When his grandmother cut his hair, his classmates teased him because it stuck out. They laughed at his hand-sewn polyester trousers, calling them flower pants.

> One day at school there was a rock throwing incident involving Kai-fong and some other boys. It was unclear who started throwing rocks at whom, but they were all caught with rocks in their hands. The other children could tell their side of the story to the teacher on yard duty. Kai-fong could not. When the incident was reported to Mother and Father, they did not understand what had happened. They

knew only that Kai-fong had gotten into trouble at school. Kai-fong was severely reprimanded by Father, Mother, and Grandmother, and he gradually began to withdraw. (Fillmore, 2000, p. 204)

Kai-fong (called Ken) learned enough English and his hair and clothing became less distinctive, but he remained an outcast at school and turned into an outsider at home. In class he was indifferent. He made friends with a small group of Asian immigrant students with similar school difficulties. At home, he stopped speaking Cantonese. When his grandmother complained, he was scolded. The more he was reprimanded, the more sullen he became. By age 10, Ken no longer understood Cantonese and rarely spoke Cantonese. At age 16, Ken no longer attends school, spends little time at home, and mostly hangs out with his friends (Fillmore, 2000).

Issues for Consideration

A critical issue, especially in the schooling of U.S. students, is what happens to the first language when school policies focus on the acquisition of English as a second language. Some children acquire English but lose their family language. Why and when does this language shift happen? Is it desirable or possible to speak one's home language while acquiring English as a second language? What is the teacher's role in reversing language loss? At what human costs should the goal of English language acquisition be met? What is the relationship between language loss, family intimacy, and individual and group identity?

Patterns of Language Loss.   There are several reasons why students who live in homes where a heritage language is spoken do not become fluent heritage language speakers, yet most acquire fluency in English. Heritage language support at school is important. Schooling language experiences in the heritage language can (a) advance vocabulary development, (b) teach reading and writing skills, (c) introduce English after children have mastered their first language (age 5 or later), and (d) encourage and value second-language learning in the heritage language.

Language experiences in the home during those critical first five years, as well as consistent opportunities to practice the heritage language throughout childhood and adolescence, are essential conditions needed to maintain and sustain a heritage language. Some of the patterns gleaned from the research show that the following factors influence accelerated heritage language loss (Fillmore, 2000; Portes & Hao, 1998):

Deliberate Parental Decision.   Some bilingual parents purposefully bring up English-speaking children because they believe their child will face discrimination in school. They might perceive that English-speaking children do better in school than bilingual students and, as such, have greater opportunities to succeed. Some may feel ashamed of their language, and some may not want their children to speak English with an accent.

Unconscious Assimilative Linguistic Behavior. These bilingual individuals develop habits of language where English is dominant. Continual English usage—learned English literacy skills in school and use in the workplace—results in a greater proficiency in English than in their heritage language. They feel more comfortable speaking English. Often, without conscious thought they end up speaking only in English to their children. These parents may speak their heritage language in social situations with other family members and in the community, but not to their children.

Heritage Language Rejection by Children. In these cases, often the parents are monolingual heritage language speakers or have a minimal command of and exposure to English. In school, these children may be subjected to excessive ridicule and discriminatory practices because of their language differences (accents, expressions, incorrect grammar), as well as their ethnic, cultural, and economic differences. They may experience a sense of shame, prompting them to suppress heritage language development by refusing to speak their heritage language. Since lack of English skills keeps them out of social situations, they see their home language as a social limitation. If they view the language of their ethnic group as having low social status, some children resist speaking their heritage language. Parents, especially if they only speak the heritage language, face serious problems trying to raise children with whom they cannot communicate, impart values, share cultural practices, and provide nurturing support (Fillmore, 2000). There are also children, adolescents, and adults who are not fluent in their heritage language and who refuse to speak their home language around other fluent speakers. They too, may fear ridicule and criticism. This lack of practice further erodes heritage language.

Preschool English Immersion Programs. Some parents are not aware of the traumatic experiences young preschool children face in English immersion programs. Unfortunately, their young children attend preschools and day care centers before their heritage language is established. English becomes their dominant language. These children and their siblings bring English into the home and stop speaking their heritage language. Sometimes there is one older sibling who serves as translator for the younger children. If these parents, who often work long hours, cannot speak English, raising children with whom they cannot communicate in their heritage language produces serious problems in terms of maintaining cultural values and beliefs.

Classroom Applications

All students are cognitively, linguistically, and emotionally connected to the language of their home. They are entitled to use family linguistic strengths in school learning experiences. Schooling that focuses on helping students transition from home to school promotes development by building upon the skills they bring to school. Effective practices design opportunities for students to demonstrate their capabilities and accomplishments. Effective instructional approaches for language learners model and explain new concepts and provide extensive practice speaking. The following suggestions maintain students' linguistic strengths. As you reflect, respond, interpret, and evaluate the needs of the students in your class, note changes in social participation patterns, growth in emerging language usage, and movement out of the stages of silence that linguistically diverse students often experience.

Valuing Students' Linguistic Knowledge

Value and use the linguistic knowledge students bring to school.

1. Acknowledge linguistic diversity as strength. Provide school experiences that enable English language learners to learn English and encourage the maintenance of their home language. Support native English learners' efforts to learn another language.
2. Use a variety of languages in learning events. Label charts, posters, books, songs, and greetings in more than one language. Learn and use sign language in the classroom.
3. Allow English language learners who speak the same language to work together so they can construct knowledge, interact socially in either language, and serve as mutual resources to practice or translate language. Anticipate ways to handle the silent period most ELL experience and applaud children who serve as a language resource.
4. Balance learning expectations for all students by giving them opportunities to demonstrate achievement in ways other than the verbal and written use of American English. Promote activities that help students develop leadership and social skills. Assess some of the students' work through creative displays in dance, art, drama, and music.

Promoting Language Development

Include instructional strategies to promote language development.

1. Provide multiple opportunities and plan specific lessons to promote vocabulary development. Use objects and pictures and explain abstract concepts through modeling. Give students multiple and diverse opportunities to practice language.
2. Adapt curriculum to recognize the needs of English language learners. Learn as much as you can about the language and culture of the students in your classroom. Inquire about the students' schooling experiences (if any) in their country of origin. Use the Internet, available library resources, and publishing catalogues to locate instructional resources.

Building Language Continuity

Build linguistic continuity between the home and school to support student's social and cognitive development.

1. Encourage parents to maintain home-language learning. Explain to caregivers that skills learned in the children's heritage language transfer to second-language learning. Advise bilingual parents that one parent should consistently use the heritage language when speaking with their child to ensure second-language learning. Tell parents not to worry if their child's language is delayed due to hearing two languages, because it may take longer to learn two languages.
2. Seek ways to communicate with parents in their home language and provide welcoming parent-teacher encounters. Invite parents to the classroom. Have notices translated before sending them home. Make home visits, if possible.

Conclusion

In an English dominant country such as the United States, loss of native languages is inevitable; however, this phenomena has far-reaching consequences. Although some may have lost their heritage language, others are fortunate to speak an ancestral language. Folk wisdom informs us of the importance to provide a schooling context that helps students maintain and sustain their heritage language while supporting them in English language acquisition. Teacher actions of this nature can reverse the language loss trends.

We might also encourage native English-speaking students' efforts to acquire a second language, especially if they live in a community where other languages are spoken. World language programs, usually at minimal cost, can begin at the elementary level. If you speak a heritage language, you might consider the responsibility of passing it on to the next generation.

RECOMMENDED READINGS

Bialystok, E., & Hakuta, K. (1994). *In other words: The science and psychology of second-language acquisition.* New York: Basic Books.

Rickford, J. R. (1999). *African American vernacular English: Features, evolution, educational implications.* Williston, VT: Blackwell.

Smitherman, G. (1999). *Talkin that talk: African American language and culture.* New York: Routledge.

8 Culturally Inclusive Content: Expanding Knowledge Acquisition

The overarching purpose of schooling is to stimulate, capitalize on, and sustain the kind of motivation, intellectual curiosity, awe, and wonder that a child possesses when he or she begins schooling.

—Sarason, 1995, p. 85

Among the multiple purposes of K-12 public schooling is to enable children to demonstrate the social behaviors and academic knowledge expected from them at graduation. The context, content, and instructional process students experience during their thirteen years of schooling are intended to result in these achievement outcomes. Ideally, all students who complete a K-12 school curriculum acquire the knowledge and skills needed to function freely and responsibly as young adults in a culturally pluralistic, democratic society. Since teachers in classrooms shoulder the major responsibility for student achievement, most would agree that teacher skill in selecting instructional materials is critical to student engagement.

This chapter addresses instructional resources. Its purpose is to help teachers (a) realize the importance of interest, relevance, and appropriateness when selecting resources; (b) develop skills to critically analyze and identify diversity elements in instructional materials; and (c) understand how to adapt, change, reframe, or modify the resources available to them. The first section familiarizes the reader with the sixth diversity pedagogical dimension, defines the terms, and describes teacher pedagogical behaviors and student cultural displays. The second section, teacher pedagogical behaviors, discusses the purpose of schooling and addresses ways to analyze, assess, and adapt curricular materials to meet the needs of diverse learners. The next part, student cultural displays, examines knowledge acquisition and academic goals and standards. Classroom applications follow.

Diversity Pedagogy Dimension 6:
Culturally Inclusive Content/Knowledge Acquisition

While this pedagogical dimension appears to be the most straightforward, it requires a considerable amount of knowledge (subject matter content and cultural knowledge), hard work, time, and commitment to consistently make culturally inclusive decisions when selecting resources and adapting material to meet the needs of diverse students. Table 8.1 describes the terms *culturally inclusive content* and *knowledge acquisition*. It discusses some of the pedagogical strategies (teacher behaviors) needed to apply this dimension in the classroom and explains how students might display signs of acquiring knowledge from multiple perspectives.

Teacher Pedagogical Behaviors

A brief overview of scholarship examining the purpose of schooling is presented in this section. It also addresses ways to select, analyze, evaluate, and adapt curricular materials to meet the needs of diverse learners. Although student and teacher contact with instructional resources cannot be separated from the ways children experience the instructional process and classroom climate and how the subsequent learning outcome develops, it can be helpful to examine culturally inclusive content separately. This information may be helpful when applying the sixth pedagogical dimension in the classroom.

Purpose of Schooling

The documentary *The Merrow Report: In Schools We Trust (1997)* describes the 150-year history of U. S. public schools and shows how historical events influence how citizens perceive the purpose of school (http://www.pbs.org/merrow/tv/trust/). This video reveals that people not only expect different things from schooling but they also disagree on what public schools should do. Multiple perceptions and expectations of schooling are complicated by (a) the growing achievement gap between ethnic White students and those from ethnic groups of color, (b) the unequal funding sources in neighborhood schools, (c) the low percentage of households with school-age children (more than 75 percent of the households do not have school-age children), and (d) the mixed messages the public sends regarding the value of children and their schooling needs. Teacher status is reflected in low salaries, high turnover, teacher shortage, and the high number of teachers working without credentials in low socioeconomic communities. In many cases, social class, race, and ethnicity segregate children, and some children attend school in substandard, poorly equipped buildings.

Scholarship examining the purpose of schooling provides a historical overview and presents the ideological perspectives that shape schooling in the United States (see Goodlad & McMannon, 1997; Hurn, 1993; Kaestle, 1983; Spring, 2001, 2002). These traditions and ideological positions influence the intention, selection, organization, and evaluation of curricular content—what is taught or not taught, explicitly or implicitly. They affect why, how, and whom we school.

TABLE 8.1 Diversity Pedagogy Dimension 6: Culturally Inclusive Content/ Knowledge Acquisition

Definition of Dimensional Elements

Culturally Inclusive Content: The culturally influenced substance, meanings, and perspectives present in the instructional resources used in the various fields of study such as literacy, mathematics, science, social studies, art, music, and physical education.

Knowledge Acquisition: The process of connecting prior cultural knowledge to new information in ways that promote new understandings and advance the development of knowledge and skills needed to reason, solve problems, and construct new insights.

Teacher Pedagogical Behaviors	Student Cultural Displays
Provides subject matter resources and classroom opportunities to extend students' home cultural knowledge and experiences to construct new knowledge and understandings. • Selects authentic information from historical, literary, and scientific viewpoints of multiple diverse cultural groups. • Acknowledges the accomplishments of diverse ethnic groups to our nations' past, present, and future economic, political, cultural, and social growth and identity, prosperity, and global status. • Uses meaningful instructional examples applicable to the experiential background of all students. • Adapts curricular resources to address the cultural and linguistic needs of diverse students.	Signs of active use of prior cultural knowledge, skills, and concepts to remember, reason, solve problems, acquire, and construct new knowledge and understandings. • Consistently demonstrates measurable academic improvement and competency in all subject areas and values understandings from multiple perspectives. • Displays knowledge of own ethnic groups' accomplishments and of those of other diverse groups to the collective national identity, economic prosperity, and global status. • Identifies with and responds to the classroom's instructional content. • Contributes to the construction of new personal and group knowledge.
Evaluates curricular content for ideological message and examines its authenticity, language, and illustrations. • Analyzes textbooks, teacher guides, videos, bulletin board materials, websites, and packaged programs used in the classroom for inclusion and exclusion of significant cultural information. • Identifies content for accuracy, stereotypes, omissions, distortions, or use of biased language.	Expressions of the analytical skills needed to critically evaluate diverse perspectives in subject matter content. • Identifies, understands and analyzes the multiple cultural, social, and political perspectives, values, and worldviews present in a given classroom resource or event. • Evaluates content for accuracy, stereotypes, omissions, distortions, or biased language.

Historical Overview. Spring (2001) points out that there is neither a single nor a correct interpretation of U.S. educational history. However, certain patterns emerge to help us interpret how past and present educational policies influence schooling and how they will undoubtedly shape the future. The four historical trends, discussed below (a) socialization process, (b) cultural conflict, (c) economic/political mandates, and (d) equal opportunity/liberal directives reveal how different people view the purpose of schooling. The trends you experienced as a student or support as a teacher are highly likely to influence how you perceive the usefulness and importance of the various instructional materials in your classroom. These experiences affect your selection and subsequent adaptation of these resources in your classroom.

Socialization Process. This vision perceives schooling as a means to "Americanize" and prepare children for their future roles in a democratic society. Children learn how to promote the common societal good, acquire the commitment to perpetuate the current society values, and develop skills to improve society. In schools, children experience an **enculturation process** (the way schools expect students to act and think) that often requires assimilation to cultural norms, cognitive patterns, communication styles, and belief systems (Pai & Adler, 2001). Thus, schools are used to transmit a set of core values. This process is one of the ways to ensure the survival of the dominant culture.

Economic and Political Mandates. Historically and presently, some people view school as the means to prepare a competent work force. The role of schools is to provide society with a critical mass of human resources and intellectual capital. Certain economic directives and political issues must shape and drive school curricular content. Therefore, schools train students to be punctual, responsible, hard working, competitive, and independent. They keep students out of the job market until they reach young adulthood and prepare them to transition seamlessly from school to work upon graduation. This is critical, if we are to advance technologically, survive economically, and maintain dominance in global industrial markets.

Cultural Conflict. The U.S. society is not a racially, ethnically, culturally, or linguistically homogeneous society; consequently, a major part of the history of schools involves conflict over which cultural group should control what happens in schools. Public, policy makers, and educators differ on what norms and values should be taught to students, who should decide the content of national, state, and district standards, and who determines valid content knowledge. Conflict emerges over what cultural knowledge is taught in public schools and how social issues of inequality such as oppression, privilege, racism, sexism, homophobia, and classism are addressed in the school curriculum.

Equal Opportunity and Liberal Directives. Advocates of this position have consistently maintained that all children are entitled to free, public K-12 schooling with the goal of improving their quality of life—to achieve the *American Dream*. Schools should cultivate children's intellect and actualize their human potential. A goal is to prepare students for lifelong learning and to learn to live amicably with others in diverse communities. Students are encouraged to reach self-fulfillment, develop critical-thinking and problem-solving skills, and gain the knowledge needed to make decisions to improve their life's conditions and those of others.

Ideological Perspectives. Since their inception, public schools were expected to transmit a particular knowledge to children. Spring (2001) refers to this function of schooling as ideological management. He maintains that schools and the media use information to influence children's minds and to determine a national culture, which in turn controls societal norms, values, and attitudes. Since knowledge is not considered neutral, there is an ongoing debate about what should be included in the instructional content. In the United States, instructional resources generally align with one of three ideologies: (a) Anglo conformity theory, (b) melting pot idea, or (c) cultural pluralism theory.

Anglo Conformity Theory. This theory maintains that individuals who are not members of the Protestant, mainstream Anglo American group benefit economically and socially from complete renunciation of their indigenous or heritage culture. These individuals must learn to adopt the behaviors and values of the mainstream group in order to succeed. Therefore, in schools, students from diverse ethnic groups of color, those from different sexual orientation groups, recent immigrant groups, and children from different religious groups or family lifestyles profit from schooling experiences that teach them English and provide them with opportunities to develop the values and norms valued by the dominant mainstream group. Thus, if they learn appropriate values and behaviors and develop independent, individualistic, and competitive skills, they will gain social inclusion, achieve academically, and improve their possibilities for future economic success.

Melting Pot Idea. In the early 1920s, people who adopted this ideology used this metaphor to imply that the inevitable union among ethnically, culturally, and linguistically diverse European American groups would forge a new, single, cultural group— "Americans." This proposed merger of Anglo Saxon people with other European immigrant groups excluded individuals from ethnic groups of color. Native Americans, African Americans, Mexican Americans, and Asian Americans were not part of the melting pot. However, in the 1960s more inclusive metaphors emerged, such as mosaic, salad bowl, tapestry, and patchwork quilt, advocating the same viewpoint. Basically, this perspective assumes that all citizens of the United States will either melt, join, or blend culturally to form a new "American" people. This new race will embrace and sustain Anglo Saxon Protestant mainstream cultural values and practices.

Cultural Pluralism Theory. A key principal of this theory is the right of all U.S. citizens to coexist equitably with their distinct cultures, languages, and identities. Everyone is entitled to preserve any aspect of their heritage as long as it does not interfere with the legal rights of others. As U.S. citizens, they benefit from degrees of communality, such as same language (American English), a common market, equal political and social status, and protected legal entitlements. Cultural pluralism encourages acculturation and rejects assimilation. It supports a democratic society that recognizes and acknowledges the cultural pluralistic nature of the United States.

Instructional Resources

As a teacher you will be required to evaluate, select, and adapt instructional resources to meet the specific academic, cultural, social, and linguistic needs of diverse students. When making these decisions, you will consider the needs of individual students, groups of children, and the requirements of the entire group. How can you respond to the diversity present in the classroom and still promote a sense of communality? How will you recognize and evaluate the ideology present in instructional materials? Which ideology will you support? The following section discusses elements of this responsibility.

Teaching includes making instructional decisions regarding what lessons to teach, which books to read, how and when to use specific materials, which posters to put up, which websites to search, and which videos to watch. These choices involve the selection of instructional content. An important skill is the ability to organize, examine, and evaluate instructional materials for classroom use. Prior to the selection of the actual instructional content used in the classroom, most teachers analyze instructional materials. This analysis can be cursory or thorough. During this analysis you will describe the characteristics of the subject matter present in the materials, determine the grade level, and identify the ideological perspectives to determine its potential usefulness.

Examination of Resources.   At different times during the school year and for distinct purpose and function, you will likely employ three types of examinations: availability, appropriateness, and ideological perspectives. Each is discussed below.

Availability.   The main purpose of this cursory evaluation is to become aware of the materials and tools available and the types of instructional support they may provide. In the beginning of the school year you will generally check all of the resources, such as adopted student texts, teacher guides, workbooks, in-class library books, supporting texts (e.g., dictionaries, thesauruses, atlases), manipulatives, maps, science equipment, and even art supplies (e.g., paper, crayons, markers, scissors). You will organize these materials for possible future use. Since there is a high reliance on textbooks, you will examine suggested activities in teacher guidebooks, worksheets, handouts, tests, and any supplementary materials that accompany student's textbooks. You will count textbooks and workbooks that you intend to use to make sure there are enough materials for every student. At this time, and throughout the year, you will determine what is available in your school's bookrooms and libraries, what can be shared with colleagues, checked out from district resources, and borrowed from local libraries. This type of continual examination most often answers the following questions: What instructional materials am I expected to use? How helpful are these materials? What is lacking or missing? Where can I get what I need?

Appropriateness.   Generally, assessing for the appropriateness of instructional resources takes more time, and the process is more thorough. If you are already informed of the availability of materials, the goal, at this point, is to evaluate how certain materials can support a lesson being taught and the ways the resource might meet individual and group student needs in areas such as ability levels, language strengths, and interest. When inspecting textbooks, you will determine if the textbook at a particular grade level is at the appropriate level of difficulty for students assigned to you. Materials are also checked for academic accuracy. If textbooks, maps, or charts are outdated they may contain inaccuracies. Supplementary materials are carefully examined because they may not be marked with a specific grade level status. You will preview films and documentaries before showing them to students and read supplementary books, pamphlets, newspapers, and archival resources for potential use. When reviewing these materials you will consider visual appeal, student interest, age-appropriate content, level of difficulty, and its value to the content being taught. This assessment most often poses the following questions: Can I use this resource for this lesson? What adaptations or changes do I need to make to make this resource meaningful to students? How can this resource enrich students' learning experiences?

Ideological Perspectives.   An in-depth critical analysis is required to examine the culturally influenced substance, meanings, and perspectives present in the instructional resources. Since the multicultural educational movement has advocated inclusion for the past forty years, you will probably see pictures of diverse people in most textbooks and current materials. You are also likely to find references to some of the contributions and accomplishments of people from diverse racial, ethnic, and gender groups. Resources including issues on topics such as gender, sexual orientation, ability differences, and poverty might also be included in some of the curricular materials. In other words, some of the instructional resources will have references to diversity. However, particular ideological perspectives will frame this content. The ability to identify the purpose of the particular ideological perspective influencing instructional content is needed to provide students with culturally inclusive resources. *Teachers must be especially alert to curricular content often considered culture-free such as science, mathematics, and technology.* These subjects are not disconnected from a cultural context in the teaching-learning process. This type of evaluation raises the following questions: How does this content facilitate new understandings? In what ways do these instructional materials connect to students' prior knowledge? Does this resource advance the development of skills needed to reason, solve problems, and construct new insights?

Limits of Inclusion

Assuming that efforts are taken to purposefully include culturally inclusive materials, this substantive content may allow students to see, hear, or read about someone or something with whom they share racial, ethnic, linguistic, or cultural attributes. But, inclusion does not guarantee that students will acquire academic skills. Some of the achievement issues underrepresented students face in the schooling process cannot be corrected by inclusion. Teachers must go beyond inclusion and exposure of materials with illustrations of people from diverse ethnic and racial groups, perspectives from diverse groups, and accomplishments of diverse groups. Inclusion supported with a teaching-learning process that helps students develop higher level reasoning skills (see Chapter 9) and implemented in a culturally safe context (see Chapters 5 and 6) has a higher probability of success.

Analysis of Ideological Perspectives

School academic knowledge found in the content of instructional resources generally expresses one or more of the following cultural positions or ideologies: Anglo conformity theory, melting pot idea, or cultural pluralism theory. Sutherland (1985) points out that authors usually take three different ideological stances when promoting their agenda:

1. Assent: These writers subscribe to the dominant cultural norms, and their work supports this position. Therefore, their work, purposefully or inadvertently, promotes either the Anglo conformity theory or the melting pot ideology.
2. Advocacy: The work of these authors endorses specific social practices. They openly support a particular ideology, and their work explicitly promotes this position.
3. Attack: These authors denigrate particular social practices through their writing. While these authors are associated with a particular ideology, their work is focused on criticizing the ideas and practices of those who differ philosophically.

Writers who support the cultural pluralistic theory may either advocate for this position or may choose to attack the status quo. These ideological stances can be identified when one is analyzing the content in instructional materials.

We do not have empirical research showing how the knowledge, norms, and perspectives found in curricular content biased toward the dominant culture affects the academic achievement of students from excluded groups. However, a teaching-learning process that devalues students and their families, causes cognitive dissonance, and fails to link new knowledge to students' prior cultural knowledge is likely to create psychological barriers that students must overcome to succeed. Since schools control whose personal knowledge and whose cultural norms are transmitted, students who are able to use their personal and cultural knowledge to make a seamless transition from home to school are highly likely to benefit. One can conclude that it is easier for students to succeed academically if their cultural knowledge is used and validated in teaching-learning events. Since we live in a culturally diverse nation and participate in a globally expanding society, you might consider promoting a cultural pluralistic theory. If you endorse this theory, you might find the following information on how to identify particular ideological perspectives influencing the curricular content helpful.

Evaluation of Instructional Content. Textbooks are one of the most important instructional resources to scrutinize, because they guide a major portion of instructional content. They are viewed as the least expensive and most reliable means to transmit knowledge. Textbook content accounts for approximately 80 to 90 percent of the school curricular content, 75 percent of student in-class work, and 90 percent of homework activities (Altbach, 1991; Honig, 1985). The reliance on textbooks increases as students move through school from kindergarten to grade twelve. The higher the grade, the more textbooks are used. Additionally, most students assume that what they read and see printed in textbooks is factual and accurate. Since the textbooks teachers use reflect particular ideologies, it is important to understand how to evaluate textbooks and know how to teach students to critically analyze their content.

Children's literature is another resource to critically examine. These books are a basic resource in the elementary level and a major supplement in middle and high school language arts and social studies classrooms. The same guidelines for evaluating textbooks and children's literature can be used to analyze other instructional materials such as videos, films, posters, guidebooks, workbooks, and websites.

Ethnocentrism, a belief that one's own culture is superior to other cultures, can shape the content of authors' work and can also influence the way resources are perceived. Hernandez (2001) explains that ethnocentrism in textbooks and other instructional materials may be difficult for teachers to identify. She points out that "a perspective consonant with one's own attitudes and values is likely to be accepted at face value and not be questioned" (p. 206). If a goal is to identify culturally inclusive instructional materials, it is important to be able to recognize when cultural diversity is promoted through (a) the purpose of the message, (b) the authenticity of the cultural knowledge, (c) the tone and substance of the language, and (d) the support provided by illustrations.

Table 8.2 provides some direction in four general categories: message, authenticity, language, and illustrations. Scrutinizing for the message involves the ability to recognize specific cultural, social, and political values embedded in the resources. There are economic benefits resulting from the sale of multicultural materials, consequently one has to be aware of exploitation or misrepresentation, especially by outsiders (individuals who write about or study a culture differing from their own). Issues of authenticity arise when writers do not accurately reflect the heritage, values, or issues of the particular group they are writing about. A glaring example of this appropriation

TABLE 8.2 Guidelines to Analyze Culturally Inclusive Instructional Materials

Message	Authenticity	Language	Illustrations
The instructional materials project acceptance of cultural, ethnic, and linguistic diversity; provide knowledge of diverse cultural groups; and support a democratic society where all citizens coexist equitably with distinct cultures, languages, abilities, sexual orientations, and identities. The work addresses social and political issues responsibly in realistic, age-appropriate ways.	The producers of the work have a worthwhile purpose and indisputable authority. They possess authentic cultural knowledge of their own groups and represent the knowledge of other groups through these groups' viewpoints, values, and norms. The authors' academic expertise in the content area and experiential wisdom are evident in the product.	Language, written, spoken, and silent, is an important part of the cultural history and ethnic identity of the speaker. When applied to instructional resources, language supports the intent of the message and adds to its authenticity by reflecting an honest, realistic, fair, accurate, and knowledgeable presentation of the topic, person, or idea.	Illustrations (if any) function as a visual representation of the intended message. Similar to language, images support the message and provide another dimension of authenticity through realistic, accurate, and knowledgeable impressions of people, cultural artifacts, places, geographical maps, scientific and mathematical objects.

of ownership can be found in Native American children's literature. Reese (1997) states that in 1995, 98.5 percent of the children's literature about Native Americans was not written by Native Americans.

Language and illustrations support the message and authenticity of the work. When examining for these components, think of how different students might integrate the visual information and language to make meaning of the content. Consider how negative, visual stereotypes or derogatory language used to describe a particular cultural group might affect children from the same cultural group and how it might shape the thinking of children who have had little or no contact with that cultural group. Galda (1998) points out that texts can function as mirrors and windows. Will the book you select be a mirror, allowing some students to see themselves accurately, or a window, enabling other students to experience vicariously what another culture is like?

Since no single resource can capture the complexities of a cultural group, what will you include in the curriculum to actively support multiple perspectives and new knowledge? You can use the checklist in Table 8.3 to evaluate instructional resources, with a rating of 1 indicating low cultural inclusiveness and 5 representing high cultural relevance.

Adaptation of Curricular Content

National, state, and district standards, state legislators, policy makers, and district decision makers (a) require mandatory attendance of children; (b) determine the length of the school year and day; (c) attempt to control what children learn through curriculum standards and textbook adoptions; (d) establish the requirements needed for graduation; (e) control which standardized testing tools measure student knowledge and school effectiveness; and (f) in some states, determine who passes to the next grade and who is retained. In spite of the multiplicity of policies and mandates, it is classroom teachers' understandings of the purpose of schooling that ultimately guide the selection and adaptation of the day-to-day subject matter content. Teachers bridge the idealistic goals of the larger society and the demands of educational policy makers to the realities in classrooms; consequently, they decide how students and society benefit from schooling.

Teachers rarely use instructional resources in the same way, and students often experience identical content differently. Therefore, before reworking materials or developing lesson plans, it is important to know the characteristics of the students for whom you are adapting materials and the context in which instruction will take place. Culturally inclusive lesson plans cannot be developed in abstraction. In fact, most lesson plans, prepared without a particular student population in mind, can rarely be applied successfully in actual classrooms with diverse students. Consider the following: Do barbers plan how to cut and style your hair prior to meeting you? Do doctors write generic prescriptions and have them ready to give to any patient with a particular disease? Do lawyers have a set, fixed parenting plan for all divorcing clients to establish child visitation rights? Do teachers create lesson plans without knowing the students

TABLE 8.3 Checklist for the Analysis of Culturally Inclusive Instructional Material

Message	1	2	3	4	5	N/A
1. **The status, accomplishments, ideals, norms, and values of a cultural group are presented as one of many groups that comprise our nation's diversity** (e.g., a particular group does not have a privileged or superior position; people of color are not presented as helpers to European Americans or as social problems with special needs, or as objects of oppression to be pitied).						
2. **The work promotes national unity** (e.g., all citizens have equitable racial, ethnic, cultural, gender, political, and social status. They all enjoy degrees of communality, such as same language, common market, and protected legal entitlements).						
3. **There is diversity within the group being discussed** (e.g., differences of people from the same ethnic group are shown in the variety of careers held and of racial markers such as skin hue, facial features, differences in skills, strengths, and needs. There are various economic levels, leadership positions, social backgrounds, and academic roles present, as well as variety in food, clothes, art, and music preferences).						
4. **The content is academically and historically accurate and presented from multiple perspectives,** including the viewpoints of all groups under discussion (e.g., there is a balance between the struggles and accomplishments of all cultural groups).						
Authenticity	1	2	3	4	5	N/A
1. **The author has authority based on insider cultural knowledge, or has expert experiential knowledge of the cultural group under discussion and is able to tell the story from that group's viewpoint** (e.g., authors are from the culture they are writing about; the ethnicity of the author is identifiable; the work does not misrepresent or exploit the cultural group; the resource is accurate in terms of history, heritage, values, attitudes, norms, and worldviews of the culture or event under consideration).						
2. **The main purpose of the work is to extend students' knowledge of culture, provide new insights, and promote understandings** (e.g., economic benefits resulting from the sale of multicultural materials do not appear to be the author's primary objective).						
3. **All cultural groups' accomplishments to the nation's past, present, and future economical, political, cultural, and social growth are presented realistically, authentically, and accurately** (e.g., people of color and other nonmainstream groups are not presented as only making contributions to the established, dominant European American society).						

(continued)

TABLE 8.3 Continued

Language	1	2	3	4	5	N/A
1. **The language is fair, realistic, accurate, and honest** (e.g., it does not demonize, romanticize, idealize, stereotype, typecast, or classify some people with substantial or token status, with meaningful or insignificant knowledge, or with invisible or silent roles).						
2. **The language is inclusive.**						
3. **Students** (consider their age and maturity) **can handle the presence of overloaded, biased, inflammatory, insulting, offensive, or prejudicial language** (e.g., does the author use expletives, racial slurs, or homophobic language? Examine the author's word choices such as slaves/enslaved people, or terrorists/freedom fighters. Members of the dominant cultural group give entitlements, such as voice and the right to vote, to others. Differences in colors, values, languages, and practices are described as strange, colorless, exotic, ugly, or foreign).						

Illustrations	1	2	3	4	5	N/A
1. **The illustrations reflect the realities of a culturally pluralistic society** (e.g., there is a balanced representation of diverse racial and ethnic groups, gender, ability differences, socioeconomic class, sexual orientation, and family lifestyles).						
2. **People, events, places, maps, and cultural artifacts are represented accurately** (e.g., unique racial, ethnic, and cultural differences are evident in the illustrations; there is not a prevalent generic model; a specific racial or ethnic group can identify people; and maps are realistically proportioned).						
3. **The pictures are not stereotypical and do not exhibit overloading of cultural symbols** (e.g., teepees are houses for Native Americans, regardless of the tribe. There is overloading, an abundance of Mexican American symbols in a single text or story, such as red, white, and green colors, a piñata, bright flowers, and tamales).						

for whom the lesson is intended and the context in which the lesson will be taught? The logical answer to all of the above is no.

Teachers need to acquire a pedagogical foundation that includes, but is not limited to, the following skills: (a) knowledge of the subject matter content and an understanding of how to teach it, (b) ability to recognize the ideological position of instructional resources, (c) understanding of how supplementary materials enhance learning,

(d) insight regarding the cultural knowledge students bring from home, and (e) competency in linking new knowledge to students' home knowledge. If you plan to use certain materials or are preparing yourself to teach you can

1. Acquire a wide range of content knowledge in the areas you plan to teach and practice identifying the ideological position of the work.
2. Realistically identify the characteristics of the student population and type of setting you are likely to teach. Do you have the required skills and commitments to accept a teaching position with this particular student population? Do you feel comfortable working in this type of setting? Think about the following:
   a. Decide on a grade level range and subject area expertise.
   b. Identify the school setting. Will the setting be in a rural, suburban, urban, private (secular or religious), or public school?
   c. Project the characteristics of the student population. Ask yourself: Will I teach in rural low-income, low-performing segregated school with a majority of poor European American children; or will I teach in an urban school with a majority of African American, Mexican American, Chinese American, or ethnically diverse children? Is it likely that I will teach mainly English language learners from multiple ethnic and racial groups; or will I end up teaching in a segregated, suburban, middle-class school with a majority of European American children?
3. Once the issues in item 2 are more or less determined, practice making up the characteristics of the students in your class. Keep in mind how the following factors and possible examples affect your lesson plan:
   a. Setting: rural school
   b. Grade level: fourth grade
   c. Class size: twenty students
   d. Gender: eight girls and twelve boys
   e. Socioeconomic status: Sixteen of the students receive free or reduced lunch.
   f. Academic ability: Half of the students are two or more years below grade level in reading and mathematics.
   g. Ethnicity: one African American, ten European Americans, and nine Mexican American
   h. Language: All of the Mexican American students need instruction as second-language learners (two are bilingual, two have acquired conversational English, two are emerging English language learners, and three are monolingual Spanish speakers
   i. Sexual orientation: One European American girl lives in a home with two mothers.
You can practice changing the setting and student characteristics, but try to keep it in line with your possible teaching assignment. When preparing lesson plans and adapting instructional materials, have a student population and setting in mind. This will help you learn how to adapt materials for a particular population.

Student Cultural Displays

Children acquire and display their knowledge and skills at home, in their communities, and at school. Teachers realize that there is a difference between the knowledge acquired through schooling experiences and that learned through their educational process. Schooling, private or public, provides students with academic knowledge and encourages certain social behaviors. Education, on the other hand, is a much broader construct. A child's education is gleaned from various sources and transmitted through multiple generations. Parents, caregivers, family members, peers, religions, and communities all serve to educate children. Through these multiple sources, children are educated with the necessary information, values, and competencies needed to participate comfortably and effectively in their extended personal familial community. This extended community also provides children with the knowledge, attitudes, and skills required to contribute, as individuals and as members of a particular ethnic group, in the community's greater public, social, and political life. The ways students use their prior knowledge in school, and their ability to connect new information to what they already know, often determines the extent to which new knowledge is acquired. This section discusses knowledge acquisition and academic goals and standards.

Knowledge Acquisition

Students remember, shape, and link their existing experiential, cultural knowledge to new concepts to acquire new knowledge involving conceptual change. They connect prior cultural sets of knowledge, cognitive processes, and social skills to new concepts in ways that promote the construction of new knowledge and advance the development of new insights. Knowledge acquisition takes place when prior knowledge comes in contact with new evidence, which results in changed information resulting in new understandings. Vignette 8.1 exemplifies this process in a young child, and Vignette 8.2 describes language growth in a high school sheltered English writing lesson.

> *Vignette 8.1*
> *Seven Ways*
> Miguelito, my grandchild, age 2, while riding in the car repeatedly announced that there were two ways, *this way* and *that way* (prior experiential knowledge based on multiple trips going either up the street or down the street). Pointing to a direction, he would state, *We're going this way* or *Let's go that way.* Grandpa would respond, "Yes, we're going this way. The store (or wherever we were going) is down the road a piece."
>
> One rainy day, in a strange town, our family was taking him to a McDonald's Play Space before settling down in the motel. We went up the street one way quite a long way and then turned and went back the other way. We still could not find it. Grandpa decided to go back to the motel. Miguelito watched and kept looking for a McDonald's sign. All of a sudden he noticed the side streets. He pointed to them and started counting out loud: *one, two, three, four, five, six, seven* (new

evidence). He quickly said, *Grandpa, go that way! There's seven ways. Go that way! You can find it.* Grandpa complied. He went down a side street and stopped at a gas station for directions. Miguelito was delighted when we finally found a McDonald's Play Space. *See, there's seven ways,* he muttered as he waited to be let out of his car seat (new understanding).

Issues for Consideration
Although both two ways and seven ways are misconceptions of the different ways to get to a specific location, this example shows that young children think by remembering prior knowledge. It also shows that sometimes, with young children, you can almost see them thinking. You can watch them process new information. In this case, Miguelito's focus on the problem and awareness of new facts (side streets) helped him modify and change his original misconception that there were only two ways. Of course he was highly motivated to help find the play space. Do you think it can be observed when he realizes that there are more than seven ways? What learning conditions were in place?

Vignette 8.2
Sheltered Instruction
This activity took place in a Building Writing Skills high school summer class. Ariza has been in the United States for one year. She could converse in English.

> Each day, when she [Ariza] entered Mr. Walker's class she would see objectives listed on the board related to the writing genre the students would practice, the skill they would look for when peer editing, and the language function or grammar feature of the day. Mr. Walker would explain these to the class. Before reading a newspaper article, Mr. Walker and the class did an activity. Sometimes they looked at photographs and described what they saw, and Mr. Walker would list their words and later suggest how they might use these words in their writing. Sometimes he acted out a scenario with student volunteers, like a reporter interviewing witnesses to a crime. Then, after they read the article, they would act out their own group scenario and write it up. Before they read about teenagers who crashed their car, student groups made a word web about peer pressure—what it leads to and how to resist it. Mr. Walker modeled how they could complete their web on the board before they got to work. After reading the article, they discussed it with a partner to form an opinion on whether peer pressure led to the crash or not and then wrote an opinion essay. . . . Ariza was pleased that Mr. Walker felt her writing was improving and gave her advice on what features [e.g., grammar, punctuation, use of passive voice] to work on in future assignments. (Echevarria & Short, 2004, pp. 21–22)

Issues for Consideration
This example demonstrates effective sheltered instruction for English language learners. Notice how language learning was promoted through modeling, social interactions, and conversation in context. How did students use their prior

knowledge when interacting with each other and with the teacher to acquire new vocabulary, build new meanings, and improve their writing skills?

Academic Goals and Standards

In K-12 schooling students are required to learn subject matter content. One of the ways schools identify the specific knowledge and skills students need to know is through the development of standards. A committee, which may include experts in the content area, district personnel, teachers, and other interested or invited parties usually develop the standards. Standards establish the highest proficiency criterion or benchmarks that students are expected to achieve. They identify, define, and delineate the knowledge, concepts, and skills that students should master at each grade level in each subject area. Students are routinely tested for performance levels on various standards. Major goals focus on (a) bringing consistency and coherence to the subject matter; (b) assuring that all students learn what is required; and (c) deciding on a set of goals and curriculum that will be used to direct student testing, improve staff development, and determine school resources. Students approach, meet, exceed or are below the standard. Standards-based schooling is a systemic, homogenized approach to the teaching-learning process that (a) expects teachers to use an established set of standards; (b) tests students' level of proficiency of the endorsed standards; and (c) links student learning, promotion, graduation, and sometimes teacher salary, to student standard achievement. This section briefly discusses the evolvement of the standards movement, the goals of the No Child Left Behind Act (2001), and teacher responsibility to the application of these standards in diverse classrooms.

Evolution of Standards. *A Nation at Risk* (National Commission on Excellence, 1983), published by the U.S. Secretary of Education, can be considered a precursor to the development and implementation of content standards. This publication questioned the quality of U.S. public schools and warned of low academic achievement. It generated a back-to-basics movement and called for systematic educational reform. This trend prompted President George Bush to convene the National Governors Association in 1989. Endorsement of national educational goals and standards was one of the results of this conference. The first curriculum standards were created in mathematics: *Curriculum and Evaluation Standards for School Mathematics* (National Council of Teachers of Mathematics, 1989). The standards-based schooling and assessment legislation *No Child Left Behind* (2001) requires that teachers use approved standards to guide instructional content to determine student achievement.

Continued backing for content standards from national, state, and district levels resulted in standards in other subject areas such as science, history, physical education, language arts, social studies, and the arts. Teachers are expected to know the adopted content standards in their school district, and students are required to learn the content in each subject area at each grade level. It is the teachers' responsibility to cover this material and to provide learning conditions and classroom activities to help students acquire, master, and test well in the specific content knowledge and skills. Because content standards are part of public schooling, many states have developed standards frameworks. These frameworks (a) clarify how instruction and assessment are linked to standards, (b) delineate sets of learning goals for each subject to match each standard, and (c) recommend inservice teacher professional support.

No Child Left Behind. The *No Child Left Behind* legislation (2001) is the principal federal law affecting schooling in grades K through 12. It is designed to improve student achievement. This legislation requires that states test students' progress in reading and mathematics every year in grades 3 through 8 and at least once during grades 10 through 12. Science will be included in the testing assessments by the year 2007/2008. Schools are required to inform parents of their students' test scores and alert parents of their children's school performance. Theoretically, parents have the option of removing their children from low performing schools and enrolling them in higher performing schools, or they can receive afterschool services such as tutoring or remedial classes. A basic premise of *No Child Left Behind* (2001) is that if some schools can produce high achievement, then all schools should be able to do so.

This federal law also defines the qualifications of teachers and paraprofessionals who work in classrooms. It expects school districts to meet or develop plans to meet the goal of having highly qualified teachers in all classrooms. Some federal funding is provided to schools, and, in exchange for strong accountability, states and local districts are given more flexibility in the use of federal education funding.

Application of Standards in Diverse Classrooms. There is much debate and controversy regarding the selection and implementation of standards, especially when applied to underserved children. Some argue that critical questions have not been fully addressed. Some concerns include:

1. Who determines if the instructional content in the standards represent diverse perspectives and include the wide range of experiences of people in the United States?
2. How do standards accommodate the different ways students construct knowledge?
3. What is the role of students, teachers, and parents?
4. How are assessments linked to standards?
5. Do standards guide or control the teaching-learning process?

Obviously, all students, including those from poverty and ethnic groups of color, can and must be expected to learn and attain proficiency in the subject matter content identified by the standards. The first steps include (a) understanding what students should know and be able to do in each subject area, (b) making instruction culturally inclusive to ensure that more students have access to learning, and (c) modifying classroom resources and creating classroom conditions to enable all students to learn.

The most compelling motivation for learning is intrinsic, thus Kohn (1999) explains that high achievement is directly related to student interest. He distinguishes between fun and interest, pointing out that mastering content of interest to students (that which they find satisfying to them) requires intense effort, concentration, and hard work. Students' interest in the subject matter creates a personal connection that drives engagement leading to competence.

Newmann (1992) points out that one of the most immediate and persisting issues for teachers is the lack of student engagement. Students' disengagement may be an outcome of meaningless instructional content that is disconnected from their experiential knowledge. However, the type and quality of student engagement must be evaluated. It is important not to mistake activity for achievement or to confuse behavioral compliance with knowledge gain. In other words, busy, well-behaved students are not necessarily learning what the teacher intended.

The following two vignettes *Chicken Egg* (Greenfield, Raeff, & Quiroz, 1995) and *Hummingbirds* (Rothstein-Fisch, Greenfield, & Trumbull, 1999) contrast the ways two teachers framed scientific content knowledge and shows how this orientation either compromised or enhanced student learning. Both of these events took place in settings with a majority of Mexican American students. The teacher in *Hummingbirds* received special preparation in how to apply Mexican American students' cultural knowledge in the teaching-learning process.

Vignette 8.3
Chicken Egg

> A kindergarten teacher was showing her class an actual chicken egg that would be hatching soon. She was explaining the physical properties of the egg, and she asked the children to describe the eggs by thinking about the times they had cooked and eaten eggs. One of the children tried three times to talk about how she cooked eggs with her grandmother, but the teacher disregarded these comments in favor of a child who explained how eggs look white and yellow when they are cracked. (Greenfield et al., 1995, p. 44)

Issues for Consideration

The child's comment about "cooking eggs with her grandmother" was a valid response to the question "to think about the times they had cooked and eaten eggs." The student described an interpersonal experience involving an egg. She linked this experiential knowledge to the question. The teacher was expecting students to describe the physical attributes of the egg in isolation, such as the shape, colors, or parts. She most likely considered this type of description scientific. Unfortunately, she did not understand why the student was responding with a story about how the egg intersected with her lived, social experiences. This scenario shows that sometimes children who do not share the same points of reference with the teacher cannot know what the teacher expects, especially if the teacher's question is ambiguous.

Does your conceptualization of what constitutes science influence what you might accept as a correct answer? Do you think that the lack of **knowledge of culture** (information about other cultural groups) affects teacher competency? What are ways teachers can acknowledge and validate the scientific content knowledge children acquire from their routine, interpersonal, cultural, and ethnic experiences? How can students' home knowledge be used to promote new scientific content knowledge? How do you think experiences of this nature on the elementary level affect students' scientific interest and achievement in middle school and high school? Do you think you can use students' home experiences to extend new knowledge and to open classroom discourse to diverse ways of knowing?

Vignette 8.4
Hummingbirds

> In preparation for a field trip to a nearby wetlands Ms. Altchech (4th–5th grade) invited a docent to visit the class. He asked, "What do you know about humming-birds?" Students began to tell stories about their family's experiences with birds, but the docent became impatient and said, "No more stories!" He expected students to use scientific language to talk about hummingbird anatomy or ecology. . . . When the children were told to stop telling stories, they became silent. (Rothstein-Fisch et al., 1999, p. 66)

When the docent left, Ms. Altchech extended the lesson. She wrote "Story Highlights" on the left side of the blackboard and "Scientific Aspects" on the right. As students shared information, she categorized student responses on one of these two sides. All responses were perceived as valid.

> In one story a child reported being in the garden with her grandmother when she noticed that hummingbirds seemed to stand still in the air. This family-based story led to a discussion about how the wings of hummingbirds must beat rapidly to sustain their apparent stillness. The children, fascinated by the topic, engaged in scientific discourse, scaffolded by the teacher, about how body mass, metabolism, and food intake are related. (Rothstein-Fisch, et al., 1999, p. 66)

Issues for Consideration
When discussing and comparing the classroom teacher and docent behavior in these two vignettes, what aspects of this event do you find most problematic? Why? Can you identify specific teacher behaviors that explicitly connect the home and school knowledge to science? In what ways did teacher behavior encourage or discourage student engagement? What teacher-created conditions enabled students to acquire new knowledge?

Classroom Applications

Classrooms operating on a single cultural model will have difficulty providing adequate schooling experiences to all children. Lessons created for mainstream children may limit learning opportunities for some children. Awareness of how culturally inclusive content advantages more children is critical. Generally speaking, adopted textbooks and pack-aged programs do not take into account the cultural diversity present in the students' unique family backgrounds nor do they utilize the prior knowledge children bring to school. The following suggestions are designed to help you incorporate culturally inclusive content and find ways to adapt any instructional resource. You are encouraged to gain knowledge of other cultures as well as develop a deeper understanding of your own experiences. Improved academic achievement and changes in your own and your students' attitudes and behaviors, as well as improved interactions with families, can help you to evaluate your program and to guide future direction.

Observing Students' Responses to Materials

Observe how children in your classroom from different racial, ethnic, linguistic, and cultural groups respond to culturally inclusive materials and to materials reflecting other ideologies.

1. Analyze instructional materials to identify the producers' ideology.
2. Adapt instructional material reflecting diverse ideological positions to meet the needs of the particular students in your classroom.
3. Examine how students respond to instructional resources. You might start by writing down the behaviors and responses of one or two students, or you can note the degree of engagement of different learners or groups of students.
4. Describe successful and unsuccessful lessons to interpret any patterns that emerge. Note levels of engagement, appraise the situation, and make needed changes in the lesson content and delivery of instruction to see if positive change occurs. Replicate successful lessons.
5. Hold discussion groups with parents to gain information from their perspectives of their child's strengths and preferences. Ask what they would like their child to learn in the classroom. Find out the students' interests and areas of expertise.
6. Take classes, read, and share materials specific to the developmental process of children from diverse ethnic, cultural, ability, and language groups. Participate in university courses or in-service training opportunities to increase your cultural content knowledge, and apply this information when working with culturally and linguistically diverse children and their families.

Acknowledging Students' Cultural Knowledge

Value the cultural knowledge students bring to school by acknowledging multiple aspects of diversity through respect, discussion, and affirmation.

1. Discuss ideas, feelings, and experiences students choose to share when responding to instructional content.
2. Use resources that reflect all kinds of family lifestyles. Be aware of children who live with grandparents, in single-parent homes, or in foster care and of children who have homosexual or biracial parents. Be cautious when planning family-related activities that potentially exclude some children, such as holding a Mother's Tea, making Father's Day cards, or creating family trees. Realize that some

children may not have baby pictures to bring to school and some may not have money to purchase required items or to pay for field trip events.

Building Home and School Relationships

Build strong interpersonal relationships between home and school to encourage open communication and increase caregivers' involvement in school activities.

1. Invite parents to share cultural knowledge such as traditional stories or songs or to demonstrate job skills or unique talents. Observe a *You Are Special Day* and have students make cards and gifts for people they love. Have children invite a significant other of their choice to a classroom curricular event, school breakfast, play, concert, or other event.
2. Collaborate with other teachers, parents, caregivers, and the community to organize workshops on meaningful topics based on common interests and needs.
3. Identify any adverse social factors, such as poor nutrition, abuse, homelessness, parental depression, violence, or drugs, that may affect families, and bring culturally knowledgeable and sensitive experts to advise staff or small groups of parents on ways to more effectively meet the needs of children exposed to these circumstances.

Exploring Cultural, Ethnic, and Linguistic Backgrounds

Explore your own ethnic, cultural, and linguistic background as well as the diversity specific to your classroom community.

1. Examine how your race, ethnicity, sexual orientation, abilities, gender, religion, class, and economic status positions you culturally, guides your perceptions and attitudes, and influences how you think and act.
2. Invite speakers to your staff meetings to explain cultural practices, ability differences, diverse religions, and lifestyles practiced in your school community.
3. Use parent conferences and community resources to increase your understanding of the various cultural groups represented in your school.
4. Construct a personal history, beginning with the surname you acquired matrilineally or patrilineally or to the lineage acquired through adoption or marriage.
5. Interview family members to find out the origins of your family traditions, beliefs, and customs.
6. If you do not speak another world language, interview family members to find out when and why the language shift occurred.

Conclusion

By using inclusive instructional content, you and your students will be challenged to define controversial abstract concepts such as power, control, abilities, oppression, privilege, entitlements, voice, personal needs, and group requirements. You are highly likely to become more alert to the cultural nuances in curricular content, especially in subject areas often considered culture-free such as science and mathematics. Thinking critically about multiple worldviews might promote the discussion of realistic and hopeful solutions and future contributions to the social and political issues facing our national and global society. You as teacher will go beyond the mere inclusion and exposure of materials with illustrations of people from diverse ethnic and racial groups to connect the teaching-learning process to its cultural context.

RECOMMENDED READINGS

Anyon, J. (1981). Schools as agencies of social legitimation. *Journal of Curriculum Theorizing, 3*(2), 86–103.

Gay, G. (2000). *Culturally responsive teaching: Theory, research, and practice.* New York: Teachers College Press.

9 Instruction: Developing Reasoning Skills

As a classroom teacher, you bring your own cultural norms into your professional practice. The extent to which your teaching behavior will become an extension of your own culture exclusively or will incorporate the cultures of the students you teach may be influenced by your perceptions of the relationship between culture and school practices, political beliefs, and conceptionalization of school learning.
—Hollins, 1996, pp. 2–3

Teaching is not separate from learning. Purposeful movement, teacher talk, evidence of planning, attempts to engage students, grading student work, or efforts to maintain order can be observed in classrooms. Teachers may express feelings of efficacy and commitment. However, if students do not learn what is intended, teaching is not taking place.

The purpose of this chapter is to help you understand the relationship among culture, cognition, teaching, and learning and to explore culturally inclusive instructional strategies that promote learning. Part I introduces the seventh diversity pedagogy dimension, instruction/reasoning skills. The second section examines structures of intellectual standards and discusses ways to reframe instruction (teacher pedagogical behaviors). The next part focuses on the culturally influenced student approaches to learning (student cultural displays). This is followed by classroom applications.

Diversity Pedagogy Dimension 7: Instruction/Reasoning Skills

This dimension promotes understanding of cognitive models and culturally inclusive approaches to learning. It examines teaching strategies needed to implement this dimension and describes how students demonstrate culturally influenced reasoning skills (see Table 9.1, pp. 146–147). Application of this dimension acknowledges a basic principle: Instruction is not generic. Students do not receive the same instruction identically. Successful lessons with one student or with a group of students may be neither appropriate nor effective with a different child or group. Teacher ability to deliver culturally inclusive instruction to diverse students is consequential to their opportunity to learn.

TABLE 9.1   Diversity Pedagogy Dimension 7: Instruction/Reasoning Skills

Definition of Dimensional Elements

Instruction: Teacher actions facilitating the construction of students' new knowledge through teaching strategies connecting students' prior cultural knowledge to new understandings, creation of a classroom context enabling student learning, and selection of culturally inclusive content.

Reasoning Skills: Ability to apply knowledge from personal cultural practices, language, and ethnic experiences to gain command of one's thinking through the acquisition and development of the thinking tools needed to gain new knowledge and take control of one's learning.

Teacher Pedagogical Behaviors

Student Cultural Displays

Exhibits knowledge of the disciplines one is expected to teach and understands the pedagogical methods required to facilitate student learning in these content areas.
- Creates and implements instruction goals for diverse student populations in specific content areas.
- Evaluates and adapts lessons for student understanding and subject matter mastery.
- Recognizes and responds to students' perceptions, interpretations, or misconceptions to subject matter content.

Signs of active use of prior cultural knowledge, skills, language, and concepts to acquire and construct new knowledge and understandings of concepts from various school content areas.
- Consistently demonstrates measurable academic improvement and competency in all subject areas.
- Identifies with and responds to the classroom's instructional content.
- Evaluates subject matter content for diverse cultural, social, and political perspectives and interpretations.

Uses instructional resources, classroom context, and teaching strategies as tools to guide student learning.
- Decides what, when, and how learning activities are structured.
- Uses a variety of instructional styles to present new concepts.
- Utilizes the evolving nature of lessons to incorporate students' cultural knowledge, cognitive preferences, language strengths, communication styles, and motivational systems to jointly produce and construct new knowledge.

Exhibits cognitive strengths in preferred learning styles and acquires skills in nonpreferred learning modalities.
- Can function socially and cognitively in diverse learning situations.
- Applies diverse learning styles to classroom learning events.
- Contributes to the construction of personal and group new knowledge, identifies cognitive and social strengths and weaknesses, and practices self-motivation and self-discipline in the acquisition of new knowledge.

Understands the purpose, value, standards, and elements of thinking; knows how thinking develops; is skilled in teaching thinking skills; creates an environment allowing students to take control of their learning; and facilitates the development of responsible lifelong learners.
- Understands how to challenge beginning thinkers.

Expressions indicating an understanding of the purpose, value, standards, and elements of thinking while acquiring the intellectual traits needed to develop, practice, and master the thinking skills needed to take control of ones' learning and mature into a lifelong learner.
- Examines and controls own thinking.

Teacher Pedagogical Behaviors	Student Cultural Displays
• Is skilled in questioning techniques that encourage higher level thinking skills. • Provides opportunity to practice advanced thinking. • Can identify and apply purposes of thinking. • Acknowledges the value of thinking. • Encourages thinking about thinking to develop higher level thinking skills.	• Acquires intellectual standards and recognizes elements of critical thinking. • Develops intellectual traits characteristic of successful thinkers. • Moves beyond dualistic thinking. • Respects the opinions and worldviews of others. • Makes thinking about thinking a priority and is consciously aware of own thinking process.

Teacher Pedagogical Behaviors

Teaching-learning events can be described as specific, jointed activities between two (or more) individuals where new understandings are co-constructed. When these experiences take place in formal schooling contexts, it is presumed that students will experience new ways of doing things in an environment that is generally different from the ways they learn in their homes. It is also assumed that some students come to school with experiences, skills, strengths, and knowledge used to perform competently within their cultural group; but these same characteristics may be perceived as peripheral or irrelevant in the classroom. To provide better services to more students, teachers must understand how culture influences cognitive and social development and know how to apply these understandings in teaching-learning situations. This section examines models of intellectual standards and discusses ways to reframe instruction.

Intellectual Standards

Models of thinking can be useful when designing teaching-learning events. Knowledge and application of intellectual standards help identify the nature of higher level, critical thinking skills. Appropriately challenging learning events for students encourage them to practice thinking at deeper levels, which improves their academic and social skills. Critical thinkers acquire knowledge about thinking and develop skills to practice thinking about thinking. Three models (tools) are discussed: cognitive objectives; scheme of intellectual and ethical development; and intellectual standards, elements, and traits.

Cognitive Objectives. Bloom (1956) developed a tool, commonly known as Bloom's Taxonomy, to delineate a hierarchy of cognitive objectives. He places thought in six levels, from simple knowledge at the bottom to complex evaluative thinking at the top (see Table 9.2, p. 148). In this model, each level subsumes those below. According to Bloom, analysis involves thinking at a higher level and includes application, comprehension, and knowledge. He points out that new ideas can only be generated in the top

TABLE 9.2   **Bloom's Taxonomy of Cognitive Objectives**

Cognitive Objective	Description
Knowledge	*The lowest level of thinking.* Recalls facts and specific information such as dates, theories, events, people, places, and chronological sequences. Recognizes patterns in the structure, content, or setting, such as categories in classes and groups. Summarizes information.
Comprehension	*The lowest level of understanding.* Accurately paraphrases and preserves the original concept. Uses information from one form to another to complete other low-cognitive tasks such as translation, interpretation, consequences, and prediction.
Application	*Using knowledge from one source in a different situation.* Utilizes concepts, ideas, or abstractions such as theories, principles, laws, or technical procedures in concrete situations and settings.
Analysis	*Beginning of higher level thinking skills.* Understands the implicit structure of the concept or work. Clarifies the relationship among ideas, identifies the purpose and intent, explains how ideas are organized, and explores the ways they are conveyed in the message.
Synthesis	*Combining parts to form a new whole.* Arranges the elements of a structure in new patterns to create new understandings from the parts or elements that were either not there before or were not clear. Formulates or tests appropriate hypothesis based on an analysis of the factors involved. Modifies assumptions based on new factors, information, or knowledge.
Evaluation	*The highest level of thinking.* Uses a standard or creates criteria to make judgments and appraisals about the extent to which the materials satisfy established criteria. Evaluates the accuracy, logic, authenticity, consistency, and quality of work based on internal evidence and external criteria. Finds fallacies and strengths in arguments. Compares and contrasts theories, generalizations, and facts about particular ideas, cultures, theories, or ideals.

Source: Adapted from Bloom (1956).

three levels: analysis, synthesis, and evaluation. Ideally, students need to function well at all levels. However students must be given multiple and consistent opportunities to practice the higher level thinking skills, if they are to develop as advanced critical thinkers.

Understanding the skills and nature of each category in Bloom's Taxonomy (Bloom, 1956) can help teachers encourage students' movement from lower levels of cognitive comfort to higher levels of thinking. However, cultural adaptations are needed when applications are made to diverse student populations because children acquire and display knowledge and skills in different ways. Students' experiential background must be used as the starting point to explore new ideas. Consider knowledge, the lowest level of thinking. According to Bloom, some of the skills in this cognitive objective include student ability to recognize patterns and categorize objects and ideas in classes. While culturally diverse students have the ability to recognize patterns in a given structure and can classify and categorize objects, they will be more successful when the specific task is relevant to their everyday practical experience. The problem may not lie in the culturally diverse students' ability to acquire, develop, and demonstrate thinking skills. It may instead reside in the students' capacity to adjust to specific tasks required in classrooms and in their teachers' ability to adapt instruction to their cultural approach to learning. Additionally, students' performance or lack of performance with a simple task should not be used to predict student ability to perform a more complex task and vice versa (Kozulin, 2004).

Scheme of Intellectual and Ethical Development. Perry (1970) viewed intellectual (and moral) development through nine positions that he grouped in four categories: duality, multiplicity, relativism, and committed relativism. When Perry documented the changes of thinking in college students, he described their thinking as a developmental process that was characterized by their personal understandings and their attitudes toward knowledge and other worldviews (see Table 9.3, p. 150).

Perry's categories are not cumulative like Bloom's; rather, each replaces the former once the individual has developed the capacity to work through each category. He theorizes that a type of paradigm shift takes place in one's psychological development.

Dualistic Thinking. Perry's (1970) theory describes a developmental process beginning with dualistic thinking. He describes **dualistic thinking** as a simplistic division of knowledge in two opposing dimensions and the inclination to divide reality into opposing parts. Binary pairs such as us/them, majority/minority, normal/abnormal, right/wrong, good/bad, young/old, win/lose, pretty/ugly, rich/poor, abled/disabled, and men/women are generated in the mind. The first one considered is generally viewed as higher, better, and more valued. This establishes a hierarchy of categories in our thinking. It often provides justification to minimize, overlook, or dominate those perceived to be members of the lower, less valuable group. Consequently, we may believe that rich people are superior to poor people. Similarly, a majority connection may be perceived as favorable, whereas association or membership in minority groups may have pejorative implications. We might even accept that certain children are entitled to higher quality schooling.

Dualism in reality, thoughts, and language is present in the normal expressions of young children. However, when this form of dualistic thinking (often unconscious) continues throughout middle childhood and adolescence, it limits students' ability to understand differences. Adolescents' cognitive skills indicate that they are capable of moving from low levels of cognitive development characteristic of dualistic thinking toward higher level thinking processes. Wigfield et al. (1996) summarize the changes in the thinking of children as they move into adolescence. During adolescence children

1. Increase their ability to think abstractly.
2. Consider multiple aspects of real or hypothetical problems at once.
3. Reflect on their actual and potential role in the issue under discussion.
4. Use more sophisticated learning strategies to acquire new information.
5. Assess their strengths and weaknesses as learners.
6. Handle complex, controversial, and advanced topics.

Adolescents do not automatically develop into better thinkers (Keating, 1990). Although students have the capability, they need multiple experiences to develop higher level thinking skills. Providing opportunities for students to view reality through

TABLE 9.3 Perry's Scheme of Intellectual and Ethical Development

Category	Intellectual/Moral Behavior
1. Dualism: Received Knowledge	Everything is right or wrong. Things are good or bad. You experience success or failure. Authorities, such as teachers and textbooks, know the correct answers. All problems can be solved. It is the learners' task to learn and memorize the correct answers and find right solutions. While some authorities may disagree with each other and some may have obscured positions, the student must select the correct answer and ignore all other positions and views.
2. Multiplicity: Subjective Knowledge	There are two types of problems, those with known and those with unknown solutions. Since solutions to most problems are not known and there may be diversity in opinions (conflicting answers), everyone has a right to trust his or her inner voice rather than rely on external authorities. Students feel they are entitled to provide personal opinions, without documentation, as probable solutions to problems. No one is wrong, and judgments cannot be made to select the right answer. Sometimes students in this position become frustrated because no one is giving them the correct answer.
3. Relativism: Procedural Knowledge	Realization that some solutions may be better than others, depending on the context and relative to available support. Reasoning methods and definite sources of knowledge are used to think about and to evaluate proposed solutions. Judgments supported by reason and evidence can reject or support ideas, values, or worldviews.
4. Commitment: Constructed Knowledge	Understanding the necessity of making choices and committing to a solution. Consciousness that knowledge is learned from others and is integrated with personal experience and reflection. Students make a commitment for the future and explore issues of responsibility, realizing that commitments are ongoing, unfolding, and evolving.

Source: Adapted from Perry (1970).

numerous perspectives helps them understand, evaluate, question, and challenge the issues inherent in concepts such as fairness, ability, ownership, racism, equality, hierarchy, democracy, privilege, oppression, and poverty. Through these experiences students can become aware of the importance of their thinking, the power of their word, and the consequences of their actions.

Perry's work can help teachers recognize and address dualistic thinkers' perplexity when faced with multiple, plausible interpretations to an issue. Teachers can develop strategies requiring students to use data to support their assumptions or opinions. Students can be challenged and nurtured to operate at a relativistic level. Teachers who acknowledge the limitations of dualistic thinking are more likely to provide experiences that move students to higher developmental stages. The critical analysis of curricular content can also help students consider other worldviews and respect differences, whereas continual conceptualization of ideas, objects, people, and attitudes at a dualistic level can be restrictive.

Intellectual Standards, Elements, and Traits. Paul and Elder (2001) maintain that we are what we think; however, most people rarely make thinking explicit. Thinking often remains at a subconscious level. Challenging students to think at higher levels is often compromised because learners are neither aware of their thinking process nor do they have the tools needed to correct poor thinking. Sometimes teachers encourage students to develop critical thinking skills without fully comprehending what this entails or understanding how to make learning about thinking a priority (see Table 9.4, p. 152).

Developing into a critical thinker is key to recognizing (a) the power of thinking, (b) the consequences of taking control of one's learning, (c) the ability to apply knowledge from one situation to another, and (d) the importance of becoming a lifelong learner. One of the most significant skills that students can learn is the intellectual competency needed to learn how to learn. Students must be taught to become critics of their own thinking, before they can evaluate and criticize the thinking of others.

Reframing Instruction

Teachers are responsible for creating optimal learning conditions that enable culturally, ethnically, and linguistically diverse children to learn. Teacher behavior in the classroom often determines who has access to teaching-learning events. Responses to the following questions are discussed below: What is involved in lesson preparation? What instructional techniques and teaching styles incorporate culturally inclusive, balanced approaches to the ways diverse students prefer to learn?

Lesson Preparation. Generally, it is more difficult to change a misconception than it is to learn a new concept. The development of lesson plans, as an element of lesson preparation, is often misunderstood. Some novice teachers think that lesson plans can be developed without identifying the characteristics, prior knowledge, and cultural heritage of the students for whom the lesson plan is intended. Some may assume that previously created lesson plans can be used with different groups of students without adaptation.

TABLE 9.4   Intellectual Standards, Elements, and Traits

The Standards	
clarity	precision
accuracy	significance
relevance	completeness
logicalness	fairness
breadth	depth

must be
applied to

The Elements	
purposes	inferences
questions	concepts
points of view	implications
information	assumptions

as we learn
to develop

Intellectual Traits	
intellectual humility	intellectual perseverance
intellectual autonomy	confidence in reason
intellectual integrity	intellectual empathy
intellectual courage	fair-mindedness

Source: Paul, Richard, & Elder, Linda. (2001). *Critical Thinking: Tools for Taking Charge of Your Learning and Your Life*, 1st edition, p. 50. © 2001. Printed by permission of Pearson Education, Inc., Upper Saddle River, NJ.

Understanding that lesson plans cannot be written in abstraction is key to effective instruction. Although you can know the content and outcome, critical elements of lesson plans are beyond your reach unless you create or adapt them for a particular group of students. Without knowledge of your students and information about the context in which the lesson will be taught, you will not know how to select the appropriate teaching tools (teaching strategies) or understand how to link students' prior knowledge to new understandings. Vignette 9.1 may help clarify this point.

Vignette 9.1
Door in the Wall
Consider planning the installation of a door in a wall. You assume that the objective (install a door), content of the lesson (steps needed to install a door), and outcome (completed installation of a working door) provides enough information. You design a plan without seeing the wall where the door will be placed.

You arrive at the location with a plan, specific tools, and strategies. You find a brick wall. Your tools are designed to cut plasterboard. Your plan does not include information to deal with the pipes and wires in the space. You have planned for the task, and you follow the steps to the best of your ability: (a) measure the space with a tape measure, (b) use a saw to cut out the space for the door, (c) implement the steps to install the door, (d) check that the door opens and closes appropriately, and (e) clean up after yourself.

Issues for Consideration

The teaching-learning process is far more complex than installing a door. This experience shares similar issues with teaching-learning process. Think of the relationship between the door lesson plan and the importance of considering the skills, characteristics, and prior knowledge of students in a specific context. Will you continue to use a tool designed for plaster board on a brick wall? Will you use teaching strategies that are inappropriate or harmful for students in your class? Will you turn the electricity, water, and gas off, cut the wires and pipes, install the door, and let someone else worry about the consequences of your actions? Will you take into consideration multiple diversity issues such as culture, ethnicity, language, gender, and ability when planning lessons? Whose responsibility is it if the house floods, burns down, or is damaged as a result of your work? Who is accountable when students do not learn? What factors remove teachers from their responsibility to teach? Are good intentions and hard work enough?

Types of Lesson Plans. As you acquire information about your students in your classroom, you will learn to plan, create, develop, implement, refine, and evaluate lessons. There are different categories of lesson planning: long-range, short-term, and daily. **Long-range lesson planning** is basic to the implementation of coherent, interdisciplinary, thematic short-term and daily lessons. Long-range lesson plans are (a) sometimes referred to as standards or goals; (b) generally yearly, quarterly, and monthly; (c) usually found in district, state, and national curriculum standards; and (d) often present in teacher guides accompanying student texts. They provide a general overview of the subject matter goals and objectives in specific subject areas. These plans can rarely be meaningfully transferred to daily classroom instruction. Although the outcome may remain the same, the content, materials selected, and teaching strategies require adaptation to the specific situation and particular students in your class.

Short-term lessons, one or two weeks in length, focus on specific concepts or short curricular units. **Daily lessons,** prepared and modified on a day-to-day basis, respond to the learning that has taken place, is taking place, or is not taking place. Novice teachers generally write long daily lesson plans describing the teaching-learning event and detailing complex teaching strategies. During this planning process, they (a) consider ways to implement culturally inclusive teaching strategies, (b) note the prerequisite skills needed to link new knowledge to students' prior skills, (c) record ways to shelter instruction for English language learners, (d) list specific questions addressing different levels of thinking, (e) identify vocabulary applicable to the lesson, (f) delineate step-by-step procedures of the actual lesson, and (g) identify ways to evaluate student learning and teacher effectiveness. As teachers gain knowledge about the skills and learning preferences of the cultural groups in their classrooms, acquire content knowledge, and internalize aspects of the teaching-learning process, written daily lesson plans may shorten in length and detail, but not in quality.

Components of a Lesson Plan.   Although there are many ways to think of lesson plans, it is helpful to identify various parts of lesson preparation (see Table 9.5). Understanding the purpose these components helps create culturally inclusive lessons and guides ways to adapt generic lessons found in textbook teacher guides, commercially prepared lesson plans, and those found in other sources, such as the Internet, teacher magazines, or handouts from professional in-service workshops.

Teaching Strategies.   **Teacher strategies** are deliberate behaviors in classrooms with the purpose of promoting student learning. Regardless of the particular teaching strategy, effective teachers use some form of explicit, culturally inclusive instruction to facilitate student learning. These culturally adaptive strategies promote teaching-learning activities that are relevant to the learners' interests, background, skills, and strengths.

Teacher centered strategies involve forms of direct instruction such as lectures, demonstrations, presentations, drills, discussions, and brainstorming. In **student centered strategies,** the teacher facilitates the teaching-learning event. This can include assisting cooperative or collaborative group learning, providing peer tutoring opportunities, preparing reciprocal peer teaching events, and guiding individual independent learning activities. Teachers who accommodate the cognitive and social needs of culturally diverse students (a) develop skills using multiple teaching tools and (b) select specific teaching strategies that promote higher level thinking skills and accommodate cultural approaches to learning.

Two teaching-learning approaches discussed below, group learning and active/affective engagement, are preferred by students from some ethnic groups of color. However, this does not mean that all students from a particular ethnic group learn the same way. Although students from particular ethnic or cultural groups may share learning regularities or patterns, we cannot assume that they share the same experiences or that preference for a particular learning approach is a fixed trait of all individuals from that particular ethnic or cultural group (Gay, 2000). That is, some African American students may prefer to work independently and others may thrive academically and socially through competitive experiences.

Group Learning.   Learning can involve individual responsibility, effort and cognition; however, it can also take place in a social interpersonal context, involving dialogue and mutual construction of new knowledge. Research shows that group learning improves the academic achievement of students who have experienced a communal or collective value orientation (Boykin, 1994; Gay, 2000; Losey, 1997; Slavin, 1995). Hofstede (1980) refers to these distinct cultural value orientations as "communications versus individualism." Triandis (1988) labels them "collectivism versus individualism." Many Asian

TABLE 9.5 Lesson Plan Components

Components	Description
Setting and Student Population	Identify the school and classroom setting. Study the student population where you plan to implement the lesson plan. Become aware of factors, such as students' cultural background, prior academic and social schooling experiences, learning preferences, grade level, age, ethnicity, race, gender, socioeconomic status, performance levels in the various subject matter areas, and language strengths and differences. Identify the knowledge students possess to determine what they know or do not know. Determine the essential prerequisite skills (what you anticipate that the students need to know) before you select teaching tools and instructional content.
Goals and Objectives	Have a clear statement of your teacher goals and student objectives (generally two or three). Identify what you want the students to learn. What is the purpose of the lesson? Why are you teaching it? How and where does it fit with curricular standards? What will the students learn as a result of the teaching-learning experience?
Resources and Materials	Examine and evaluate the variety of resources available to you. Become aware of any content or instructional constraints. Identify established curricular standards in each subject area for the particular grade level. Select culturally inclusive instructional resources from a variety of sources, such as written texts, audio and visual aids, and hands-on artifacts. (See Chapter 8 for suggestions on ways to determine the appropriateness of instructional materials and resources.)
Teaching Strategies	Become conscious of your behavior prior to the lesson, during the lesson, and after the lesson. Acknowledge the needs of the students involved in the lesson. Know what students who are not involved in the lesson will do. Think of ways to evaluate the learning of the students who participated in the lesson. At this point, begin writing the actual lesson plan. A lesson plan is a description of what you will do during the teaching-learning experiences. Address the following: (a) lesson introduction; (b) subject matter content; (c) sequence the various parts of the lesson; (d) teaching strategies, thinking tools, and instructional resources; and (e) extended activities beyond the lesson such as seatwork and homework.
Student Assessment and Teacher Competency	Evaluate established goals and objectives, appropriateness of instructional resources, and effectiveness of teaching strategies. How will you know what was learned by students? Were the instructional resources culturally inclusive? How will you determine the degree of student interest, motivation, and participation? How can you improve the delivery of this lesson? (See Chapter 10 for more information.)

American, African American, and Latino American students show preference for group learning because they have been socialized in a collective, interpersonal, and relational cultural context. These students regard themselves as part of a group and community. They value social bonds, support group achievement, and accept group responsibility. Teacher comments such as "Help your classmate" and "We are a community" support this orientation. European American students, socialized with an individualistic value orientation, generally prefer a competitive and independent learning context and process. They see themselves as individual personalities, prefer to achieve autonomously, value individual accomplishments, and accept responsibility for their own efforts. These students may respond to statements such as "You need to help yourself" or "The person with the highest score gets a star."

Two types of group learning, cooperative and collaborative, share similar characteristics and retain distinct elements. **Cooperative learning** involves students working in small groups. These groups are often controlled and manipulated by the teacher. Teachers often (a) decide who participates in the various groups and the number of participants in each group; (b) use group learning to promote cross-cultural, cross-ability, and cross-gender social interactions; (c) separate students who they predict may have behavioral issues when working in groups; and (d) evaluate students individually. They may assign individual roles, such as leader or note taker within the group. In cooperative groups, it is possible for students to work independently and create individual products or pieces that are later combined in a group outcome such as a group oral presentation or project. Sometimes cooperative group learning experiences are competitive in nature. When this is the case, teachers replace individual competition with group competition. Generally, cooperative learning groups function at a lower level of group cohesiveness and engagement.

In **collaborative learning groups,** interpersonal interactions are at a higher level of personal involvement. Group responsibility is enhanced, participation is more focused on learning and sharing, and the process takes place in a more natural learning context. This type of interaction often creates what Boykin and Bailey (2000) call communalism, priority placed on the social bond and responsibility to the group. Teachers generally (a) allow students to self-select their working groups, (b) evaluate the group process as well as the individual and group product, and (c) expect group efforts to produce a superior outcome that would not have been possible individually or completed without the meaningful contribution of each group member.

Consider the following when preparing students for group work:

1. Encourage movement from cooperative to collaborative group process.
2. Allow students to self-select group members.
3. Minimize competition.
4. Endorse the development of social bonds and friendships.
5. Focus on responsibility to the group.
6. Promote equal participation in the learning process.
7. Design open-ended learning activities.
8. Practice group communication skills.
9. Apply negotiation and problem-solving skills.
10. Develop self-evaluation skills on group process and product.

Active and Affective Engagement. Gay (2000, p. 169) explains that the inclusion of multiple sensory stimulation in an instructional strategy involves creating learning situations that are "active, participatory, emotionally engaging, and filled with visual and physical stimulation." Studies show that teaching strategies that (a) place emphasis on emotions and feelings, (b) put together sensory stimulation, (c) incorporate high levels of energy, (d) allow for individual personality expressions, (e) promote oral and aural communication, and (f) encourage spontaneity in behavior are effective with many African American students (Boykin, 1994; Boykin & Bailey, 2000; Walton, 1997). These teaching strategies support active and affective engagement; include opportunities for rich oral conversation; may use dramatic performances, movement, music, and dance to promote academic understandings; and encourage peer support in a group learning context and process.

Boykin and Bailey (2000) suggest that you consider the following when developing teaching strategies to support students' active and affective engagement:

1. Express thoughts, ideas, and emotions openly.
2. Share knowledge and materials.
3. Use purposeful, expressive movement.
4. Incorporate music, dance, and rhythm in cognitive tasks.
5. Support heightened levels of physical stimulation.
6. Encourage social orientation, interconnectedness, and bonding.
7. Recognize the rhythmic orientation manifested in speech patterns.
8. Include multiple and varied stimulus, activities, and elements in the environment.
9. Acknowledge multitask competence.
10. Endorse cultural practices originating in the home.

Teachers who value what students know and how they know provide a balanced approach to learning. Designing a variety of learning events to accommodate different learning preferences helps students develop learning flexibility. Understanding how to use general information on cultural learning characteristics of diverse groups is important; however, use caution so that these learning characteristics acknowledge within group differences. Realize that it is not reasonable to think that every individual of a particular ethnic group will display the same learning preference. Notice how Lois (teacher) in Vignette 9.2 uses instruction to respond to children's understandings.

Vignette 9.2
Who Would Like to Go?
This event took place in a kindergarten classroom with immigrant, first generation children from different countries, and native born children from diverse ethnic groups. Carlos selects a book about a Japanese American family from the classroom's "Reading Center."

> Before Lois begins to read the story, she tells the students a little about this ethnic group, like the proper name, its country of origin, some symbol of its culture (they eat a lot of different kinds of noodles), and where large numbers of its members

live in the United States. She asks if anyone can find Japan and California on the maps. She helps the group locate these places. As the students return to their places and settle down for the story, we hear Lois asking, "If we wanted to go to the places where there are a lot of Japanese Americans, how would we get there? Who would like to go?" Several hands pop up quickly at the thought of such an imagined journey. Incidentally (maybe not), the book Carlos chose to read is about a little boy taking his first airplane ride with his parents to go visit his grandparents who live far away. Once this "context setting" is completed, Lois proceeds through a dialogic reading of the book. She pauses frequently to probe the students' understanding of associated meaning prompted by the narrative text, to examine their feelings, and to predict upcoming developments in the story. (Gay, 2000, pp. 41–42)

Issues for Consideration

Lois is described as a teacher who has the "ability to make their instruction personally meaningful and culturally congruent for students" (Gay, 2000, p. 205). Can you describe how Lois responds to and incorporates the children's cultural learning preferences? Explain why Lois's "context setting" helped personalize the story for the children. How did her questioning techniques support diverse children's understandings? What aspects of this event can be classified as intellectually invigorating? How did Lois integrate children's affective knowledge?

Student Cultural Displays

During the formal teaching-learning process, you will initiate learning events and make specific cognitive and social demands on your students. Teachers who understand that students respond differently to classroom conditions and learning experiences are more likely to recognize the ways children connect new situations with familiar ones. This section discusses understanding of how children learn, cultural variations in students' approaches to learning, characteristics of cultural learning preferences, and types of intelligence.

Understanding How Children Learn

Knowledge of the current literature on how children learn and awareness that they acquire complex skills and knowledge before coming to school lets us know that the problem does not lie in children's capacity to learn. Students' school achievement often depends on the quality of the teacher's skills. Bransford et al. (1999) describe general characteristics of children as learners. Children:

1. Learn rapidly and readily. They have a strong disposition to learn.
2. Have reasoning ability; however, they may lack knowledge and experiences. They reason facilely with the knowledge they possess.
3. Hold misconceptions that may impede school learning. Teachers must pay attention to children's incomplete understandings.

4. Reveal prior understandings (cultural knowledge) and demonstrate competencies shaped by their environment and cultural experiences. Teachers must be aware of the ways in which children's cultural knowledge influences what they know and understand. They can help children make connections between new situations and familiar ones. Children's prior knowledge (skills, beliefs, concepts) influence what they notice and how they organize it. The same stimulus (teaching activity) can be perceived and understood differently depending on the prior knowledge children bring to the situation.

5. Possess privileged domains, such as causality, numbers, language, and physical concepts, and nonprivileged domains such as learning how to read and other school knowledge. When children are required to learn in nonprivileged domains they need to develop strategies of intentional learning.

6. Need to understand what it means to learn, to become aware of who they are as learners, and to determine for themselves if they understand. They need to develop **metacognitive skills**—the ability to monitor one's current level of understanding and to decide when it is adequate and when it is not.

7. Are problem solvers and problem generators. They attempt to solve problems and seek new challenges.

8. Persist when acquiring new knowledge and skills, because success and understanding are motivating in their own right.

Cultural Variations in Approaches to Learning

Differences in the ways children display cognitive and social skills are influenced by the variations present in the cultural context in which they are socialized (Ochs, 1997; Vygotsky & Luria, 1930/1993). Children's knowledge and competencies are shaped by their home cultural experiences and value orientations. Sometimes teachers ignore, underestimate, or misinterpret the competencies of diverse students. Teachers who design culturally inclusive teaching-learning events (a) recognize the ways culturally diverse students display their competencies, (b) respond to the ways they prefer to learn, and (c) realize that a group's cultural practices and norms and culturally influenced ways of knowing may not be applicable to every student from that group.

Styles of Inquiry. Gay (2000) uses the term "styles of inquiry" to describe how the inquiry preferences of many students from ethnic groups of color differ from those traditionally used in classrooms. For instance, the ways students respond to teacher questioning techniques may differ. Gay (p. 93) explains that "students of color, who are strongly affiliated with their traditional cultures" tend to respond to divergent (open-ended) questions and favor communication modes where more students have opportunities to respond. Yet, most teachers ask convergent (single-answer) questions involving an interaction between the teacher and one student at a time, usually in a whole group setting.

Questioning techniques expecting correct responses within a controlled set of knowledge can also value objective knowledge over relational ways of knowing gained through experiences. Greenfield et al. (1995) found that teachers sometimes inadvertently discredit answers given by students who use cultural, social information. In their study, Mexican American children were asked to describe eggs by thinking about the times they had cooked and eaten them. *"One of the children tried three times to talk about how she cooked eggs with her grandmother, but the teacher disregarded these comments in favor of a child who explained how eggs look white and yellow when they are cracked"* (Greenfield et al., 1995, p. 44).

Teachers may use inquiry methods that emphasize deductive approaches to learning, analytical examinations of details or parts, or the solving of problems by examining the relationship of one part to another (Witken, 1962; Irvine & York, 1995). This linear model, moving sequentially from the specific to the general and examining objects/concepts without a context may not be the preferred approach to learning for some children from groups of color. Students of color often use a more inductive problem solving and reasoning process. They may use observed instances in context to generate an idea or a concept. They move from whole to part and from the general to the specific.

When teachers privilege convergent thinking and focus exclusively on deductive processes to form conclusions, they may inadvertently dismiss the thinking process of students who think divergently and inductively. Questions such as "How many people are in the picture?" "Do the people look happy?" help students combine details that may eventually lead them to form a conclusion. However, questions focusing on the whole such as "What's happening here?" or "Have you ever seen this?" are also intellectually stimulating. Heath (1982) found that African American students responded actively when divergent (open-ended) questions focusing on the big picture and incorporating personal experiences were asked.

Characteristics of Cultural Learning Preferences

Gay (2000, p. 150) views learning style as "the process one habitually uses for cognitive problem solving and for showing what one knows and is capable of doing." These responses or learning preferences are determined by the individual's upbringing and are dependent on their prior cultural experiences. They may or may not reflect general cultural learning patterns preferred by other members of their cultural group. Although learning styles are not static, traits they can explain how children process culturally influenced ways of learning. Gay explains:

> By the time children begin their formal school career at five years of age, they already have internalized rules and procedures for acquiring knowledge and demonstrating these skills. These cognitive processing protocols are learned from their cultural socialization. They may be refined and elaborated over time, even superseded on occasion for the performance of certain tasks. But the core of these culturally influenced rules and procedures continues to anchor how individuals process intellectual challenges for the rest of their lives. (p. 150)

Children use their learning styles to demonstrate the ways they tend to engage with learning tasks. Gay (2000) points out that acknowledging diverse cultural ways of knowing provides teachers with evidence of the ways ethnically diverse students (a) approach learning tasks; (b) express oral and written thoughts; (c) select preferred content; (d) feel comfortable with the physical and social classroom context; (e) organize their work space; (f) perceive sensory stimulation for receiving, processing, and transmitting information; (g) interact and relate with others in social and instructional settings; and (h) choose incentives and stimulations that evoke learning and motivate accomplishments. Theoretically, learning styles help teachers examine when their approach to the teaching-learning task is compatible with students' learning needs.

Learning style is distinct from intelligence. Learning style refers to how students prefer to learn whereas intelligence refers to what or how much they know. Learning style theory examines the ways students see and process information, and some of the scholarship on learning style attempts to explain why some students do better in school than others (Irvine & York, 1995). Differences in the ways students acquire new knowledge and how they prefer to demonstrate their learning can explain why some students easily adapt to school and succeed and others do not. Matching teaching strategies with students' learning preferences and providing a balance of instructional approaches to meet the needs of diverse students are likely to foster greater opportunity for more students to learn.

Vignette 9.3 shows how children, when given the freedom to discover and teach others, can direct lesson content and process. This incident also demonstrates how students' prior cultural knowledge can be used to develop higher level thinking skills.

Vignette 9.3
Make Them the Same

This event took place in late September in a kindergarten classroom, located in a low-performing, high-poverty public school. Most of the children were second language learners and all received free or reduced lunch.

On a Wednesday, the children entered the room from lunch recess, sat on the rug in the front of the room, and formed a circle. The teacher explained the math assignment. The small group lesson schedule was written on butcher paper. Along with the math worksheet, the children were asked make five sets of ten, using red quarter-size plastic disks. The teacher told the children that this would give them practice counting from one to ten. She would later meet them at their tables, check the piles, and everyone would count by tens out loud: "ten, twenty, thirty, forty, fifty." While the teacher worked with small groups, she observed how the children counted the disks but did not comment or interfere.

Lance (Laotian American) counted the first set of ten disks; then, without counting, he proceeded to make four other columns equal in height. Noticing that Bobby (Laotian American) was still counting disks, Lance told him how to do it quickly. Bobby had to be convinced that this problem-solving technique was right. Bobby double-checked the second column. He measured the height against the first, took it apart, recounted the disks, and remade the column. Smiling, he quickly completed the other three columns without counting.

Seemingly delighted with the discovery and noticing that the other children were methodically counting plastic disks, Lance and Bobby walked around the room, showing others an easier way. Soon, at various tables, children were teaching others how to do it. They all quickly completed this tedious, time-consuming task.

On Thursday, the children were given the same task, but this time it was a planned whole group activity and the task involved making ten sets of ten. Only a few students counted each pile. Most counted the first, measured for height, and made the nine other piles. Teacher and children discussed the process of counting and measuring. Children were asked if this problem-solving technique worked with other materials, such as blocks, cubes, and other pieces of things such as puzzle and tangram pieces. Could things be weighed? Would volume work? Could they predict, project, estimate numbers or volume? Students then worked individually and in small groups on aspects of this problem using other materials.

On Friday, the teacher planned an integrated math and science lesson, involving three activities: (a) Children were asked to estimate the number of jelly beans in a large jar. They were each given a small baby food jar full of jelly beans (to keep) and count. Would this experiential knowledge help or not be of consequence in their estimation or prediction? They counted, ate, and wrote their predictions on scraps of paper. (b) They watched while the teacher put a cup of rice and two cups of water in an electric rice cooker. Children were to predict how full the pot would be when the bell went off indicating the rice was cooked. What would happen to the water? (c) The third activity involved pinto beans and water. The teacher alternated putting cups of raw pinto beans and cups of water in a medium-sized pot. She asked the children to tell her when to stop adding beans or water to make sure the pot would not overflow.

The Asian American children immediately and accurately responded to the rice event. One child said that when he was 4, it was his job to measure rice and water, put them in the rice cooker, and make rice every night for dinner. The Latino American children told the teacher to put more water and to stop putting in beans after the second cup full. The children were asked how their prior knowledge (what they learned at home) helps them learn in math and science in school. Ten key vocabulary words (jelly beans, cup, rice, beans, water, volume, evaporation, estimate, predict, and problem solve) were listed on butcher paper. These words were read out loud a couple of times and the word meanings were discussed. The children were given a small 3-by-5-inch pieces of paper with these ten words. Their homework was to read these ten words to or with three or more people, circle one of them, and draw a picture on the back showing the meaning of the circled word (Sheets, 1998).

Issues for Consideration
High interest in his choice activity might have prompted Lance to quickly finish his required math tasks. He and a group of boys went directly to a box containing unfinished, high-priority Power Ranger paraphernalia, such as belts, buckles, badges, and arm cuffs. However, teaching others how to complete a task supports the social and interactive nature of the ways children learn. Lance discovered and

shared his knowledge that ten disks could be measured rather than counted once you had one pile made.

The teacher behavior indicates awareness that student's cultural knowledge can be used to extend new understandings. Conditions in this classroom both instructional and contextual encouraged children to discover, to create, and to use prior knowledge during classroom events. What was necessary for a simple busy-work activity to evolve into a more complex math and science lesson? How was students' cultural knowledge used to introduce scientific and mathematical concepts? What were some of the teacher strategies used to promote language development? Why was teacher observation of student behavior critical in this learning event? Why did the teacher explicitly link the children's prior cultural knowledge to new understandings in math and science?

Types of Intelligence

A type of intelligence is different from a learning style. However, Gardner's (1985) construct of multiple intelligences is often applied in practice as a learning preference, rather than a perceived ability (see Table 9.6). Gardner theorizes that students possess different types of intelligences or perceptual modalities. Attention to these individual strengths presumes that all students should not be treated the same.

According to Gardner (1985), there are seven intelligences or modalities: linguistic, logical mathematical, spatial, musical, bodily kinesthetic, interpersonal, and intrapersonal. Gardner believes that the development of these intelligences is dependent on the experiences and values provided by the families and the cultural experiences of the child. Children exposed and encouraged to participate in the bodily-kinesthetic domain, such as ballet lessons and involvement in sports, have more potential to develop strengths in that area. This theory of multiple intelligences provides the teacher with a framework to recognize and affirm students' diverse strengths. Teaching to the different modalities also ensures a balance of learning experiences and teaching strategies.

TABLE 9.6 Multiple Intelligences and Student Characteristics

Modality	Characteristics and Strengths
Linguistic	Word oriented. Good storyteller, reader, and writer. Loves verbal play.
Logical/Mathematical	Conceptually oriented. Good math student. Loves logical patterns.
Spatial	Image oriented. Daydreamer, artist. Attracted to visual media.
Musical	Rhythm and melody oriented. Sings or plays musical instruments.
Bodily Kinesthetic	Physically oriented. Excels in athletics or fine motor areas like dancing.
Interpersonal	Social oriented. Strong leadership skills. Enjoys group work.
Intrapersonal	Intuitively oriented. Strong willed and self-motivated. Prefers solitude.

Source: Adapted from Gardner (1985).

Classroom Applications

Current research on cognition points out that, although learning is a basic adaptive function, children's cultural experiences create prior knowledge that must be used to construct new knowledge. Teachers who design effective lessons and create optimal learning conditions make appropriate linkages between the capacities, skills, and experiences particular children bring to school and to the intended learning activity. Thus, designing classroom events, creating learning conditions, and recognizing the role of culture in schooling are mutually dependent and inseparable in the teaching-learning process. The teaching-learning process, where knowledge develops, is not distinct or neutral from culture.

Promoting Intellectual Growth

Acknowledge the ways in which teaching and learning about how to think about thinking are essential to promoting intellectual growth and to enhancing the development of intellectual standards, elements of critical thinking, and intellectual traits.

1. Familiarize yourself with multiple models of thinking and systematically use them when designing teaching-learning events. Incorporate intellectual standards when planning instruction. Develop culturally inclusive questioning techniques that help advance students' cognitive development and displays of higher level, critical thinking skills. Design appropriately challenging learning events for students to encourage thinking at deeper levels. Identify and respond to low levels of dualistic thinking.
2. Teach thinking skills explicitly as essential tools for learning how to learn. Provide multiple opportunities for students to develop awareness of their thinking processes. Have students take ownership of their own learning by creating learning conditions where students consistently use intellectual tools to practice metacognitive skills to purposefully monitor their own thinking.

Incorporating Students' Learning Preferences

Plan, create, and use teaching strategies matching students' learning preferences, and use diverse strategies providing a balance of instructional approaches to consistently foster greater learning opportunities for more students.

1. Observe how students in your classroom from different racial, ethnic, linguistic, cultural, and socioeconomic groups respond to the various instructional strategies and use this information to adapt teaching approaches. Notice how individuals and groups of students handle competitive versus collaborative learning events. Identify problematic or positive elements in individual and group work to enhance the benefits of these experiences for more students. Observe how students react to various teaching tools, such as visual, oral, hands on, modeling, and participatory.

2. Analyze the participation structures in your classroom to include more inclusive discourse opportunities. Use teacher-student, student-student, student-led discussions, and small group discourse.

3. Adapt generic lesson plans available from commercial sources to reflect diverse learning needs of the particular students in your classroom. Examine the prerequisite skills implied in the lessons and determine the level of significance the activity plays in the lives of the students.

4. Examine how students respond to your instructional methods. You might start by writing down the behaviors and responses of one or two students or by noting the degree of engagement of different learners or groups of students. Describe successful and unsuccessful lessons, and interpret any patterns that emerge, such as level of engagement and motivation. Appraise the situation and make changes in delivery of instruction to see if positive changes occur. Replicate successful lessons.

5. Conference with individual or groups of parents to gain information from their perspectives of their child's strengths and preferences. Ask what they would like their child to learn in the classroom.

6. Take classes, read and share materials specific to the cognitive and social developmental process of children from diverse ethnic, cultural, ability, and language groups. Participate in university courses or in-service training opportunities to increase your cultural content knowledge, and apply this information when working with culturally and linguistically diverse children and their families.

Using Prior Knowledge in Learning Events

Gain information about students' prior cultural knowledge, strengths, and skills, and incorporate these understandings and competencies into learning events.

1. Include language objectives in lesson plans that take into account cultural and linguistic differences in students' vocabulary levels, concept development, and prior knowledge in specific lessons. Identify vocabulary and concepts that need further clarification and use specific techniques to clarify these words or terms, such as hands-on manipulatives, multimedia, illustrations or visuals, demonstrations, real-life objects, and adapted texts.

2. Prepare learning events that link to students' prior experiences. Provide authentic learning experiences that are neither simulated nor contrived. Promote learning conditions that encourage collaboration. Include interpersonal interactions and expect a deep level of exploration, reflection, and internalization. Involve multiple voices and perceptions of students to extend, validate, and affirm students' self-discoveries.

Conclusion

As a teacher you will constantly think, judge, and make decisions. You will determine the classroom context, select instructional methods, choose textbooks, decide time on task, delineate the purpose and goals of instructional events, pick specific instructional content, and grant or influence the social and academic status of the students in your classroom. You will implement your educational philosophy, make resources accessible or inaccessible, control social interactions, judge student behavior, define competence, monitor the time allotted for classroom events, establish evaluation criteria, and frame curricular content.

You will decide to change children's behavior, or you will view yourself as the subject of change. You will adapt instruction to meet the particular needs of the students in your classroom, or you will use generic lessons. The incredible power that you will have as a teacher is only equal to the phenomenal power that your students have as active participants in the teaching-learning process. Can you change your patterns of thinking in ways that support mutual accommodation?

RECOMMENDED READINGS

Echevarria, J., Vogt, M., & Short, D. J. (2004). *Making content comprehensible for English learners: The SIOP Model* (2nd ed.). New York: Pearson.

Paul, R., & Elder, L. (2001). *Critical thinking: Tools for taking charge of your learning and your life*. Upper Saddle River, NJ: Prentice Hall.

10 Assessment: Encouraging Student Self-Evaluation

> *Whether they [students] are white, black, Hispanic, Native American, or Asian American will, to a large extent, predict their success in school, whether they go to college, and how much money they will earn as adults. . . . The disparity in school performance tied to race and ethnicity, known as the achievement gap, shows up in grades, test scores, and college completion.*
>
> —Johnson & Viadero, 2000, p. 1

Assessment is closely connected to the teaching-learning process. However, one cannot assume that the appropriate selection of testing instruments or the modification of assessment tools translates to students' having equitable opportunities to achieve. Ultimately, it is the teachers' responsibility to teach all students. One of the ways teachers monitor their teaching skills is by measuring student knowledge gain through a variety of instruments. The purpose of this chapter is to help teachers understand the relationship among culture, assessment, and the teaching-learning process. Assessment strategies and tools that promote learning are explored through the development of student self-evaluation skills.

The first part of this chapter introduces the eighth diversity pedagogical dimension, assessment/self-evaluation. The second section, teacher pedagogical behaviors, discusses the achievement gap and classroom assessment strategies. The next part, student cultural displays, suggests ways to help students self-evaluate. This is followed by classroom applications.

Diversity Pedagogy Dimension 8: Assessment/Self-Evaluation

This section uses the scholarship on assessment and metacognition to point out possible pedagogical strategies (teacher behaviors) needed to apply this dimension in the classroom (Madaus & Clarke, 2001; Pintrich, 1995; Zimmerman & Schunk, 2001). Student cultural displays show how students might demonstrate ability to apply metacognitive skills to help them understand what they know and what they need to know to function competently in academic events and social situations. Table 10.1 (p. 168) describes the terms *assessment* and *self-evaluation*.

TABLE 10.1   Diversity Pedagogy Dimension 8: Assessment/Self-Evaluation

Definition of Dimensional Elements

Assessment: Organized, structured, ongoing, varied methods used to observe, document, record, evaluate, and appraise the level and quality of individual and group student work and knowledge gained in a given activity or subject, to (a) improve student learning, (b) determine what students know and what they are able to do, and (c) evaluate how student performance matches teacher expectations and standards.

Self-Evaluation: Self-appraisal through reflection, review of thoughts and analysis of personal and group behavior to (a) monitor academic and social goals, assess progress, and identify competencies and weaknesses, (b) plan, assume ownership, and take responsibility for one's learning, and (c) evaluate the strategies used to maximize the acquisition, retention, and performance of new understandings.

Teacher Pedagogical Behaviors

Applies a variety of assessment techniques at an individual and group level to respond to cultural cognitive preferences, monitor student learning and adapt instruction accordingly, and provide opportunities for students to practice metacognitive skills.

- Uses multiple methods and approaches—oral, written, performance, observation checklists, anecdotal records, homework, tests, quizzes, contracts, rating scales, portfolios—to collect assessment data to evaluate student progress.
- Minimizes competitive classroom interactions and encourages collaborative group work.
- Applies assessment knowledge to design, change, or adapt learning events.
- Adapts instruction in response to student assessment information.

Facilitates classroom events and encourages the development of students' self-evaluation skills in individual and group settings.

- Provides multiple opportunities for students to evaluate their knowledge, skills, strengths, gaps, and weaknesses.
- Promotes thinking about thinking and explains metacognitive strategies.
- Clarifies and models appropriate thinking and problem-solving strategies.

Maintains open communication with parents regarding students' academic growth, social skills, linguistic strengths, cultural competencies, and responses to diversity concerns.

Student Cultural Displays

Signs of applying metacognitive skills to understand what one knows and what one needs to know to monitor personal learning and identify areas of strengths and weaknesses in order to function competently in a given subject matter and social situation.

- Uses self-monitoring techniques such as frequent checking and goal setting to evaluate personal and group growth, identifies and corrects inconsistencies in thinking, learns from errors, and shows awareness of cognitive preferences.
- Recognizes and evaluates problems in learning as an individual and group member.
- Consciously applies problem-solving strategies and evaluates their effectiveness.
- Understands why particular decisions are made under certain conditions.

Demonstrations of responsibility, ownership, and conscious control in planning and directing own learning.

- Applies new understandings of cognitive strengths and weaknesses when performing and displaying new acquired knowledge.
- Understands the value and purpose of thinking about thinking.
- Is self-motivated to acquire, use, and retain new thinking strategies.

Indications of sharing new understandings and knowledge with family members, while respecting and valuing the cultural knowledge learned in the home.

Teacher Pedagogical Behaviors

Equity (treatment characterized by fairness and impartiality) in assessment does not necessarily reside in the selection or even in the content of assessment tools themselves. Rather, equitable assessment depends on teacher accommodations of the learning conditions that enable students to learn what is intended. This section examines the current achievement gap and discusses classroom assessment strategies.

The Achievement Gap

The **achievement gap,** disparity in school performance associated with race and ethnicity, shows up in test scores, grades, high school graduation and dropout rates, and college completion. It is one of the most urgent problems and damaging phenomena in public schooling. Johnson and Viadero (2000) explain that researchers can use race and ethnicity to predict the schooling outcomes of millions of children by the end of their kindergarten year. By 2019, at age 24, European American children entering kindergarten in fall 2000 "will be twice as likely as their African American classmates, and three times as likely as Hispanics, to have a college degree" (Johnson & Viadero, 2000, p. 1).

Achievement Gap Patterns. The term **high stakes,** when used in reference to standardized tests, indicates that test results are used to set policy; reward or punish districts, schools, educators, and children; and involve the public by openly reporting school, district, and state scores. Districts can implement curricular programs for particular students based on their test scores. School districts can be denied federal funding. Low-performing schools can be **reconstituted** (taken over by the state). Teachers can be fired or rewarded monetarily. Principals can be removed, children can be forced to repeat a grade, and some students are denied high school graduation diplomas. Using information from the National Center for Educational Statistics (NCES), and the National Assessment of Education Progress (NAEP), states, local districts, and scholars report the following achievement patterns, applications, explanations, and results of high stakes standardized tests (Haycock, 2001; Madaus & Clarke, 2001; Rosenshine, 2003):

1. Between 1970 and 1988, the achievement gap between European American students and African American students was cut in half, and the gap between European American students and Latino American students decreased by one-third; however, since that time the achievement gap has either grown or remained stagnant.
2. In mathematics and reading at the end of high school, African American and Latino American students demonstrate skills equal to those of European American eighth graders.
3. Approximately 76 percent of European American graduates and 86 percent of Asian American graduates go directly to college compared to 71 percent of African

American and 71 percent of Latino American graduates. However, only one-half of African Americans and one-third of Latino Americans are as likely as European American students to earn a college degree.

Applications in Classrooms. Scholars point out that the data available from standardized tests generally do not positively affect the teaching-learning process (Goodwin, 2002; Jones & Whitford, 2002). Although school districts may establish goals for overall test score improvements, information from standardized tests are rarely used to modify instruction, adapt learning conditions, or assess student progress for the children who are most adversely affected. Poor test results are often used to pressure teachers to teach to the test in inappropriate ways, thus changing instruction and learning. Tests given in the past often define the instructional content of what is currently being taught. Teachers determine the skills or the type of thinking required by the test, and then they prepare students to meet these demands. Teachers are not only influenced by the content of the test, but they often strive to copy the form. Thus, kindergarten children are taught to fill in the bubble. Students are taught to memorize facts and select from a possible set of answers rather than to produce their own responses. Test performance becomes more important than learning. Additionally, teaching to test content and focusing on test preparation maintains low-level cognitive skills. Examinations also increase competition and sometimes encourage cheating on the part of schools, teachers, and students. Tests do not enhance home-school communication, because parents usually receive a test score with no other information.

Explanations for the Achievement Gap. Scholars who examine explanations for the achievement gap identify factors such as flaws within the tests themselves, presumed characteristics inherent in low-performing students and their families, and possible inadequacies of classroom teachers (Gay, 2002; Orfield & Kornhaber, 2001; Madaus & Clark, 2001). They point out that flaws within the tests themselves challenge their validity. For example, tests are unfair and culturally biased. They do not test what is being taught and learned in school. They are not aligned with state and school standards or with textbook content.

Some assign blame to students and their families. Individuals holding this viewpoint argue that low-performing students are poor, unmotivated, unskilled, have parents that do not care, do not have books in the home, come from single-parent households, are linguistically deficient, and watch too much television. These critics believe that students may dismiss the rewards or punishments attached to tests and may put forth minimal effort. They think that low-performing students are not motivated to take the test. Cultural variations in parenting, differences in cultural values and practices, and diverse linguistic skills are viewed as deficit factors affecting school achievement.

The responsibility is also placed on teachers. Those who blame teachers maintain that teachers may not have strong academic backgrounds in the subjects they teach and may not know how to teach their assigned subjects or grade level. Teachers in low-performing schools are more likely to be uncredentialed, have low expectations, teach less because they spend most of their time handling disciplinary issues, rarely teach reasoning skills, and do not offer students rigorous curricula.

Testing Results. The data suggest that districts requiring students to pass an exit exam to graduate from high school have the highest drop out rates for students from ethnic groups of color and for those from low-income families (Goodwin, 2002). This same student population also experiences the highest grade retention rates. Additionally, a significant portion of the district and school budget and classroom time is spent on tests and test preparation materials. Monies for instructional resources are used to purchase test preparation programs. Class time, generally reserved for instruction, is spent taking tests or preparing students to take tests. Curricular programs for underperforming schools often include low cognitive level scripted programs in math and reading based on the deficit model, which maintains that something is wrong with the child (Irvine, 1991).

The achievement gap, even conceding that standardized tests are flawed, clearly shows that schooling conditions for many students from groups of color and poverty are problematic. Focusing on the achievement gap is of no use, unless efforts are made to minimize and eliminate it. An assumption that the schooling conditions for children of color and poverty would be worse if some form of accountability were not in place is highly probable. If European American children demonstrate achievement on imperfect standardized tests, then students from groups of color and poverty should likewise display similar signs of competency. States, districts, schools, and teachers should be accountable for student learning. There must be consequences for those who do not or cannot provide equitable services to all children. Students are required by law to attend school; they ought to be guaranteed access to quality schooling experiences.

Classroom Assessment Strategies

One of the ways to close the gap and to improve student learning is to understand how teacher assessment and development of student self-evaluation skills intersect with the teaching-learning process. Appropriate and meaningful assessment procedures, in and of themselves, do not automatically remove barriers to student learning. However, the results of authentic assessment must be used to examine the teaching-learning process. This implies changes in thinking, attitudes, instructional strategies, learning conditions, and appropriateness of instructional content. It also means that students must be explicitly taught skills to evaluate their own progress. They need multiple opportunities to take control, responsibility, and ownership of their learning. Ultimately, teachers must concede—if students are not showing growth in what they intend to teach—in these cases, for these particular students, they are not teaching. Teaching is inseparable from learning.

Teacher Assessment Skills. Knowledge of specific assessment techniques to measure student learning provides the foundation needed to create, use, and adapt evaluation tools. Understanding how to evaluate the learning growth of culturally diverse children requires sharp observational skills with close attention given to the cultural nuances present in students' cognitive and social preferences. To enhance student learning, teachers must understand how, when, and what pedagogical changes address the issues present in data collected from student assessment. Vignette 10.1 illustrates how a teacher responds to an assessment result and shows how this information influenced her behavior.

Vignette 10.1
Spelling Test

Marco, a Mexican American third grader, attended a low-performing high poverty school with a majority of African American students. He was the only Mexican American student in the class, and as an emerging English language learner he often had problems understanding his assignments. This school had no services available for English language learners. Ms. Wallace, an African American first-year teacher, was committed to issues of diversity, but felt she did not have adequate skills to meet the needs of linguistically diverse students, especially those with minimal English skills.

Marco failed the spelling test, again. Only three of the ten words were spelled correctly. The students worked quietly at their seats, writing each of their misspelled words five times. When approached, Marco appeared ashamed that he did not do better. He indicated that he had studied the words "a long time" the night before. When asked, he could neither read the misspelled words nor did he know the meaning of the words when read out loud to him.

He explained that he looked for Spanish words in the English word and that he had looked for patterns in the sequence of letters and tried to memorize these patterns. He saw the Spanish word *si* (yes) in the English word since. Marco studied *rooster* by remembering *rst*, the order of the alphabet, and just put two *o*'s between the *r* and the *s* and put *er* at the end. He recognized *rooster* when the teacher called it out, spelled it correctly on the test, but did not know what this word meant. The word *once*, with the same spelling, pronounced in Spanish means *eleven*. When asked why he missed *once* since he could spell it, he replied (in Spanish), "I didn't understand it when the teacher said it."

Issues for Consideration

As a result of this event, Ms. Wallace and the other third-grade teachers developed a sheltered language arts program for Marco and the other Spanish-speaking students in their classrooms. In terms of spelling, Marco selected the ten words to study for his weekly spelling test. He could read and understand the meanings of each word. The third-grade team also met with the principal and requested help. They suggested that Pablo, an only-Spanish-speaking student in another third-grade classroom, be transferred to Ms. Wallace's classroom. Parental permission was given and Pablo was moved into the classroom, providing both boys with a linguistic resource and possible friendship connection. Within a month, due to teacher insistence and principal support, a Spanish-speaking paraprofessional was hired to assist primary teachers with English language learners. How were some of the changes in the teaching-learning process and conditions for learning taking place in Marco's classroom related to assessment? Can you identify some of the pedagogical changes made by the teacher? How was Marco involved in self-assessment?

Since student evaluation is an integral part of the teaching-learning process, books on tests and measurement provide extensive information on specific techniques, such as how to organize assessment data, different methods of data collection, and explanations on how to evaluate written assignments. These valuable resources explain that meaningful evaluation procedures (a) are planned, continuous, diagnostic, varied, fair, and confidential; (b) provide meaningful feedback to students; (c) can be used to communicate student growth with parents; and (d) reflect on teacher ability to meet instructional goals and subject matter objectives (see Crooks, 1988; Ebel & Frisbie, 1986; Natrillo & Dornbush, 1984).

Blame for low student achievement cannot be placed on the issues associated with standardized achievement tests or with limitations in teacher-made assessment tools. Data garnered from assessment of student achievement at the classroom level should result in significant changes in instruction. Assessment should yield useful information for improving instruction. It should provide teachers with the information needed to quickly respond to the problems students might be experiencing and to identify ways to connect instruction to students' strengths.

Student Cultural Displays

Meeting the needs of students also requires that they have opportunities to self-evaluate their learning growth. Access to meaningful instruction, especially in areas of need as identified by the student and teacher, is also required. This section discusses student self-evaluation including motivation, goal setting, knowledge acquisition, and thinking skills.

Student Self-Evaluation

Encouraging students to become involved in assessing their knowledge growth increases their level of responsibility and ownership for learning and potentially contributes to their ability to structure and control their overall learning process. Generally, an immediate benefit is their increased motivation to succeed, visible enthusiasm in teaching-learning events, and heightened self-expectation for their ability to display competency. Self-knowledge about one's own knowledge process is an important first step in thinking about thinking about their performance.

The scholarship on metacognition clearly establishes the powerful role it plays in promoting students' active role in the teaching-learning process (see Paris & Paris, 2001; Pintrich, 1995; Zimmerman & Schunk, 2001). Developed and practiced metacognitive skills help students to realistically and openly evaluate their progress in terms of level of self-motivation, awareness of their acquisition of new understandings, degree of knowledge retention, ability to set realistic and attainable goals, and candid evaluation of their performance in relationship to established standards. These skills help students identify how their attitudes, beliefs, and behaviors affect their learning. Vignette 10.2 illustrates how a fourth-grade teacher expected students to be responsible for their learning.

Vignette 10.2
Ding Ding
This event took place in an ethnically diverse urban fourth-grade classroom with a majority of Pilipino American students. The students were preparing for a field trip to a salmon hatchery in a nearby town. The discussion centered on the habitat needs of the salmon from egg to adult and how natural conditions differed from those in a hatchery. When Ms. Cooper, a European American teacher, used the term *watershed,* two soft *ding dings* were heard. The teacher immediately wrote *watershed* on the blackboard and asked children to define the term. She did not move to the next topic until everyone understood *watershed.*

Issues for Consideration
In this classroom, students were encouraged to say *ding ding* when they did not understand any aspect of a lesson. The teacher's immediate response was incorporated into the flow of the lesson. Why do you think techniques of this nature places responsibility on the learner? What other signals can be used?

As a teacher, you can share and model metacognitive skills. You can create a climate that fosters the development of self-regulation. Students can learn that skillful thinking and thinking about thinking helps to evaluate and track their academic and social progress. Metacognitive strategies useful to students must be explicitly taught, practiced, and linked to self-assessment. A basic goal when teaching metacognitive skills is helping students understand that learning involves learning how to learn.

Motivation.   Since motivational factors are critical to self-regulation skills (Zimmerman & Schunk, 2001), teacher recognition and response to these student cultural displays is crucial. Attitudes toward and interest in a subject influences student learning. Students' motivational orientation—how they feel about a subject, beliefs about their ability to do well, and past experiences in a particular subject area—facilitates and supports their efforts. Students can be encouraged to identify negative thoughts, experiences, and feelings. They can work on recognizing gaps in their learning and identify areas of strength. Students can become aware of available resources, such as teacher, peers, parents, and supplementary materials. They also need to understand the purpose of the lesson and the value of what is learned. Development of specific study habits to improve academic skills in a given subject area, such as how to break up content into smaller pieces or steps, how to use the textbook effectively, ways to establish a consistent study time, and knowing when and how to ask for help from teacher and peers, is fundamental to experiencing success.

Goal Setting. High-achieving students generally demonstrate the ability to self-regulate. They establish personal, academic, and social goals and exhibit strategies to meet these objectives. Self-assessment is an essential component of all teaching-learning events. Teachers can focus instruction and organize work periods in ways that encourage individual, small group, and whole group goal setting. Procedures can be developed to help students personally monitor the degree to which they meet established targets. An emphasis on learning rather than grades is more likely to encourage the development of lifelong learning. Opportunities for students to evaluate why they make decisions and how choices promote and direct their progress toward stated goals are essential. Students who are provided opportunities to manage their time can learn to use their time more effectively.

Knowledge Acquisition. Constructing and acquiring new information can be frustrating for students, especially if they have had prior difficulties in a particular subject area or skill. One of the first steps to self-regulation involves helping students recognize that learning happens through mistakes, and it is important for students to identify and examine learning problems. Providing students with opportunities to evaluate how various metacognitive techniques improve their ability to learn new concepts and skills can advance attitudes of self-efficacy. Students can evaluate differences in understandings when they preread material before the lesson or prior to oral whole group reading. They can examine what happens when they use varied and supplemental resources addressing the same topic. Discuss how and why small study groups help or what happens when students prepare questions when they do not understand the material. Does highlighting and marking material or taking notes of key ideas help? Explore why taking time to review material or creating mnemonic devices helps them remember material. Examine factors underlining issues such as test anxiety and help them identify ways to relax and demonstrate what they know.

Thinking Skills. Learning to think at higher levels is difficult for students who have not had consistent practice or who have not been taught the standards of thinking (see Chapter 9). Deliberate efforts can be made to encourage reflection before, during, and after a learning event. Students can be shown how to recognize inconsistencies in their thinking, misconceptions, and assumptions. They can (a) examine how and when specific problem-solving strategies are most effective; (b) acknowledge how thinking influences their decision-making process; (c) consciously track the steps in the thinking used to arrive at a particular conclusion or solution; and (d) learn how to make predictions, understand how to ask questions, and consciously transfer knowledge from one situation to another.

Classroom Applications

High-stakes standardized testing shows that students and schools are expected to be accountable for achievement. However, the achievement gap indicates that classroom instruction and subsequent assessment procedures may not always serve the purpose they are designed to accomplish. Classroom teacher assessments and student self-evaluation skills are mutually dependent and inseparable in the teaching-learning process. The following suggestions might help you combine the information from multiple assessment tools and student self-evaluations to promote optimal learning opportunities for more children.

Improving Instruction through Assessment

Acknowledge the ways in which assessment improves instruction and promotes accountability for student achievement.

1. Familiarize yourself with multiple types of assessment instruments and understand how to select appropriate tools to evaluate your teaching and student learning. Use multiple sources (students, peers, parents) to assess student growth. Refine assessment strategies, such as tests, oral and written assessments, collaborative group work, individual problem-solving projects, homework, observational records, rating scales, portfolios, and student self- and peer assessments, to measure student performance and knowledge gain. Observe and evaluate how students respond to your instructional strategies, classroom context, and instructional materials. Purposefully and carefully align curricular standards, teacher goals, and student learning objectives to assessment content and outcome.

2. Create, develop, use, and refine reliable, balanced, comprehensive, and dependable information from various assessment tools to guide your decisions of the changes needed to promote high academic achievement. Recognize when a particular assessment tool provides credible or limited information. Develop multiple tools to be used in tandem with observational data to determine the degree of student knowledge gain or to identify possible approaches and solutions to problems or ways to replicate and transfer successful assessment techniques to other classroom events. Balance the ways students are asked to demonstrate knowledge, skills, and abilities.

Addressing Diversity in Assessment

Observe how children in your classroom from different racial, ethnic, linguistic, and cultural groups respond to assessment techniques and adapt teaching strategies, classroom climate, and instructional materials accordingly.

1. Examine how students respond to specific types of assessment instruments. Notice if and how knowledge displays change or are significantly influenced by the type of measurements used. If students are more successful in written assessments versus oral experiences, you might consider changes in the ways you teach writing, discussion, and presentation skills. Appraise planned learning events to make appropriate changes in the lesson content and delivery of instruction to see if learning gains take place. Replicate successful assessment tools. Apply assessment information to meet individual and group needs.

2. Make realistic inferences, valid interpretations, and fair conclusions from the assessment data. Understand how cultural variations in students' home-rearing practices might affect assessment measures, but do not use cultural information to limit students' opportunities to learn or to shift responsibility for low achievement. Become aware of how stereotypes might affect what you expect from diverse groups of students. If you believe that Chinese American students are not creative or that they are weak in oral presentation skills, you might avoid using evaluation tools that measure these skills and thus deny them opportunities to express, develop, and strengthen competencies in these areas. If you think African American students excel in oral expressions, you might choose to use this form of assessment without balancing it with other types, thus limiting their prospects to strengthen and display their skills in other forms or to develop strategies to excel in different ways. Or, if you overcompensate by allowing Mexican American children to work exclusively in cooperative and collaborative groups, they will not be given opportunity to practice and develop skills in independent problem-solving projects.

3. Take classes; read and share materials specific to assessment strategies for children from diverse ethnic, cultural, ability, and language groups. Participate in university courses or in-service training opportunities to increase your knowledge of assessment strategies, and apply this information when working with culturally, ethnically, and linguistically diverse children and their families.

4. Make accommodations in the assessment tools for second-language learners and for students with particular, identified learning differences. Provide additional time if necessary. Allow practice opportunities prior to actual assessment. Include adult or peer helpers who serve as translators to participate in the assessment activity.

Building Home and School Relationships

Build strong interpersonal relationships between home and school to encourage open communication and increase caregivers' involvement in their child's assessment and achievement.

1. Communicate regularly with parents and caregivers in responsible and meaningful manners. Hold discussions with individual parents or with groups of parents to gain information from their perspectives of their child's skills, strengths, and preferences. Ask what parents would like their child to learn in the classroom. Keep them informed of their child's academic and social progress. Translate, if necessary, student progress reports and homework requirements into the parents' home language. Acknowledge the necessity to escalate reporting student progress to parents of students who are having difficulties and to listen to parents' suggestions.

2. Collaborate with other teachers, district personnel, parents, caregivers, and the community to organize workshops on the achievement issues affecting meaningful topics based on common interests and needs. Bring assessment issues up at

scheduled faculty meetings. Request services and explanations of assessment procedures from district personnel. Use community resources to address student achievement. Create an interdisciplinary group to collect data and suggest solutions to achievement issues present in your school. Develop schoolwide assessment policies.

Involving Students in Self-Evaluation

Involve students in authentic self-evaluation by explicitly teaching metacognitive skills and providing them with opportunities to practice these skills.

1. Explain the purpose and intent of self-evaluation skills. Keep students fully informed of the ways in which they will be evaluated. Explain how and why you are evaluating student growth and discuss their role in the process. Be precise on the rationale for assessing specific skills or processes. Include explicit performance criteria so students can identify their own growth, weaknesses, errors, and strengths in a particular skill or process. Make sure students understand what is needed for short-term and long-term knowledge gains. Discuss the benefits of homework, describe how study habits develop, and explain the benefits of peer collaboration. Help students identify what they know and do not know. Teach students different ways to (a) organize their materials, (b) ask for teacher and peer assistance, and (c) select group members. Explain the cumulative affect of daily, weekly, and monthly grades in terms of final term grades. Discuss the association among grades, standards, and learning objectives in a given subject. Students will vary on the time needed to conceptualize and apply self-evaluation techniques. Allow for the time needed for students to acquire and practice these metacognitive skills.
2. Make explicit linkages between the teachers' goals, objectives, content, and assessment procedures and the students' responsibility and opportunity to learn what the teacher intends. Provide students with opportunities to self-monitor their understanding of what is expected and to check their knowledge gain. Report assessment results to students as quickly as possible. Discuss how your limitations in teaching and students' level of effort affect knowledge gain. Point out individual and group strengths as well as areas requiring more attention. Focus on ways students can self-monitor their knowledge gain. Encourage student participation by involving them, when possible, in setting achievement standards and making choices of assessment methods.
3. Schedule regular conferences with students to discuss progress.

Conclusion

Authentic and reliable assessment of one's teaching skills and students' knowledge gain requires (a) extensive planning when creating assessment instruments, (b) considerable time grading to evaluate student growth and to report results to students and parents,

(c) specific skills to help students develop self-evaluation strategies, and (d) extensive knowledge of culture to make the needed pedagogical adjustments to enable more students opportunities to learn. Acknowledge that poor student performance is not a consequence of their cultural heritage, linguistic abilities, or the economic status of their parents. You, as a teacher, stand at the front line of the teaching-learning process. In terms of access to equitable opportunities to learn, you are, at best, the greatest resource and, at worse, the most consequential liability in the school life of students.

If students are held accountable for achievement, schools must create conditions that enable them to learn. The achievement gap evident in standardized tests, even when instruments are viewed as flawed, clearly shows that something is wrong. Low-performing students are often a result of a series of low-performing teachers. Achievement issues do not reside in culturally diverse students' potential, ability, and capacity to learn; they lie in our skills to teach.

RECOMMENDED READINGS

Darling-Hammond, L. (2000). Teacher quality and student achievement: A review of state policy evidence. *Educational Policy Analysis Archives, 8*(1). Retrieved from http://epaa.asu.edu/epaa/v8n1.

Orfield, G., & Kornhaber, M. (Eds.). (2001). *Raising standards or barriers? Inequality and high stakes testing in public education.* New York: Century Foundation.

Zimmerman, B. J., & Schunk, D. H. (Eds.). (2001). *Self-regulated learning and academic achievement: Theoretical perspectives.* Mahwah, NJ: Erlbaum.

PART THREE

Classroom Applications

11 Cultural Strengths of African American Children

[Children] come to formal education with a range of prior knowledge, skills, beliefs, and concepts that significantly influence what they notice about the environment and how they organize and interpret it. This, in turn, affects their abilities to remember, reason, solve problems, and acquire new knowledge.
—Bransford et al., 1999, p. 12

In *The Dreamkeepers: Successful Teachers of African American Students*, Gloria Ladson-Billings (1994) describes how expert teachers of African American students tap into the cultural, cognitive, and affective aspects of the teaching-learning process and use what Foster (2000, p. 6) calls the "substance of the children's lives and their communities." Lee (2000, p. 12) also maintains that classroom teachers must give attention to the "everyday practices, language uses, and routines that are the stuff of ethnic experience." These scholars argue that drawing extensively on students' ethnic experiences and acknowledging the cultural aspects of cognition may increase the potential to link new knowledge to children's prior knowledge. This chapter examines the ways African American high school students were able to apply their prior cultural knowledge, ethnic experiences, and linguistic strengths in a six-week language arts unit that culminated in an extraordinary dramatization (Sheets, 1998a).

The chapter begins with a description of a language arts high school urban classroom and documents how a six-week unit evolved. The curricular content of this unit focused on aspects of the African American culture. The second part of this chapter describes classroom events, teacher behaviors, and student cultural displays through the eight diversity pedagogy dimensions delineated in Chapters 3 through 10 of this text.

Language Arts Mass Media Class

This study took place in an urban high school's newly created language arts class called Mass Media (Sheets, 1998a). This language arts section began two weeks into the semester; consequently, most students used this class to make up credit for previously failed language arts classes. Some were pulled out from other language arts classes for behavioral reasons, and a few were advised to take this new class as a way to fulfill a graduation English requirement. The twenty-six students in the class included nine African Americans (five females, four males), two Mexican Americans (two females), three Chinese Americans (two females, one male), eight Pilipino Americans (one female, seven males), two European Americans (two females), one Japanese American (male), and one Vietnamese American (male). The principal, counselors, and most teachers viewed these students as low-achievers and disciplinary problems.

In this class, students were involved in selecting the topic of study; developing the rationale, goals, and objectives; and determining measurable outcomes for each unit. They worked collaboratively, read and wrote extensively, and participated in student-led discussions. The first three-week unit involved film as a medium. Students selected films around specific social issues. They watched films, read reviews, made oral presentations, and wrote critiques. The next three-week unit focused on literature. Students examined multicultural children's literature and then focused on Maya Angelou's poetry.

Mass Media was in session approximately two months prior to *The Project*, a six-week unit described in the next section. During the first two months, African American students attended regularly, exhibited cooperative, positive classroom behavior, participated in class discussions, and completed assignments at an acceptable level; but evidence of collaboration, self-motivation, and ownership in their learning process did not surface consistently. *The Project* describes the genesis of an incredible experience where African American students demonstrated and applied their cultural knowledge to acquire new understandings.

The Project

> I was taking a doctoral seminar entitled *Educating the Black Inner City Child* while teaching a language arts course, Mass Media, in high school. The African American students in this class were asked if they would help me meet a course requirement. Students knew that this project was a major part of my grade. I would document and present selected aspects of the project at the university. If they chose, they could attend the university class session and participate in my presentation. They agreed to help.

Weeks One and Two. During the first two weeks of the class a bound reader with eight of the university course readings (Baber, 1987; Bennett, 1990; Boykin, 1986; Fordham & Ogbu, 1986; Gay, 1987a, 1987b; Kochman, 1981; Pasteur & Toldson, 1982) was given to each student. Over the next two weeks, they read, discussed, reviewed, and reported on the content of different articles. Students quoted different authors' perspectives to support their positions and easily dismissed others. They openly expressed high interest in the readings' content. They applied cultural knowledge, provided significant experiential data to support critiques, and demonstrated high levels of personal interest. Students proposed goals and activities, which were dated and recorded on butcher paper. They wrote required summaries and short critiques.

Week Three. The third week was spent planning and selecting project activities. Three groups were working simultaneously on different topics, so it became impossible to spend entire class periods exclusively on the African American project. Through readings and discussions, the students acquired a common knowledge base. I invited them to a working lunch to develop the rationale, goals, objectives, and measurable outcomes. Seven of the nine African American students from the Mass Media class attended. Without informing me, they invited seven other African American students (five who were in my Spanish classes, and two whom I knew but were not in any of my classes). Most of these students had read most of the articles. The fourteen students verbalized and actualized new roles and status. Leaders emerged, and the traditional teacher-student relationship changed. The students took control of the unit, and the teacher became a facilitator. The working lunch committee met three times during the third week. At the end of the third session, the students said they would develop the goals, adding that their friends and family would help. I was summarily told to draft a rationale and objectives and to write the agreed to measurable outcomes on a chart by tomorrow. Luther smiled and reminded me, "You're the one getting the real grade at the university."

The next day, Jamila came in and wrote three goals on blue butcher paper. These goals would guide the unit. Since I had not been part of the goal-setting discussion, I, along with the rest of the class, read the goals for the first time.

> Goal 1: To touch the intangible, the African American soul.
>
> Goal 2: To feel the unconscious, the cultural richness of our creative, spontaneous, vulnerable power called style.
>
> Goal 3: To hear and see the undeclared, invisible message implicit in the struggle.

From a teacher's perspective, this was the moment that the African American students assumed ownership of the content, climate, and process. Using red butcher paper, I posted the rationale, objectives, and measurable outcomes on the wall (see Table 11.1).

TABLE 11.1 African American Cultural Unit

Rationale	Objectives	Measurable Outcomes
Students are central in the curricular content.	1. Understand, appreciate, and value self. 2. Respect ethnic and cultural diversity at the individual, group, and societal level. 3. Use knowledge from multiple perspectives.	1. Read and critique a minimum of three articles. 2. Participate collaboratively in group activities. 3. Perform in at least one creative interpretation of the unit's central theme. 4. Write one reflective essay (minimum 200 words) on ethnic identity using a word processor.

A student-led discussion followed. In a **student-led discussion,** the person speaking has the floor until he or she calls on another person, who then takes control of the discussion until he or she calls on the next person, and so forth. The teacher, with the same status as the students, has to raise her hand and be acknowledged before speaking. In this type of discussion, students do not often call on the teacher. During this conversation, student leaders explained the goals, objectives, and requirements. Small groups formed and decided the specific activities, which included (a) a student-produced poster artistically expressing student reaction to the total experience, (b) a video documentation of selected classroom activities, (c) a literary monograph containing student reflections on their ethnic identity development, (d) an afterschool reform rap session, and (e) a student recitation at the university of *And Still I Rise* by Maya Angelou (1986). Students who emerged as cultural leaders assigned tasks to the members in their respective groups. The project was in student hands. I merely provided the necessary resources.

Weeks Four and Five. These weeks were spent discussing core values, communication styles, racial identity, ethnic identity, cultural shifting, African American English, prejudice and racism, and the African American collective identity. Students wrote reflections on their ethnic and racial identity and prepared for the student-selected, culminating activity, which would be videotaped. Orally, students participated in thematic discussions centered on the identification, analysis, evaluation, and synthesis of African American cultural values. They used drama to interpret the various stages of ethnic and racial identity, confrontational student-teacher interactions, and frustrating schooling experiences. Student-selected activities included recreated current events and cultural vignettes, such as the Rodney King event, poetic readings, male posturing, and the "walk."

Week Six. During the last week of the unit, students prepared for their self-selected, in-class mini-dramatizations and the culminating activity—*A Church Scene.* Once the date was selected, special invitations were made and hand delivered to all of the African American students in the school, approximately eighty-five students.

The Church Scene

The church service was complete with a preacher, deacon, choir, collection, and blessing. The unity, spirituality, and celebration of this event came forth as a major production, without a single prior practice performance. The African American principal was invited and was in attendance. Choir robes, an electric piano keyboard, podium, microphone, speakers, and over eighty African American students dressed in "Sunday Best" seemed to materialize out of thin air. While remarking on the dramatic excellence of the culminating event to a group of students, I inquired—"How did you get everybody together to practice?" Shaundra explained, "It just happened. We don't have to practice. It came naturally. It's just one of the unique talents Black people have." As the laughing, excited students quickly filed out, Runako paused and reached out for a quick hug, and said, "Rosa, I will never forget this day. You allowed us to be Black. It never happens." Her soft voice was different from her usual, carefree, spirited remarks. Those sixteen words at the end of the first day of filming created an unexplainable emotion, an intangible lump in my heart, reinforcing my perception that something incredible had just happened.

This six-week unit examining some aspects of the African American culture was a powerful experience for students, the teacher, and the school. Almost all of African American students enrolled in the high school "cut" their fifth period to join our Mass Media class. As they filed in, I asked, "Do you have a pass?" and when the students indicated "yes," they were allowed entrance (I knew most of them did not have their teachers' permission). These unofficially invited visitors, attracted by the cultural content and welcomed by the Mass Media students, stood, sat on tables, and chairs, and stuffed the room with an emotionally charged vitality. The classroom climate was creatively uncontrolled, yet culturally governed, kept in check by student directed nuances that changed effortlessly as the leadership role and power status emanated individually from the collective group.

When the principal (African American), who was invited to the final presentation, saw the African American student visitors in Mass Media, he assumed that they had permission to attend. However, later, in response to teacher complaints, he asked to see me. He applauded me for providing the African American students a meaningful experience and then ordered me to not allow unregistered students in my class again. I quickly agreed, since the activity had already taken place. I had already chosen to take professional risks when I did not adhere to existing policies and procedures for admitting unassigned students to class. Although I experienced a dissonance, a clash between institutional expectations and instinctive actions rooted in cultural values, I knowingly chose to meet my personal values and beliefs.

Diversity Pedagogy Dimensions

This section describes selected culturally influenced behaviors, attitudes, and knowledge that the students disclosed. As theorized, you will notice that complex developmental processes involving both student cultural displays and teacher pedagogical behaviors show that these dimensions rarely occurred in isolation, and, at times, some dimensions were more prominent than others depending on the classroom event.

Dimension 1: Diversity/Consciousness of Differences

This student-controlled project dispelled prevalent stereotypes and prejudicial attitudes regarding African American people and culture. Students shared and gained knowledge about the cultural values, attitudes, and behaviors of African Americans. This knowledge appeared to minimize discriminatory behaviors. Tony commented:

It wasn't just an African American unit. It was a chance for everyone to get insight about our culture as well as their own. Sometimes what you learn about others makes a reflection on who you are. You become a better more open person. I really feel that's what happened.

All of the students in the class used oral and written forms to express an increased acceptance and understanding of their own and other ethnic groups. They became more aware of the need to learn and understand other cultural groups. Students from ethnic groups of color begin to view their White peers in and out of the classroom as individuals and as members of the White racial group.

The African American students were aware of the discriminatory practices directed at them at school and they wanted change. They decided to have an afterschool function as a final activity with student selected issues. They scheduled, planned, and ran a Reform Rap Conference to discuss their concerns. Whereas the students were not fully aware of the process and procedures needed to bring about institutional change, they readily identified the limitations and obstacles to their schooling opportunities. For example, students explained that it was difficult to win school offices because Asian American students, a majority in number, voted for other Asian American students. They pointed out even in sports "we stink" because, although African American students participate, the majority of Asian American students competed mainly in swimming, golf, and tennis. This eliminated the depth and experience needed to be athletically competitive in the sports they liked—football, basketball, and track. For the most part, they did not feel their well-being was a priority in the school.

> Here at Leschi, I don't feel that I fit in. Not as a person in general, but as a Black person. Asians are the majority here and you never forget it. They have their clubs and organizations. What do Black people have? Nothing. Nothing but pride. (Tia)

Twana's experience was similar:

> I can say for a fact, if you were to talk to an African American, and ask if they truly felt valued in this school, they would probably answer "No."

The students criticized teachers. Other than three African American teachers who taught Science, Social Studies, and Marketing, the Chinese American teacher who taught Chinese and Japanese languages and ESL, and a Chicana American who taught Spanish and Mass Media and Social Studies, the entire staff was European American. Whereas the teachers were not all "mean and unfair," students felt that they were not committed to their welfare either. They enumerated their problems with the European American faculty without mentioning names. They commented:

> They think we're dumb and can't learn. All we do are worksheets and answer questions at the end of the chapter. (Kenneth)

> Teachers don't really care if you are ever going to be a success. White teachers, not all, but the majority, use a lot of racial slurs to put down Black students. They say things like: "You are only going to amount to burger flippers. All Blacks are going to be dead real

soon. No Blacks are going to succeed! All Black people are trouble, always causing a big commotion." (Jamila)

They treat us all the same, not realizing that we are individuals, with different skills and different personalities. (Tia)

They listed solutions on poster paper during the last half hour. The posters were left on the classroom walls, and in the days immediately following the Reform Rap Conference, African American students invariably wandered in to read and comment on the solutions section. Some of the students proudly claimed ownership for a particular solution idea. Some of the items on the list included:

1. Ask the principal to hire young African American teachers.
2. Attend the district's interview training and participate in new staff hiring.
3. Demand a Black Studies program to learn about the African American culture.
4. Involve family in the PTA.

The Reform Rap Conference was productive in meeting the students' needs to voice frustrations and anger in a safe, nurturing environment, but it did not move them beyond the identification stage. Students were not demeaning or disrespectful when expressing concerns about staff members. They were respectful of each other and listened carefully. Affirming, supportive statements often followed longer statements— "Yep," "I heard that," and "That happened to me too." The four hours spent at the conference quickly vanished.

There was not enough time to formulate how, when, and to whom future action would be directed. It was my perception that being able to talk about issues important to them was enough for now. They had experienced discourse as a reform strategy. In spite of the heavy, depressing content of the session, the students were in good spirits as they moved to the school's PTA Multicultural Dinner scheduled that same evening.

Dimension 2: Identity/Ethnic Identity Development

In schooling students are often conditioned to conceal ethnic behaviors. In Mass Media, African American students were able to freely display ethnic knowledge, behaviors, and values. Curricular activities, high expectations, and student written and oral products met students' emotional, social, creative, and cognitive needs without compromising their ethnic integrity.

African American students in Mass Media experienced what I call a **collective ethnic encounter,** a significant ethnic group happening, while not unusual in a home or community context, that occurs infrequently in classrooms. The spontaneous participation of the entire African American student population was an impressive outcome. The African American critical mass seemed to add a spiritual consciousness to the church scene. This new majority appreciated, respected, and validated the student production, and in turn the students' oratorical style and rich oral language enhanced the call-response dialogue.

These students actively participated in a nurturing, self-directed activity that was ethnically and culturally compatible. Students described their experience:

> We felt free to do what we wanted without having to worry about fitting into someone else's standards of decorum. We didn't have to worry about what other people would say or their perception of our behavior. It was our time to be us. It goes back to an old '70s expression, "Being Black sure ain't easy, but living Black sure feels good." (Jamila)

> At that moment the whole class felt as if we were in a world of our own. I am sure that I speak for the whole class when I say we felt very important. No teacher has ever taken the time or has even had the interest in African American students. (Tia)

Students were given Cross's (1991) racial identity and Gay's (1987a) ethnic identity stage theory research. It was explained that Cross's racial stage theory model was designed for adults, while Gay's ethnic identity stage theory model could be applied to adolescents. The difference between the constructs of race, ethnicity, racial identity, and ethnic identity were discussed along with the limitations of stage theory.

In small groups, students shared personal experiences and described situations that could be classified in the various stages of ethnic identity. Students recreated probable behaviors and attitudes prevalent during the various stages of ethnic identity. They produced dramatic skits, musical interpretations, poetic raps, as well as reflective essays addressing ethnic identity affiliation. Selected excerpts from essays follow:

> To me, being African American is a lifestyle and a way of life. Being African American determines how I act, speak, and think. It also determines how I live, how I'm perceived, and how I'm treated. The first thing people notice when they see me is my skin color, whether they realize it or not. Some people allow skin color to determine their behavior. I've seen it happen plenty of times. They look at you a certain way or talk to you a certain way that is not the way they normally talk to members of their own race. (Tony)

> I feel secure knowing that I am African American. I am proud to be a part of a culture that has a rich and colorful background. I don't let negative images, opinions, or beliefs about my ethnicity affect me. I pass them off as ignorance. That doesn't mean I ignore or tolerate them. I look at it like this. It's not my job to educate or raise anybody. I can only say how I feel about it. It would be easy to go off on that particular person, but I choose not too. I choose to counter ignorance with intelligence. (Jamila)

> To be Black, to act Black, and to live Black are all different. Being Black to me is more than physical. It is the essence of spirituality, soul, intelligence, and a deep creativity that exceeds beyond reality. My experience of being Black has been very positive, except when I am exposed to the ignorance of others. (Runako)

> I am proud to be a young Black man. . . . Some people look at my skin color and think that I'm nothing but a troublemaker, but they are wrong. That's a problem; everybody judging each other by their cover and not taking time to find out what others are really about. As an African American I am happy, but not happy about the way we get treated, because it is not right. I feel good in some ways and bad in some ways. I mostly feel bad that African Americans have to face a lot of prejudice. I feel good about all the talent we

have and our ways of living. Being Black is a challenge, a challenge that needs to be accepted by Black people. (Jason)

Dimension 3: Social Interactions/Interpersonal Relationships

Teachers can play a significant role in helping children develop the social skills necessary for initiating and sustaining friendship as a critical resource (Hartup, 1996). They can create classroom conditions that enable students to forge friendships, promote group solidarity, and build community through collaborative learning activities. Teachers can provide opportunities for repeated social encounters in the classroom.

In this classroom, students were able to self-motivate and self-govern classroom interactions. This required a change in the traditional teacher-student role and status. The teacher provided access to classroom resources, and students assumed greater responsibility in their learning process. Students actively participated in nurturing, self-directed activities that reflected beliefs, values, prior knowledge, and social conventions from diverse cultures. They were able to participate in culturally relevant social interactions which resulted in (a) multiple opportunities to develop and display leadership roles in curricular events; (b) active participation in learning experiences involving collaborative interactions with others that demanded deep levels of exploration, reflection, and internalization; and (c) spontaneous involvement in the Mass Media cultural vignettes and church scene that promoted bonding with the other African American students in the school. Runako's comment is representative:

> I had the opportunity to study African American culture. During the process of gathering information, I had the chance to work with others to learn, have fun, and share our culture. I feel that the African American population here at Leschi High School has grown together and has bonded, throughout this great learning experience.

Dimension 4: Culturally Safe Classroom Context/ Self-Regulated Learning

The overall classroom mood honored student entitlement to respect voice and freedom. It provided multiple opportunities to practice self-regulated behavior. Expected high levels of student social and academic competence used friendship, family, and community as resources and explicitly affirmed students' cultural heritage. There was a teacher belief that the students had the capability and the desire to demonstrate positive behavioral patterns; therefore, efforts were directed toward enabling students to (a) internalize self-control; (b) share space; (c) develop skills to better understand and monitor joy, anger, freedom, and conflict; and (d) encourage a willingness to become a member of the community.

Because discipline was a student-selected topic for the Reform Rap Conference, the differences between the constructs of discipline and classroom management were explained. **Discipline** (self- or other-imposed) was defined as student or teacher actions and decisions made to meet personal needs. A **disciplinary action** by a teacher is a decision that judges student behavior unacceptable. **Classroom manage-**

ment was described as a teacher management plan that includes practices, routines, techniques, and skills to create a positive classroom climate conducive to teaching and learning.

Similar to a regular conference, students who attended received a student-prepared Discipline Packet that included (a) Boykin's (1986) previously read article entitled "The Triple Quandary and the Schooling of African American Children"; (b) data on the disproportionality of disciplinary actions toward African American students in their school, district, and nation; and (c) information on the school district's disciplinary appeal process. Students' general response to this information included anger and outrage at the injustice and inequitable treatment directed against them as members of the African American ethnic group.

Working in small groups, students analyzed how differences in communication styles; allegiance to a collective identification; and individual and group personal choices made to ignore, comply, or resist Eurocentric behavioral norms, such as tone, volume, and purpose of voice, impacted how disciplinary issues affected them. They were aware that their choices could result in personal and group harm. Focus was placed on developing strategies to enhance negotiating and problem-solving skills that promoted self-control.

After brainstorming disciplinary issues and recording ideas and suggestions on colorful butcher paper, students broke into groups to prepare skits depicting student-teacher behavioral confrontations and student-administrator referral sessions. Students spilled out into the hall and staircase. Skits were performed on a makeshift stage and videotaped. Whole group discussion followed the skits. Students voiced their concerns in a forum where they felt they were being heard and understood. They also expressed support and empathy for their peers whom they perceived to be unfairly disciplined. Although this topic produced the most personal and group anger, it was also the most comical, as students role-played actual situations about themselves, teachers, administrators, and parents.

Dimension 5: Language/Language Learning

Teachers who acknowledge the functions of language beyond direct exchange of information are often more successful with students from diverse linguistic groups. Every language embodies both the historical experience of a particular cultural group and the group's conscious effort to transmit its collective values (Vygotsky, 1962). Native speakers of a given language utilize not only its grammar and vocabulary, but also its distinctive verbal customs, patterns of thought, and styles of learning. Students' linguistic displays also have value and meaning to identity development, academic competence, and social behavior.

Students are cognitively, linguistically, and emotionally connected to the language and culture of their home. They are entitled to use the strengths of their family's linguistic and cultural backgrounds in school learning experiences. Most educators can recognize the need to respect and maintain the language of children who speak European and Eastern languages. They also understand the need to modify instruction to meet the needs of English language learners. However, what is not generally clear is the need to adapt the teaching-learning process to the language issues facing many African American children who must negotiate the ways of school language.

The schooling problems of students learning a new language and the difficulties African American children, who speak American Black English, encounter in classrooms are not analogous (Perry & Delpit, 1998). In fact, scholarship shows that different cultures, even those sharing the same language, use language in different ways (Cole & Schriber, 1974; Villanueva, 1999). Some point out that even the rhetoric (and writing) of monolingual English speakers from a culture different from the mainstream retains ancestral cultural influences (Villanueva, 1999).

American Black English, as a language, and its subsequent association with the achievement outcomes of African American children remains controversial, because it is often erroneously judged substandard. Gay (2002) maintains that this was evident in the public contest surrounding the American Black English controversy in Oakland, California, during the 1996–1997 academic school year. In summarizing some of the issues, Gay (2000) points out the following:

1. The policy statement in Oakland, in part, argued that African American students possessed a recognizable language system discrete from American English and that children should not be dehumanized, stigmatized, discriminated against, or denied opportunities to learn because of the language they speak.
2. Supporters of the Oakland policy argued that the real issue was not about the language itself, but about the role of language and the validity of African American experiences in the schooling process. A critical goal in Oakland was to build bridges between language, culture, and communication styles of African American students and those of the school for the purpose of improving literacy achievement.
3. Tactics used by critics of the Oakland policy on Ebonics involved distortions and media sensationalism. Assumptions were made that Ebonics would be taught instead of American English, and that it would be imposed on all African American students.
4. Many individuals who spoke against Ebonics were uninformed. They confused Ebonics with slang, rap, illiteracy, and incorrect, broken English. This misinterpretation was influenced by negative values and stereotypes attached to the language strengths and communication styles of African Americans, especially those who live in high-poverty urban settings.

African American students in Mass Media engaged in multiple modes of discourse, such as small group, large group, teacher-directed, student-led, call-response, conversational dyads, dramatic presentations, monologues, orations, and debates, in the language of their choice. Their verbal ability to convey ideas, state positions, share knowledge, and assume verbal leadership was acknowledged. Students did not have to address schooling perceptions of what is acceptable vocabulary, communication styles, pitch, volume, or intensity. The acquisition of new vocabulary and the maintenance of their home language were evident in their classroom participation and student products—reading, writing, and speaking.

The following comments show that students understand how language is linked to their culture, ethnicity, achievement, and pride:

> We demonstrated to all the way Black people communicate, dress, walk, and overall deal with each other. People that were not Black were amazed at how smart, sophisticated, and unified Black people are once we are in accord with each other. We showed others how we could speak to each other in a coded language. No one who was not Black would understand what we were talking about. All of the people that came to the class [for the church scene] were amazed at how we all behaved in such a loving, caring, and fun way. (Shaundra)

> I enjoyed the activities in class. It was a time for us to express ourselves without being reprimanded for doing what comes naturally. People always say that African American people, in general, are always loud. What is loud to them is expressive to us. Being expressive is natural in our culture. (Jamila)

Dimension 6: Culturally Inclusive Content/Knowledge Acquisition

The teaching-learning process that took place in this culturally inclusive six-week unit explored African American content from the perspective of African American scholars and students. The cultural, social, and academic content elements of this unit event endured over time. Students who were not enrolled in Mass Media brought essays and poetry, completed on their own time, for possible publication in our *One Image of Our Message* publication. These students requested and usually received credit from their Language Arts teachers for these quality products. The student social communication network uncharacteristically focused to some degree on academic school concerns. Students discussed issues and ideas that were occurring in Mass Media in the halls, cafeteria, and in other classes. Some students requested copies of particular articles by African American scholars for their friends and family. African American students, especially males, without a fifth period class (they believed they had already failed, so they did not attend assigned classes) came to Mass Media regularly and, without teacher demands, completed daily class assignments and projects.

The readings, written from an African American perspective, and the overall success of the activities provided students with a greater understanding, respect, and acceptance of the African American culture. This knowledge base, along with students' experiences, cemented ethnic affiliations for African American students. Many students expressed surprise that scholars at universities studied their culture, indicating that students had not experienced insider perspectives in instructional resources.

High student and teacher learning expectations and high-status, university-level content, rather than remedial, below grade-level material, provided students with a quality experience resulting in student learning at a high achievement level. One of Kenneth's poems, entitled *Knowledge*, expresses his depth of cultural knowledge, socially responsive rage, community, and accomplishment:

Knowledge
The knowledge that I'm spitting contains facts
on the culture which I call Black

Being a Black Man in America
it seems,
the White man is daring ya
to try to come up, and when you do
you get stomped on by the mighty White shoe.
Every time I walk the streets I have to think
Why is the man trying to put me on the blink?
We're losing it 'cause we don't understand
their game plan
We need to get together and just take a stand.
You know the White man or should I say devils?
They think they're higher up looking from the next level
I guess they're blind and can't see what's evident
that the Black Man is highly intelligent
I have a plan to make it in society
I'm going to lean on you brother
And you'll lean on me.

Dimension 7: Instruction/Reasoning Skills

When making teacher instructional decisions to enhance children's reasoning skills, most teachers' prior knowledge on human development is based on a body of scholarship produced by the dominant culture and based on the norms and behaviors of European American middle-class children. Therefore, without modification, these instructional decisions may not be applicable to children from groups of color. Consider how most classrooms separate emotion and cognition, focus on the individual at the expense of the group, pursue objective analysis versus personal scrutiny, and rely on written documents over oral productions.

In Mass Media, African American students used higher level learning skills in different modalities—emotion, recognition, creativity, evaluation, control, analysis, posturing, synthesis, music, performance, and modeling—to integrate new information from the readings to their prior knowledge rooted in personal cultural wisdom and ethnic realities. The instructional design allowed students freedom to apply their cultural knowledge, language uses, and ethnic habits. Balanced instructional strategies created conditions, individually and collaboratively, for students to experience higher level critical thinking.

As a result, students were free to work collaboratively to apply experiential knowledge, critical thinking skills, and ethnic habits of mind to produce exceptional products. Students made posters; wrote narratives; made speeches; and created, recited, and dramatized poetry. A monograph, containing artwork, essays, and poetry, was published and given to friends and family members. Discussions and essays irreverently dismantled or proudly embraced scholars and theoretical constructs. When discussing Fordham and Ogbu's (1986) notion of "acting White" as a reason for lack of achievement, they were aghast someone "smart" could come to that conclusion. Luther's poem, simply entitled *Poem*, summarized the general feeling:

Poem
They put it together without a thought
It wasn't a lie, but it was a plot
To piece the puzzle in an aftermath
Astounded me so much,
I had to laugh, they miss the truth
and lack knowledge from the roots.
Although you heard it from someone else
It makes no sense cause it's only true
to myself.

Students also created mini-dramas and skits reflecting their analysis of various issues affecting them. Jamila, when reflecting on the "Rodney King Enactment" in her statement below, does not compartmentalize the cognitive and affective domain. Her use of the pronoun *we* may indicate that she may not perceive learning exclusively as an individual phenomena:

> We decided to re-enact the Rodney King beating. We all sat around and laughed afterwards. Not about the issue itself, but about how funny Tony [acting as Rodney] was. Then after all the fun and games, we sat down and talked about the real situation and how it affects the African American community. We all participated in a serious group discussion. We talked about everything from how we feel about being the ethnicity that we are to how we feel about being part of American culture. I feel proud and secure knowing that I am African American. I am proud to be a part of a culture that has such a rich and powerful background. Negative images, opinions, or beliefs don't affect how I feel about my ethnic group. (Jamila)

Dimension 8: Assessment/Self-Evaluation

It can be argued that students can be included in the assessment process, as long as the teacher has a mastery of the curriculum, holds high expectations, and uses accelerated content. Based on my extensive experience teaching in K-12 urban public schools, I have found that students who are traditionally underserved are also harmed through assessment policies and procedures in schooling. As a result, they often develop highly sophisticated coping skills to maintain psychological well-being, in spite of the teachers' low assessment. As a teacher, I always try to convey the idea that both of us—students and teacher—are evaluated according to how we accomplish specific academic outcomes. If they do not learn what is intended, then I am not teaching. Conversely, if they do not learn through meaningful experiences what is mutually agreed, then grades are meaningless.

The grade for Mass Media was based on a point system that included attendance, participation, reciprocated respect, and assignment completion (each worth 25 points). Students were involved in determining the categories, the point worth, and the total evaluation of their peers in two of the categories—reciprocated respect and participation. In written assignments points were not taken off for writing quality, such as spelling, grammar, or punctuation, if the procedural requirements were met. Procedural requirements included items such as length, due date, summary, analysis, application, headings, having been typed, font size, and double spacing. However, students received extensive feedback and were encouraged to resubmit an edited version as a replacement for future assignments. For example, if ten essays were required, a resubmitted edited paper would count as one of the ten. Self-motivation and self-pride, as well as interest in the specific strengths and areas for improvement suggested in the teacher comments and peer evaluations, were a greater incentive to improve writing skills than a more traditional teacher-imposed grading scale. All of the students exceeded the total number of required written assignments. The number of rewrites was influenced by their determination to be published in *One Image of My Message*, a student publication.

Although students received full completion points for all required assignments meeting minimum grade requirements, all work submitted for possible publication in the *One Image of My Message* monograph was subject to multiple drafts and extensive editing for punctuation, spelling, sentence structure, and clarity by the student editors prior to acceptance for publication. Mini-posters throughout the school advertised and solicited work for this publication. It was a refereed monograph, and being published became a high priority. The editorial team solicited the cover design by the best artist in the school, who happened to be a star on the basketball team, but was not enrolled in Mass Media.

Conclusion

This classroom experience shows that it is possible to create teaching-learning conditions that produce excellence in student performance and social development. During this six-week unit, African American students took ownership of an accelerated curricular content by critically reading and analyzing university graduate-level articles and book chapters. Throughout the semester they used friendship connections, collaborative skills, leadership abilities, and linguistic strengths to succeed socially and academically.

The description of the learning that took place in Mass Media documents student learning at a high level of competency. It also points out that student learning may depend on the teachers' ability to provide students with the resources needed to transfer prior knowledge to new knowledge and to make decisions that benefit students—even if these choices potentially place teachers at risk.

RECOMMENDED READINGS

Cross, W. E., Jr., Strauss, L., & Fhagen-Smith, P. (1999). African American identity development across the life span: Educational implications. In R. H. Sheets & E. R. Hollins (Eds.), *Racial and ethnic identity in school practices: Aspects of human development* (pp. 29–48). Mahwah, NJ: Erlbaum.

Ladson-Billings, G. (1994). *The dreamkeepers: Successful teachers of African American teachers.* San Francisco: Jossey-Bass.

Moses, R. P., & Cobb, C. E. Jr. (2001). *Radical equations: Math literacy and the civil rights.* Boston: Beacon Press.

CHAPTER

12 Linguistic Strengths of Mexican American Students

Textbooks . . . often become the curriculum itself; the teacher's goal is to cover the material, not to uncover what students want to say or what is important to them. Problems are seen as residing in students, not in the materials.

—Valdés, 2001, p. 156

Two major concerns facing Mexican American students are the subtractive nature of schooling experiences and the progressive nature of their underachievement. **Subtractive schooling** refers to the cultural and linguistic losses students endure during the schooling process (Valenzuela, 1999). The **progressive nature of underachievement** speaks to the generational decline of achievement as documented by grades, test scores, dropout rates, and disciplinary actions (Valenzuela, 1999). First- and second-generation Mexican American students perform at a higher level than third- and later-generation students (Portes & Zhou, 1993; Suarez-Orozco, 1991). The longer they are in school the lower they achieve. Thus, what begins as a minor problem in primary school becomes acute in high school. The research in this chapter shows a reversal of this trend. This study examines the successful classroom experiences of a group of Mexican American high school students over a three-year period (Sheets, 1995a).

This chapter* describes the changes that took place in a high school Spanish class that enabled Mexican American students to succeed academically and socially. In this class, Mexican American students used their native language skills, experiential knowledge, and cultural resources to achieve academically. The second part of this chapter screens teacher behaviors and student cultural displays through the eight diversity pedagogy dimensions.

*This chapter is adapted from Sheets, R. H. (1995). From remedial to gifted: Effects of culturally relevant pedagogy. *Theory Into Practice, 34*(3), 186–193. Copyright by The College of Education, The Ohio State University. All rights reserved.

Advanced Placement Spanish Class

This study took place in an urban classroom. Mexican American students, a minority in number, were generally assigned to ESL classes. Fabiola and Lupe, fluent native-born Spanish-speakers, were the only Mexican American students enrolled in the second-year Spanish class. After the first few weeks of school, they stopped coming to class. They could neither read nor write in Spanish. They ended up failing the second-year Spanish course. Their student records indicated serious nonattendance patterns resulting in academic failure in most of their classes. One of the reasons for failure was poor attendance. However, it made absolutely no sense for Spanish-speaking students to fail a beginning-level Spanish course. What happened when I examined the extent of my responsibilities as teacher and reflected on who is ultimately accountable for student failure?

¿Qué pasó?

I used to believe that if I gave my best and some students chose not to learn, it was not my fault. I prepared and presented excellent lessons. The majority of my students succeeded. I mentored and helped students beyond class time. My classroom was comfortable, disciplined, and interesting. Students were actively involved and they often told me that they enjoyed my class. However, my assessment of self as a good teacher included the principle that I was exempt from student failure. If students did not attend, did not engage, or were not motivated, it was their doing. Maybe their parents needed to take more responsibility.

Teaching in Seattle had removed me from my culture and my people. It was a new experience to have two Mexican American students in my Spanish class. Almost from day one, I knew I was not meeting their needs. The academic failure of these friendly, likable, and polite girls and their truant behavior made me question my grammatically, textbook-driven Spanish instruction designed to teach native English speakers Spanish. I was determined to make changes to include the needs of native Spanish speakers learning Spanish. It shouldn't be difficult I told myself; after all, we routinely teach native English speakers twelve to thirteen years of English in language arts classes.

I actively recruited Fabiola, Lupe, and three other Spanish-speaking students for an advanced Spanish class offered spring semester. Naturally, they did not want to enroll. "How can we pass an advanced class?" they reasoned. "We can't even pass Spanish II." "You will. It's my fault you didn't pass last semester. I promise. You'll pass. All you have to do is try and come everyday." After quite a bit of persuasion, followed by a few home visits, they finally agreed. Spring semester, five Mexican American students enrolled in the class. This time, textbook content and grammatical concepts did not decide success.

At the end of the spring semester, all five passed the College Board Advanced Placement (AP) Spanish Language exam, earning college credit while sophomores and juniors in high school. A year later, they passed the prestigious AP Spanish Literature exam, comparable to a third-year college literature class. Over a three-year period, as a result of intervention, these Mexican American students, previously labeled at-risk, performed at a level expected of college-bound honor students. *¿Qué pasó?*

Year One: 1989–1990. I knew that course content, instructional process, and classroom context had to change if native Spanish speakers were to succeed in Spanish classes. The solution was to enroll them in my advanced Spanish class, which traditionally enrolled a small number of students. The focus would be conversation through literature and culture instead of reading and writing through grammar. I rationalized that the language fluency of the other students would increase with native speakers in the class, and the ability to speak Spanish could technically count as three years of high school Spanish. No one knew that five native Spanish-speaking students, with only one or none of the prerequisite Spanish courses, were enrolled in this advanced Spanish course. In large urban public school systems, asking permission generally means the stifling of ideas. I knew I would be told "no" with the justification that ESL programs met the needs of linguistically different students.

All five students qualified for the Federal Reduced or Free Lunch Program; three were from single-parent homes, and two were on welfare. All were a year or more behind in school grade based on credits earned, and all had serious nonattendance patterns. Other than attendance issues, they did not experience disciplinary problems. None participated in extracurricular school activities, and three held part-time jobs. All came from homes where parents spoke little or no English. Although Spanish was their first language, they had never been taught to read or write in Spanish.

The first thing they learned was that they possessed a valuable skill, the ability to speak Spanish. In the small groups with regular students, they used their linguistic and cultural knowledge to describe, translate, and explain concepts in Spanish. This verbal dexterity placed them in high demand during group work. They quickly sensed that along with their peers, I, too, believed they were capable. Within a short time, they began to acknowledge their strengths. The change was incredible. By March, their success and enthusiasm in the classroom, the yearly notice from the District Testing Office to register students for the Advanced Placement Tests, and the desire to create a challenge for them, as well as for myself, prompted me to ask them if they wanted to register for the AP exam in May. I explained that the test was difficult. We watched *Stand and Deliver*, the movie documenting the success of Mexican American students in East Los Angeles and their teacher Jaime Escalante in AP Calculus. I made it clear that it was impossible to prepare adequately in two months with only one class hour per day. They knew we would have to spend many hours after school and on Saturdays. I would call their families and, if necessary, make home visits to obtain permission. We could work around their work schedules.

During these study sessions, they learned where to place accents. They wrote many 200-word essays in Spanish, practiced two-minute orals, listened to ten-minute lectures, and answered multiple-choice questions. We were determined. Surprised that it was fun to study, they often laughed and commented, "Can you imagine! Me! Studying? *¡Es increíble!*" Then one Saturday in April, we came early to school to take a mock five-and-a-half-hour 1985 version of the Spanish Language test. Their points indicated high passing scores. It was exciting to watch them run and scream up and down the empty halls, throwing test scores high in the air.

The school counselor used the Saul Haas Fund to pay the required test fees. The Saul Haas Fund paid for specific school expenses for students who would be denied participation because of the costs involved. In May, five students took the exam. Notices in July from the Advanced Placement College Board indicated that everybody passed. The College Board scores students on a one-to-five scale, with three being the lowest and five the highest score, guaranteeing students college credit nationally. Miguel and Fabiola received fours, earning ten college credits. Lupe, Carmen, and Luis each received perfect fives, worth fifteen college credits. Lupe, Miguel, and Fabiola were only sophomores in high school. Carmen was a senior who had no chance of graduating with her class due to past, excessive absenteeism, and Luis was a junior.

Four of the five students who passed the AP Spanish Language test wanted to take another Spanish class, so it seemed logical to prepare for the AP Spanish Literature exam. Since the school could not provide basic funds for instructional materials, I wrote a proposal for a Partners in Public Education (PIPE) grant. PIPE awarded financial assistance to worthwhile innovative educational projects on a competitive basis. In June, we were awarded a $3,000 PIPE grant. With this money, I quickly ordered and scrounged for material for the AP Spanish Literature course. I spent the summer reading the literary works of the five required authors: Gabriel García Márquez, Jorge Luis Borges, Ana María Matute, Federíco García Lorca, and Miguel de Unamuno. That summer I took the sample literature exam. I barely passed with a low three.

Year Two: 1990–1991. Fall semester of the second year of the program, five new native speakers and four non-native Spanish speakers joined the four students (one of the original five was a senior) who had passed the College Board AP Spanish Language exam, for a total of thirteen. The PIPE grant provided funds for test fees, field trips, and curricular materials. I knew the academic program would take some students one to three years to accomplish, but other gains such as Spanish literacy, ethnic identity development, and interpersonal relationships would be immediate. The students gave each other positive peer support. The class provided a natural mentoring environment, and we unwittingly became a *familia.*

Two weeks into spring semester, the principal decided that thirteen was too low a number to generate a section of advanced Spanish, especially since the bulging numbers in the first-year Spanish classes required another section. In this high school, with a majority of Chinese American students, most college-bound students took French, Chinese, or Japanese as their fourth year of a world language. Most students took only two years of a world language to fulfill graduation requirements. My choice was to drop the class or combine the thirteen students with another Spanish section. So, fall semester the thirteen students were combined with thirty-two first-year Spanish students, making it a total of forty-five students in one class period. Learning and teaching were difficult; however, the thirteen advanced Spanish students were assigned a separate class spring semester.

This group, although similar to the original group ethnically, linguistically, economically, and culturally, was different due to the leadership and status of the original four. These students attended all of their classes, won school academic achievement awards, and joined extracurricular school activities. We formed a touring *Ballet Folklórico*. The students choreographed traditional Mexican folk dances, designed authentic costumes, and performed for their peers and students in the greater Seattle Area.

The *West Seattle Herald*, a neighborhood weekly, and *La Voz*, a Washington State monthly Spanish newspaper, ran articles and pictures of their successes. As members of the yearbook staff, Honor Society, soccer team, and volleyball team, they no longer felt insignificant. They did not hug the walls as they moved silently from class to class. I remember Lupe's loud voice and happy laughter in the halls and recall the strange pain I felt when she casually stated,

> You know, I used to be afraid to walk down the middle of the hall. I didn't belong. I used to touch the wall with my finger or walk around the building on the outside, even in the rain. But now everybody knows me. They say, "Hi."

As May approached, students prepared for either the AP Spanish Language or the AP Spanish Literature Exam. A teacher strike in April took away valuable school time. Without access to the school, important information carefully recorded on disks was useless without computers. Although we met regularly, the three to four hours scheduled to study were lost to the constant interruptions encountered at the places and spaces where we met. I constantly worried that I was not adequately preparing them. We had basically lost fall semester and now a strike.

In May, only Lupe and Marisol were ready for the difficult literature test. Marisol, a new student in Year Two, was preparing to take both the language and literature test. We spent the evening before test day studying until 11:00 P.M. at Marisol's home. We reviewed all five authors, five novels, three plays, thirty or so short stories, and thirty to forty poems. They knew characters, themes, literary terminology, and the structural analysis and writing style of all five authors. They also had a basic understanding of the era in which each author wrote and the major cultural and historical influences in their lives.

The literature exam was scheduled for the early afternoon. Excused from classes, they spent the morning sitting on the floor outside my room munching donuts, cramming, and waiting for my substitute to arrive. We had no time for lunch. The exam was administered in a small conference room in a downtown district office. I waited, the proctor watched, they worked, and five long hours later the exam ended. I watched as they walked out softly. Carefully and casually on the ride to Ivor's Salmon House to celebrate, I inquired, "How was it? I'm really proud of you guys!" I made sure my tone indicated that the journey mattered, not the result. Marisol had taken the AP Spanish Language exam the week before (she felt she did well) and had prepared for both simultaneously. She crossed her arms over her chest and held her shoulders lightly as she spoke in Spanish, softly and poetically. "Rosa, it feels like a heavy cloud has been lifted from my soul. I can't express how glad I am to have it over with."

Lupe was expressive and realistic. She worked thirty to forty hours a week at McDonald's, bought her own clothes and food, helped raise her brother, and even paid part of the rent. Laughing, she responded, "I'm glad that stupid test is over, Rosa. Now you can't mess with me! If I had known it was going to be this hard, I would have never done it. It was pure hell!" "Do you think you passed?" I asked timidly. Marisol tried to recall the test as she responded tentatively, "I don't know. Parts of it . . ." "Who cares!" interrupted Lupe, "Let's go celebrate! Where are we going?" Lupe then reached into her pocket and handed me the dreaded blue sheet with the three forty-five minute (each) essay questions.

In July, lime half sheets from the College Board indicated that all five students passed the Spanish Language test. One received a four and the other four had perfect fives. A score of four for Lupe and a three for Marisol meant they both passed the Spanish Literature exam! Marisol was pleased with her perfect five on the Spanish Language test.

Since it was an opportunity to learn to teach AP Spanish Literature, I applied for and was awarded a Mellon Grant designed to train AP teachers working in inner city schools. That summer I attended the University of Northern Colorado for an intensive two-week workshop on AP Spanish literature. I, the only scholarship teacher, joined teachers from exclusive prep schools across the nation. I was stunned to learn that we had prepared for one of the most prestigious AP exams taken by very few students across the United States, and my workshop classmates were equally surprised that students from an inner city urban setting had actually taken this exam. This exam had a high failure rate for mainstream students (18 percent) and an even higher failure rate for Mexican American students (22 percent). Most of the students taking the AP Spanish (and French) literature tests attended fifth-year private prep schools with access to instructional resources I could only dream about. In May 1991, only 3,146 students took the AP Spanish Literature exam compared to 23,643 students taking the AP Spanish Language exam (AP Program, 1992). Had I known in September what I found out in June, I might not have even attempted the literature exam in May. We were the only students in the entire state of Washington taking this exam.

Year Three: 1991–1992. The five-hour mock practice test in March indicated that fifteen students would be ready to take the College Board Advanced Placement exams in May. Feelings of pride were mixed with fear and knowledge that many long hours would be spent studying. No one chose to back out. Lessons were held every day for different groups after school during March and April. Sometimes I provided snacks. On the days that we stayed late, parents brought warm food. A traditional highlight was an all-day Saturday study session at my house complete with Godfather's Jalapeño Pizza.

In the third year of the program, four students passed the Spanish Literature exam, and four passed the Spanish Language exam. Two students scheduled to take the language exam were unable to do so because of personal issues beyond their control, and three students moved prior to exam day. Over a three-year period, twenty out of twenty-nine Mexican American students who participated in the program received college credit by passing national AP exams. All of the non-native Spanish speakers enrolled in this advanced Spanish class who took the AP Spanish Language test during their fourth year of Spanish also passed. The next section describes aspects of the teaching-learning process that helped make this possible.

Diversity Pedagogy Dimensions

This program enabled Mexican American students who could speak but not read and write Spanish access to AP Spanish Language and Spanish Literature courses. These classes are usually designed for and offered to gifted or honors-level native English speakers. At no time were the students who participated in the program tested for or identified as gifted. The class was in the World Language Department. It was not part of the ESL program. *¿Qué pasó?* What happened when what's happening in the classroom is important to students? The following discussion examines teacher pedagogical behaviors and student cultural displays through the eight diversity pedagogy dimensions. These dimensions, as theorized, do not happen in isolation. Although distinguishable, they merge and blend during classroom events.

Dimension 1: Diversity/Consciousness of Differences

Mexican American students were the majority in number in the class. Although this form of linguistic segregation provided valuable resources and measurable benefits, it was important for these students to see themselves as an integral part the whole school community. The acceptance of ethnic, linguistic, and cultural differences in self and in others was modeled purposefully through various activities. Some included interactions with ethnically diverse students. When field trips were taken, students representing all ethnic groups participated. Students had breakfast with and were publicly praised by the famous Puerto Rican lawyer and talk-show host, Geraldo Rivera, when he was in town. They attended motivational lectures by Jaime Escalante and Henry Cisneros. When Cesar Chavez came to *El Centro de la Raza* (local community center) the students attended. Since I was the advisor for the cheerleaders and required to attend various sporting activities, I sought and was given permission from parents to take them to basketball and football games and to the school dances that followed these events. This was especially enjoyable for the Mexican American girls who had never participated in these extracurricular school activities and who would not be allowed to go unescorted.

Discussions on issues such as discrimination, stereotypes, historical perspectives, cultural preferences, and linguistic skills about self and other groups of people were expected components of the instructional content. Ethnic, linguistic, and cultural differences were affirmed, but sometimes students perceived these differences as negative. *Real Spanish* describes an incident that occurred in this school. Although you will undoubtedly experience emotions at either end of the continuum—joy and anger—in the classroom, the difficulty resides not in the normal emotions themselves, but in the ways these feelings can be channeled to benefit students. Professionalism requires teachers not to criticize other teachers; however, misconceptions can be clarified or a different point of view can be presented.

Real Spanish

When students mentioned that they were silent in other classes, I encouraged them to participate. Lupe openly stated she was ashamed of her accent when she spoke English, then added that one of the ESL teachers told her that she didn't "even speak real Spanish." The students' expressions led me to believe that these were typical feelings and experiences. Perhaps they could sense the anger I felt as I quietly pulled down the world map and pointed out all the places in the world where Spanish was the dominant language. I explained how elements of a living, spoken language varied depending on the geographical location. In other words, the Spanish in Barcelona is different from that in Sevilla, from the Spanish spoken in various parts of Mexico, Argentina, and the United States. But they were all linguistically considered Spanish. Likewise, the English spoken in Britain is different from American English and aspects of American English differed in New York, Texas, and Montana. Yet, it was all English. Students were encouraged to be proud that they were bilingual and to openly thank their parents for this priceless gift. I pointed out that all of the students in the class spoke at least two languages, American English and either Spanish, Tagalo, African American English, or Chinese. I emphasized: "An accent only proves that you can speak at least two languages. There is no need to be ashamed of a linguistic skill that many people value, work hard for, and often go to college to acquire."

A lively, student-led discussion took place regarding the difference between Mandarin and Cantonese Chinese, why linguists categorize American Black English as a language, and the various languages and dialects of the Pilipino ethnic group. Ian, a Chinese American student in the class, was asked to write different Chinese characters on the board. Later in the week I noticed that all of the students had their name written in Chinese characters on their notebook covers.

Gender issues were of particular interest to these students. Students felt that the majority perspective of gender roles did not match their own cultural experiences. Rita's remark during a discussion of gender roles in Garcia Lorca's *Bodas de Sangre* generated spontaneous laughter and serious reflection. Rita stated that Latinas are brought up to "first serve our father, then our husbands, and finally our sons." Lupe agreed, but felt she could do more or less whatever she wanted according to the situation; however, in her father's home she willingly showed him and her brothers respect. Not to do so would show ignorance. She explained, *"No quiero parecer tonta"* (I don't want to look like an idiot). She did not see her behavior as contradictory; rather, she learned to apply her gender role situationally, depending on the event and context. Luis felt that he could accept Latinas' rights to more freedom, but he wanted his future wife to teach his children the "correct gender roles." When pressed, Luis pointed out that, yes he would help with household chores, but at family gatherings and around their families he wanted his wife and family to be *bien educados,* to honor cultural values. In the Latino culture, the cultural nuance embodied in the construct *educación* and the need to be considered *bien educado* in the Latino community may be at the heart of understanding how to bridge home and school for Latino students.

Educación is bounded by group mores, cultural norms, and values. This cultural knowledge shows people how to live responsibly and respectfully. Resistance and rejection of *educación* is perceived as an affront to one's culture and an insult to family. A person considered *bien educado* displays cultural, moral, social, personal, and group responsibility, respects the dignity of others, and demonstrates competency in multiple social situations. This person is self-disciplined, well mannered, and, most importantly, reflects positively on family upbringing. Conversely, a person perceived as *mal educado* is seen as disrespectful of self, family, and others. The amount of academic schooling knowledge that this individual may (or may not) possess is irrelevant, if the person is not able to use this knowledge gain, or cognitive skills, in acceptable ways of being in the world as a Latino. When taken to the extreme, *mal educados*, those who disgrace the family honor, merit the ultimate insult, to be known in the community as *desgraciados*. Teachers who link school knowledge to the Mexican American or Latino culture build on children's familial identities and focus on helping them develop caring, respectful, interpersonal relationships with others.

Dimension 2: Identity/Ethnic Identity Development

Because these students had a history of damaging school experiences, the development of self-esteem through ethnic identity development was an important element of the program. **Self-esteem,** a personal judgment of one's worthiness, capability, or success, was directly related to their ethnic identity development. Both individual and group ethnic identity were enhanced with an awareness of the strengths, skills, and values learned from their ethnic heritage.

Student interviews from this study generated perceptions about ethnic identity, self-esteem, personal academic expectations, and home-cultural expectations. Students felt this class allowed them to be themselves and to experience a place where no one laughed at their level of English competency and where everyone supported each other. They felt they could take pride in their ethnic heritage and linguistic abilities. Students remarked:

> I think my pride for being Latino was the most important thing that happened to me. That made me study as hard as I could to be the leader in that program. (Luis)

> I feel part of my culture in this class. I was proud when I learned to read and write all those hard words in Spanish. I didn't even know there were so many hard words in Spanish. (Fabiola)

Of additional interest, in terms of identity, were the students' responses to the questions that asked "What does gifted mean to you?" and "Do you think you are gifted?" This was the first time the word *gifted* was used explicitly. Some of their responses are summarized below:

A person who knows a lot thinks a lot and knows almost everything. Who knows? I might just be so. I am intelligent. I only need to develop my capacity. (Marisol)

A child that has superior qualities, more than others of his age and sometimes more than adults. I think so, not in an intellectual aspect but in my self-value and in the power of my self-determination. In terms of my intellect I function at an adequate level. (Fabiola)

A gifted student for me is a student who always reaches his potential. This person knows how to learn. Yes, I think so. Well maybe not but I do know I can pass the test because I studied hard and I tried to do the best I can. (Miguel)

The students were aware of their nationally recognized, academic outcomes. Local papers ran articles and pictures of their success. *Focus* (1992), the monthly newsletter for the Seattle Public Schools, referred to them in "Stand and Deliver: Seattle Schools-Style," stressing their linguistic strengths. Marc Ramirez (1992), a *Seattle Times/Seattle Post-Intelligencer* newspaper reporter, followed them throughout the year and reported their ultimate success. They were featured on the cover and dominated the September 1992 back-to-school issue of *Pacific Magazine*, the *Seattle Times/Seattle Post–Intelligencer* Sunday magazine. Ramirez emphasized how hard they studied. He described how they used their first-language strengths and culture as resources rather than hindrances. He documented their vulnerability, fear, and nervousness on test day. He also captured their feelings of family, buoyancy, excitement, expectation, and joy, while, as a group, they ripped apart the envelopes containing their passing AP scores.

Dimension 3: Social Interactions/Interpersonal Relationships

The traditional roles and status of teacher-student relationships were altered. Working as a family team, we were all equally responsible, committed, and involved in the instructional content, teaching strategies, and assessment criteria. Students determined the focus of the lessons. I provided opportunities through materials, resources, and experiences for them to learn. As active participants in the learning process, they decided whether to take the AP tests. They taught each other and determined the level of excellence required. Student literary analyses on specific works were bound into booklet form to be used for cramming weeks before the exam. Students graded the essays and determined which ones would be accepted for booklet inclusion. They helped develop the class syllabus by selecting the content and sequence of instruction.

After school, students scheduled study groups. In the typical three-hour after-school grueling study sessions, students argued, openly debated, and confronted each other, supporting their opinions with citations. They laughed, took copious notes, expressed their fear of failure, and contemplated future opportunities. Carmen remarked at the end of one of these study sessions: "I used to worry about whether or not I would ever finish high school. Now I worry if I can get enough money to go to the University. I want to go to Berkeley. Maybe be a lawyer."

In the first year of the program students learned to work collaboratively. They helped each other learn to read and write and seemed at ease seeking peer help. In the second year of the program, the addition of the thirty-two, first-year students in the advanced Spanish class created a natural situation for the development of strong student-student relationships. The first-year students, as expected, demanded, commanded, dominated, and required teacher contact time. The Mexican American students were unable to work independently; lacked the necessary skills to read; and could not attend to task assignments without the interpersonal relationship they wanted, needed, and expected from me.

To accommodate the first-year students, three days per week the advanced students worked as tutors with the beginning Spanish students. In return, the beginning Spanish students did seatwork or worked on orals the other two days per week, so that I could devote this time to the advanced students. This worked only as a schedule on the blackboard. In reality, a semester was lost for the advanced students. However, the lack of continual student-teacher interaction resulted in a natural peer mentoring process. The student-selected motto *Sí queremos, podemos*, roughly translated to mean *if we want something, we can achieve it*, reflected their feelings of togetherness, unity, oneness, community, and family. This class was never an individual effort!

Dimension 4: Culturally Safe Classroom Context/ Self-Regulated Learning

The freedom to make mistakes was fundamental. Although students believed I expected performance at an optimal level, at the same time, they were promised security and success. This climate of acceptance promoted confidence and supported motivation to excel. They understood that I believed they had boundless abilities and resources.

> I liked it when Rosa said I was brilliant. It made me want to work harder. I wanted to be the best in the class. This was hard because everyone wanted to be the best. So we just worked together and studied harder. (Miguel)

> Being in this class was a tough challenge, but I knew that I could make it. We were very supportive of each other and willing to help and then we were ready to take the test. I knew I was going to pass the exam. (Sara)

Self-motivation and the desire to learn were prerequisites to class lessons. Learning to read, like everything else in this class, required students to first express their interest to learn a skill and then request a lesson. Of course, once a lesson was requested, anyone could attend (or not attend). The following scenario is representative of the general style and mood of the learning climate that prevailed.

Student: Rosa, why am I being marked down on "organization of ideas"? What do you mean? It's almost four pages long!

Teacher: You're not using paragraphs to show a change of ideas. The paragraphs you use don't have a main idea or supporting sentences. Read my comments. You guys better get it together. I'm running out of ink!

Student: I indented. See, I indented here. Then I indented here.

Teacher: But, *mi amor*, that's not a paragraph.

Student: What's a paragraph?

Teacher: Do you want to know? (He nods) Now?
Student: *¡Sí!*
Teacher: OK. Anyone who wants to know how to write a paragraph, come up.

It was evident they thought a paragraph meant indent, write a little, indent, and write a little bit more. These high school students, schooled in remedial ESL classes with English language acquisition as the major focus, did not know the basic elements of a paragraph, a concept usually taught on the elementary level. Nor did they know what a main idea was or what supporting sentences were. They thought a paragraph was physical or spatial. It took less than fifteen minutes to master the elements in paragraph writing when students identified need and determined the time and place for teaching and learning. Their enthusiasm, insatiable desire to learn, and the excitement created when new skills were mastered, especially knowing that they had a choice whether to attend these informal sessions, established a pattern of ownership crucial to the learning climate. Students appeared hungry for writing mechanics and reading skills. One evening, Luis exclaimed,

> I can't believe it! This is fun. It feels like when I first learned how to drive. I remember I could hardly wait.

Dimension 5: Language/Language Learning

This dimension in this particular classroom situation is demonstrated throughout this chapter. All classroom interactions were conducted in Spanish. For most students, this was the first time they were together in a class where they could openly speak Spanish. Along with the obvious growth demonstrated by their performance on the AP Spanish Language and Spanish Literature tests, the use of Spanish as the medium of instruction resulted in greater parental involvement.

Repeatedly, students related how amazed they were at the pride their parents expressed because they were studying literature in their own language. Since their parents rarely came to school, the students were surprised when they became involved in and attended various school functions. Parents and extended families attended functions such as *Ballet Folklórico* performances, academic achievement assemblies, and University of Washington MeCHA (Mexican Chicano Association, a university student organization) award presentations. Parents often provided unsolicited snacks for the late afterschool sessions. I was always invited for coffee when driving the students home in the evenings.

Students were proud of their family's involvement and noted that their parents bragged to everyone—the grocery store clerk, *la comadre*, the priest, *la tía*, the neighbors and even the postman—about this class. Fabiola commented:

> My Mom and Dad always want to know what happens next in the story. I even caught my Dad trying to read *El General en su laberinto*. I liked it when my whole family, even my aunt, came to see us dance *El Jarabe*. My dad bought me a red carnation. My mom tells everyone that I can read and write in Spanish.

Dimension 6: Culturally Inclusive Content/Knowledge Acquisition

The instructional content, similar to that for other Advanced Placement classes, was academically rigorous. It was also culturally inclusive. Students applied their prior knowledge to new learning. The following are examples of the content that students eloquently expressed in art, music, drama, verbal discussions, and written narratives. Students clarified their thoughts, assumptions, and feelings by

1. Discussing the traditional role of the mother, the concept of family honor, and the influences of Catholicism. They were asked to synthesize by identifying, comparing, analyzing, and inferring similar themes in Federico García Lorca's trilogy *Yerma, Bodas de sangre,* and *La casa de Bernalda Alba* (Josephs & Caballero, 1988).
2. Analyzing the influences of the Harlem Renaissance literary period and the American economic depression on García Lorca's poetry. Identifying themes in Gabriel García Márquez's work that reflected the political and economic unrest in South America, U.S. imperialism, the African American Caribbean influence, and his socialistic political orientations.
3. Examining concepts such as existentialism, metaphysics, immortality, fatalism, solitude, circular and linear time, fanaticism, the supernatural, sexual frustration, power, magical realism, violence, and spiritual beauty in relationship to literary themes, protagonists, and individual tone and style of an author.

The ability to write coherent, analytical, and concise essays was required in one part of the AP Spanish Language test; however, this proficiency was central to passing the AP Spanish Literature exam. Although it was evident that these students needed instruction in this area, I waited until they decided they wanted to learn specific writing skills. Language Arts content or basic skills, such as decoding, spelling, vocabulary building, grammar, punctuation, paragraph construction, outlining, and essay writing, were never taught in isolation, as separate disciplines, nor were they determined by teacher decision regarding perceived student deficiency. I modeled reading and decoding by writing student inquiries on the overhead projector or on scraps of paper. The connection from verbal to written form was made whenever possible. In a speech at a nearby school district, I explained how literacy was addressed:

> I honored the fragile game we played. They pretended they knew how to read. I pretended I didn't know they couldn't read.

As students demanded to know how difficult words were pronounced, why accents appeared, the structure of a paragraph, or why various phonetic spellings occurred, it was explained. Difficult words were broken down into syllables, and phonics was slipped in as students struggled to read as much as possible. They continued teaching and learning from each other. When they finally asked to be formally taught to read, they transferred English reading skills to Spanish and applied what they had learned through multiple incidental, contextual experiences. Their conscious, self-motivated desire to learn to read allowed them to master reading in Spanish in two classroom sessions.

Dimension 7: Instruction/Reasoning Skills

The goal and substance of each lesson were embedded in higher level thinking skills using a variety of learning strategies and styles and incorporating literary concepts to actively engage the students both intellectually and emotionally. Students were taught how to work in groups, how to think critically, and how to participate in student-led discussions. They worked collaboratively in small groups and decided their contribution to the group activity. The level of proficiency in reading and writing was consequential to this student decision. All written work, such as exams, literary critiques, and reflective essays, was a single document produced by a collaborative group effort. Emphasis was placed on the development of intellectual competence by actively involving the student in critical reflection, analysis, and interpretation of literature through literary discussions using appropriate terminology. For example, they understood, identified, and discussed primary and secondary themes; and they used and applied literary terms such as paradox, hyperbole, onomatopoeia, juxtaposition, ellipse, and alliteration. By reasoning, weighing evidence, and thinking originally, they discussed the structural elements of the author's work including writing styles and literary periods, as well as the influences resulting from the historical, cultural, and political era in which the author wrote and lived.

Initially, the students could not read Spanish. They listened or followed the text as I read. Little by little they learned to read and write words, phrases, and sentences in Spanish. They helped each other translate, summarize, and write analytical papers in Spanish. Their work was filled with spelling and grammatical errors, but it was intellectually sophisticated. They drew conclusions from the literature and conducted in-depth analyses using their own intuitive frames of reference. They did not appear to feel inadequate or unaware of what they could do intellectually.

Part of the teaching strategy included exposure to out-of-school experiences. They went to dance and music performances at the University of Washington and visited selected university classes to help them realize that a college education was possible. Spanish literature professors allowed them to participate in third-year college literature classes and told them their own college students might not be able to pass the AP literature test.

Dimension 8: Assessment/Self-Evaluation

Whereas students were intellectually challenged, they were not subjected to situations where failure was possible. Tasks were designed to be verbal, and students were assessed orally until they mastered reading and writing. When the discussion of assessment took place, we quickly realized that learning, not grades, was the issue. We decided that all students who attended class and turned in assignments would receive an *A* on their high school transcript. However, the more important measure of success for both of us would be the AP test score. I evaluated the critical essays written by students on a nine-point scale using the College Board AP assessment rubric as agreed. Students received two grades on all assignments. One was an assignment completion grade that included specific requirements (e.g., such as due date, page length, content elements); the other grade reflected AP standards. The student's goal was to narrow the gap between the two scores. Students were more concerned with figuring out how to encourage each other to decrease the point spread in their scores than competing for the highest grade. They helped each other identify weak areas in their essays before addressing the needed revisions. Competition, if any, was self-directed. Ultimately, we accepted that students would be evaluated as proficient if they passed the AP exam; likewise, I would be deemed competent if my students passed.

Conclusion

The students in this Spanish class developed and refined metacognitive skills. Collectively, they were able to monitor their own learning, decide what they did not know, and determine when it was important to learn. In this class, students took ownership for their learning during all aspects from inception to evaluation. By choosing to take the College Board AP exams, involving their parents in the literary works, and working collaboratively, they determined the degree of intensity and significance each classroom learning event took in their lives. Equally important was the maintenance of their ethnic integrity and previously held perceptions of what it means to obtain an *educacíon* and be *bien educado.*

In addition, responding to the learning and teaching of skills based on student perceived need not only decreased the amount of time needed to master particular skills, but also demonstrated that a fragmented, decontextualized approach to teaching basic skills may not be pedagogically sound. The change that occurred in these students resulted in equity of educational opportunities and in equitable academic outcomes. Most importantly, it affirmed and validated ethnic identity and language maintenance. *¡Si queremos podemos!*

RECOMMENDED READINGS

Gonzalez, G. G. (1990). *Chicano education in the era of segregation.* Philadelphia: Balch Institute Press.

Reyes, M., & Halcon, J. (Eds.). (2001). *The best for our children: Critical perspectives on literacy for Latino students.* New York: Teachers College Press.

Valenzuela, A. (1999). *Subtractive schooling: U.S.-Mexican youth and the politics of caring.* New York: SUNY.

GLOSSARY

Acculturation. Changes that occur when individuals from minority groups acquire and accept the dominant cultural group's norms, values, and behaviors.

Achievement gap. Disparity in school performance associated with race and ethnicity.

Assimilation. The change that takes place when minority group members adopt the dominant cultural group's norms, attitudes, and values and reject or distance themselves from their own cultural group.

Classroom management. The personal technical skills and management proficiencies teachers acquire to advance the teaching-learning process. A teacher's management plan that includes practices, routines, techniques, and skills to create a positive classroom climate conducive to teaching and learning.

Cognitive dissonance. Discord between behavior and belief.

Collaborative learning groups. Instances where interpersonal interactions are at a higher level of personal involvement, participation is more focused on learning, and the process takes place in a more natural learning setting.

Collective ethnic encounter. A significant ethnic group happening that may occur often in the home and community but takes place infrequently in classrooms.

Committed compliance. A willingness of a child to embrace the mother's, father's, teacher's or other caregivers' agenda and accept it as one's own.

Conditionalize. The application of knowledge or of a skill set in a specific situation and context.

Cooperative learning. Students working in small groups that may be selected, controlled, and manipulated by the teacher.

Cultural discontinuity. Differences in language, experiences, values, lifestyles, and practices between the school culture and the home culture, that often produce stress, conflict, and cognitive dissonance.

Cultural knowledge. Information gained in one's socialization in one or more specific social groups. This includes the skills and competencies, such as language, values, belief systems, and **norms** (concepts of appropriate and expected behaviors) of their particular social group.

Cultural tools. Culturally mediated devices, such as language, prior experiences, and knowledge, that students use in the process of reshaping a situation so they can enter and participate effectively.

Culturally safe classroom context. A classroom environment where students feel secure and comfortable, culturally, linguistically, academically, emotionally, and physically.

Daily lessons. Lessons prepared and modified on a daily basis. They explicitly respond to the learning that has taken place, is taking place, or is not taking place.

Decision making. A judgment and choice.

Declarative. Knowledge that is goal or rule driven.

Disciplinary action. Steps taken by a teacher as a result of unacceptable behavior by a student.

Discipline. The interpersonal interactions between students and teachers, involving self-regulatory decisions of either or both to ignore, comply, or acquiesce to specific behavioral demands. Student or teacher actions and decisions made to meet personal needs (self- or other-imposed).

Discrimination. To act on the basis of prejudice, to show unfairness, or to reveal hostility toward an individual or group.

Diversity pedagogy. An ideology that views the relationship among culture and cognition as essential to understanding the teaching-learning process. It focuses on the ways teachers' and students' behavior influences the co-construction of new knowledge.

Dualistic thinking. The simplistic division of knowledge in two opposing dimensions and the inclination to divide reality into opposite pairs.

Emotional control. Feelings affecting the choice of behavior.

Enculturation. The process of being socialized to a particular culture.

Enculturation process in schooling. The way schools expect students to act and think.

English language learners (ELLs). Students whose first language is not English.

Equality. Same treatment given to all members of a given group.

Equal. Identical value or having the same privileges, rights, status, and opportunities as others.

Equitable. Fair and impartial treatment, given to all members of a certain group.

Equity. Treatment of individuals and groups characterized by fairness and impartiality.

Ethnic group. A distinctive social group in a larger society who set themselves apart or who are set apart by others due to distinctive cultural patterns, beliefs, histories, values, attitudes, languages, national origins, and physical traits.

Ethnic identity. A personal process, influenced by membership in an ethnic group. It forms within the child and develops throughout the lifespan. Ethnic identity has individual and group components, is not necessarily limited to one group, and can be internally driven, externally imposed, or both.

Ethnic socialization process. Direct and indirect messages children receive from parents, peers, and ethnic community.

Ethnicity. A part of peoples' personal and cultural history. This category includes all of the cultural, psychological, and social phenomena associated with a particular group. It focuses on the ways social and cultural practices intersect during interactions among diverse groups.

Friendship. A mutual selection in which a child chooses and is simultaneously chosen by another as a preferred friend.

Gender bias. Showing unfairness or discrimination based on gender.

Gender constancy. The recognition that one's gender is not only permanent but is also constant and remains throughout one's lifetime, regardless of outward appearance.

Gender identity. The personal sense of being male or female.

Gender roles. The public expressions of gender identity displayed through choices, actions, and sex roles.

Gender stability. Comprehension by a young boy or girl that his or her gender is permanent, usually acquired around age 4 or 5.

Habits of the mind. Automatic, internalized thinking patterns and routines.

Heterosexual. Having sexual desires for or sexual relations with members of the opposite sex.

High stakes. When used in reference to standardized tests, this indicates that test results are used to set policy, reward or punish districts, schools, educators, and children, and to involve the public by openly reporting school, district, and state scores.

Homophobic. Showing an irrational hatred, disapproval, or fear of gay and lesbian people and their culture.

Indexically. The role language plays in preserving the terms and expressions appropriate to the groups' artifacts, realities, concerns, needs, and interests. Only the language historically and intimately associated with a given culture is able to transmit their interests or name the things of that culture.

Invisible culture. Culturally determined patterns of behavior in everyday life that, for the most part, are outside one's conscious awareness.

Learning styles. Psychologically and culturally influenced characteristics that individuals use to receive and process new information.

Motivation. Why people think and act as they do.

National identity. Individual and group membership as a citizen of a nation.

Norms. Concepts of appropriate and expected behaviors.

Part/whole fashion. The cultural specificity of language and the two-way relationship between the part/whole of a particular language and its culture. For example, some expressions, sayings, and figures of speech are difficult to translate because their meaning evolves from a cultural context.

Peer acceptance. The degree to which members of a group like another group member and want to spend time with him or her.

Prejudice. A preformed opinion or an irrational strong feeling, usually unfavorable, about someone or something. Prejudicial attitudes are formed unfairly and before all the facts are known.

Privatization. Restricted, furtive, and, at times, forbidden public use.

Procedural. Knowledge that is strategy or technique driven.

Progressive nature of underachievement. The generational decline of achievement as documented by grades, test scores, dropout rates, and disciplinary actions.

Racial identity. A sense of group or collective identity based on one's perception that he/she shares a common racial heritage with a particular racial group.

Racism. Prejudicial attitudes and discriminatory actions against people who belong to another race.

Reconstituted. Low-performing schools taken over by the state.

Resistance. Self-regulatory behavior to meet personal goals.

School identity. The ways in which students perceive themselves and how others view them as student and peer.

Self-concept. A cognitive appraisal of one's social, academic, and physical competence.

Self-efficacy. A belief of one's ability to control their own behavior when setting goals and making decisions to meet and to reach these goals.

Self-esteem. An emotional response to self or a personal judgment of one's worthiness, capability, or success.

Sexual orientation. The direction of one's sexual interest toward members of the same, opposite, or both sexes.

Sheltered English. One of the instructional approaches used to teach ELL students. Teachers who use this strategy often segregate (shelter) English language learners from the English speaking students and provide content area instruction in English with a focus on developing English language skills.

Social content of gender. Culturally appropriate ways of behaving.

Socialization process. The ways human infants, born without any culture, acquire the cultural knowledge of their parents and caregivers.

Stereotypes. Oversimplified images or ideas held by a person or a group toward another person or group.

Student-centered strategies. Places the teacher in the role of assisting or facilitating the teaching-learning process. Examples of student-centered strategies include cooperative or collaborative learning, peer tutoring, reciprocal peer teaching, and individual independent learning activities.

Student cultural displays. Observable manifestations of the norms, values, and competencies children learn in their homes and communities that provide valuable insights to who they are, how they act, and what they know.

Student-led discussion. Discussion wherein the person speaking has the floor until he or she calls on another person, who then takes control of the discussion until he or she calls on the next person, and so forth.

Subtractive schooling. The cultural and linguistic losses students endure during the schooling process.

Symbolically. Associations that outsiders and insiders make among a person, language, and culture.

Teacher-centered strategies. Various forms of direct instruction used in the teaching-learning process, such as lectures, demonstrations, presentations, drills, discussions, and brainstorming.

Teacher pedagogical behaviors. The classroom actions and attitudes teachers express related to the act of teaching.

Teacher strategies. Deliberate behaviors in classrooms with a planned purpose of promoting student learning.

Unit of analysis. How something is examined.

REFERENCES

Aboud, F. E. (1984). Social and cognitive bases of ethnic identity constancy. *Journal of Genetic Psychology, 145,* 227–229.

Aboud, F. E. (1988). *Children and prejudice.* New York: Blackwell.

Adams, D. W. (1988). Fundamental considerations: The deep meaning of Native American schooling, 1880–1900. *Harvard Educational Review, 58*(1), 1–28.

Advanced placement program, The college board: National and Washington state summary reports (1992). New York: College Entrance Examination Board.

Alba, R. D. (1990). *Ethnic identity: The transformation of white America.* New Haven, CT: Yale University Press.

Allen, W. R., & Jewell, J. O. (1995). African American education since "An American Dilemma." *Daedalus, 124*(1), 77–100.

Altbach, P. G. (1991). The unchanging variable: Textbooks in comparative perspective. In P. G. Altbach, G. P. Kelly, H. G. Petrie, & L. Weis (Eds.), *Textbooks in American society: Politics, policy, and pedagogy* (pp. 237–254). Albany, NY: SUNY.

America's Children 2001. (2001). Available on the web at http:/childstats.gov/ac2001/.

America's children: Key national indicators or well-being (2003). Available at http://childstats.gov/americaschildren.

Amir, Y., Sharan, S., & Ben-Ari, R. (1984). *School desegregation.* Hillside, NJ: Erlbaum.

Angelou, M. (1986). *And still I rise.* New York: Random House.

Asher, S. R., & Renshaw, P. D. (1981). Children without friends: Social knowledge and social skill training. In S. R. Asher & J. M. Gottman (Eds.), *The development of children's friendships* (pp. 273–294). Cambridge, MA: Cambridge University Press.

Atwater, E. (1996). *Adolescence* (4th ed.). Upper Saddle River, NJ: Prentice-Hall.

Augustine, J., Jackson, K., & Norman, J. (2002). Creating inclusive programs. *Transitions, 14*(4), 6–7.

Austin-Carter, I., Brown, J. C., Deligiorgis, D., Dixon-Eberhardt, J., & Sheets, R. H. (2000, April). *Effects of teacher response to cultural displays: Implications to student academic and social competence.* Paper presented at the Annual Meeting of the Educational Research Association, New Orleans, LA.

Baber, C. R. (1987). The artistry and artifice of Black communication. In G. Gay & W. L. Baber (Eds.), *Expressively Black: The cultural basis of ethnic identity* (pp. 75–108). Westport, CT: Praeger.

Baker, K. (2002). Life of the mind. *San Francisco Chronicle,* p. 4 M 2, column 2.

Bandura, A. (1977). *Social learning theory.* Englewood Cliffs, NJ: Prentice Hall.

Bandura, A. (1986). *Social foundations of thought and action: A social cognitive theory.* Englewood Cliffs, NJ: Prentice Hall.

Bandura, A. (1993). Perceived self-efficacy in cognitive development and functioning. *Educational Psychologist, 28,* 117–148.

Barrett, R. A. (1984). *Culture and conduct: An excursion in anthropology.* Belmont, CA: Wadsworth.

Bell, S. (2000, April 18). *San Francisco Chronicle,* pp. A14.

Bennett, C. I. (1990). *High and low context cultures: Comprehensive multicultural education* (2nd ed.). Boston: Allyn & Bacon.

Bentley, G. C. (1987). Ethnicity and practice. *Comparative Studies in Society and History, 29,* 24–55.

Berlitz International, Inc. (1991). *1991 Annual report.* Princeton, NJ: Berlitz International.

Bernal, M. E., & Knight, G. P. (Eds.). (1993). *Ethnic identity: Formation and transmission among Hispanics and other minorities.* Albany, NY: State University of New York Press.

Berndt, T. J. (1984). Sociometric, socio-cognitive and behavioral measures for the study of friendship and popularity. In T. Field, J. L. Roopnarine, & M. Segal (Eds.), *Friendship in normal and handicapped children* (pp. 31–45). Norwood, NJ: Ablex.

Bialystok, E., & Hakuta, K. (1994). *In other words: The science and psychology of second-language acquisition.* New York: Basic Books.

Bloom, B. S. (Ed.). (1956). *Taxonomy of educational objectives: The classification of educational goals.* New York: David McKay.

Boykin, A. W. (1994). Afrocultural expression and its implications for schooling. In E. R. Hollins, J. E. King, & W. C. Hayman (Eds.), *Teaching diverse populations: Formulating a knowledge base* (pp. 243–256). Albany: SUNY.

Boykin, A. W., & Bailey, C. T. (2000). *The role of cultural factors in school relevant cognitive functioning: Description of home environmental factors, cultural orientations, and learning preferences (Report 43).* Washington, DC, and Baltimore, MD: Howard University and John Hopkins University, Center on the Education of Students Placed at Risk (CRESPAR). Available at www.csos.jhu.edu.

Boykin, W. (1986). The triple quandary and the schooling of Afro-American children. In U. Neisser (Ed.), *The school achievement of minority children: New perspectives* (pp. 57–92). Hillsdale, NJ: Erlbaum.

Branch, C. (1999). Racial identity and human development. In R. H. Sheets & E. R. Hollins (Eds.), *Racial and ethnic identity in school practices: Aspects of human development* (pp. 7–28). Mahwah, NJ: Erlbaum.

Branch, C., & Newcomb, N. (1986). A longitudinal and cross-sectional study of the development of racial attitudes of black children as a function of parental attitudes. *Child Development, 57*(3), 712–721.

Bransford, J. D., Brown, A. L., & Cocking, R. R. (Eds.). (1999). *How people learn: Brain, mind, experience, and school.* Washington, DC: National Academy Press.

Brembeck, C. S., & Hill, W. H. (1973). *Cultural challenges to education.* Lexington, MA: Lexington Books.

Brown, R. (1973). *A first language: The early stages.* Cambridge, MA: Harvard University Press.

Brown, R. J. (1995). *Prejudice: Its social psychology.* Cambridge, MA: Blackwell.

Bruner, J. (1986). *Actual minds, possible worlds.* Cambridge, MA: Harvard University Press.

Carver, C. S., & Scheier, M. F. (1990). Origins and functions of positive and negative effect: A control-process view. *Psychological Review, 97,* 19–35.

Cazden, C. B. (1988). *Classroom discourse: The language of teaching and learning.* Portsmouth, NH: Heinemann.

Child Poverty Fact Sheet. (2001). New York: National Center for Children in Poverty, Columbia University.

Chomsky, N. (1957). *Syntactic structures.* The Hague: Mouton.

Chomsky, N. (1972). *Language and mind* (2nd ed.). Orlando, FL: Harcourt Brace.

Clark, M. L., & Ayers, M. (1988). The role of reciprocity and proximity in junior high school friendships. *Journal of Youth and Adolescence, 17,* 403–411.

Coie, J. D., Belding, M., & Underwood, M. (1988). Aggression and peer rejection in childhood. In B. B. Lahey & A. E. Kazdin (Eds.), *Advances in clinical child psychology.* New York: Plenum.

Cole, M. (1996). *Cultural psychology: A once and future discipline.* Cambridge, MA: Belknap Press of Harvard University Press.

Cole, M., & Scribner, S. (1974). *Culture and thought: A psychological introduction.* New York: Wiley.

Corno, L. (1993). The best laid plans: Modern conceptions of volition and educational research. *Educational Researcher, 22*(2), 14–22.

Corsaro, W. A. (1979). We're friends, right? *Language in Society, 8,* 315–336.

Crooks, T. J. (1988). The impact of classroom evaluation practices on students. *Review of Educational Research, 58*(4), 438–481.

Crosnoe, R. (2000). Friendships in childhood and adolescence: The life course and new directions. *Social Psychology Quarterly, 63*(4), 377–391.

Cross, W. E., Jr. (1991). *Shades of Black.* Philadelphia: Temple University Press.

Cross, W. E., Jr., Strauss, L., & Fhagen-Smith, P. (1999). African American identity development across the life span: Educational implications. In R. H. Sheets & E. R. Hollins (Eds.), *Racial and ethnic identity in school practices: Aspects of human development* (pp. 29–48). Mahwah, NJ: Erlbaum.

Crystal, D. (1987). *Cambridge encyclopedia of language.* London: Cambridge University Press.

D'Amato, J. (1988). "Acting": Hawaiian children's resistance to teachers. *The Elementary School Journal, 88*(5), 529–544.

Debold, E. (1995). Helping girls survive the middle grades. *Principal, 74*(3), 22–24.

Derman-Sparks, L. (1995). Children and diversity. *Early Childhood Today, 10*(3), 42–45.

Dewey, J. (1916). *Human nature and experience.* New York: Holt.

Dilg, M. A. (1999). *Race and culture in the classroom: Teaching and learning through multicultural education.* New York: Teachers College Press.

Dodge, K. A. (1989). Problems in social relationships. In E. J. Mash & R. A. Barkley (Eds.), *Treatment of childhood disorders* (pp. 222–246). New York: Guilford.

Doll, B. (1996). Children without friends: Implications for practice and policy. *The School Psychology Review, 25*(2), 165–183.

Dopke, S. (1992). *One parent, one language: An interactional approach.* Philadelphia: John Benjamin's.

Doyle, W. (1986). Classroom organization and management. In M. C. Wittrock (Ed.), *Handbook on research on teaching* (3rd ed., pp. 392–431). New York: Macmillan.

Dutton, S. E., Singer, J. A., & Devlin, A. S. (1998). Racial identity of children in integrated, predominantly white and black schools. *Journal of Social Psychology, 138*(1), 41–53.

Ebel, R. L., & Frisbie, D. A. (1986). *Essentials of educational measurement* (4th ed.). Upper Saddle River, NJ: Prentice Hall.

Eccles, J. S., & Midgley, C. (1989). Stage-environment fit: Developmentally appropriate classrooms for young adolescents. In C. Ames & R. Ames (Eds.), *Research on motivation in education* (Vol. 3, pp. 139–186). Greenwich, CT: JAI Press.

Echevarria, J., & Short, D. J. (2004). Using multiple perspectives in observations of diverse classrooms. In H. C. Waxman, R. G. Tharp, & R. S. Hilberg (Eds.), *Observational research in U.S. classrooms: New approaches for understanding cultural and linguistic diversity* (pp. 21–47). Cambridge, UK: Cambridge University Press.

Edwards, C. P. (1986). *Promoting social and moral development in young children.* New York: Teacher's College Press.

Engfer, A. (1993). Antecedents and consequences of shyness in boys and girls: A 6-year longitudinal study. In K. H. Rubin & J. B. Asendorpf (Eds.), *Social withdrawal, inhibition and shyness in childhood* (pp. 49–79). Hillsdale, NJ: Erlbaum.

Epstein, J. L. (1989). The selection of friends. In T. J. Berndt & G. W. Ladd (Eds.), *Peer relationships in child development* (pp. 158–187). New York: Wiley.

Erickson, F., & Mohatt, G. (1982). Cultural organization of participation structures in two classrooms of Indian children. In G. B. Spindler (Ed.), *Doing the ethnography of schooling: Educational anthropology in action* (pp. 132–174). New York: Holt, Rinehart & Winston.

Erikson, E. H. (1950). *Childhood and society.* New York: W. W. Norton & Company.

Erikson, E. H. (1968). *Identity: Youth and crisis.* New York: W. W. Norton & Company.

Festinger, L. (1957). *A theory of cognitive dissonance.* Stanford, CA: Stanford University Press.

Fillmore, L. W. (2000). Loss of family languages: Should educators be concerned? *Theory into Practice, 39*(4), 203–210.

Fishman, J. A. (Ed.). (1966). *Language and loyalty in the United States.* The Hague: Mouton.

Fishman, J. A. (1991). *Reversing language shift: Theoretical and empirical foundations of assistance to threatened languages.* Philadelphia: Multilingual Matters LTD.

Fiske, A. P., Kitayama, S., Markus, H. R., & Nisbett, R. E. (1998). The cultural matrix of social psychology. In D. T. Gilbert, S. T. Fiske, & G. Lindzey (Eds.), *The handbook of social psychology* (Vol. 2, 4th ed., pp. 915–981). New York: McGraw-Hill.

Focus. (1992, October). Stand and deliver: Seattle schools-style. p. 2.

Fordham, S., & Ogbu, J. (1986). Black students' school success: Coping with the burden of acting white. *The Urban Review, 18*(3), 176–206.

Foster, M. (2000, April). *Teaching black students: Best practices.* Paper presented for the Commission on Research on Black Education.

Freeman, D. J., Brookhart, S. M., & Loadman, W. E. (1999). Realities of teaching in racially/ethnically diverse schools: Feedback from entry-level teachers. *Urban Education, 34,* 89–114.

French, D. C., & Tyne, T. F. (1982). The identification and treatment of peer relationship difficulties. In J. P. Curran & M. P. Monti (Eds.), *Social skills training: A practical handbook for assessment and treatment* (pp. 280–308). New York: Guilford.

Freud, S. (1940). An outline of psychoanalysis. In J. Strachey (Ed. & Trans.), *The standard edition of the complete psychological works of Sigmund Freud.* London: Hogarth.

Galda, L. (1998). Mirrors and windows: Reading as transformation. In T. E. Raphael & K. H. Au (Eds.), *Literature-based instruction: Reshaping the curriculum* (pp. 1–11). Norwood, MA: Christopher-Gordon.

Garcia, R. (1978). The multiethnic dimension of bilingual-bicultural education. *Social Education, 42*(6), 492–494.

Gardner, H. (1985). *Frames of mind.* New York: Basic Books.

Gay, G. (1981). Interactions in culturally pluralistic classrooms. In J. Banks (Ed.), *Education in the '80s: Multiethnic education* (pp. 42–53). Washington, DC: National Education Association.

Gay, G. (1987a). Ethnic identity development and black expressiveness. In G. Gay & W. L. Baber (Eds.), *Expressively Black: The cultural basis of ethnic identity* (pp. 35–74). New York: Praeger.

Gay, G. (1987b). Expressive ethos of Afro-American Culture. In G. Gay & W. L. Baber (Eds.), *Expressively black: The cultural basis of ethnic identity* (pp. 1–16). Westport, CT: Praeger.

Gay, G. (1999). Ethnic identity dimensions and multicultural education. In R. H. Sheets & E. R. Hollins (Eds.), *Racial and ethnic identity in school practices: Aspects of human development* (pp. 195–212). Mahwah, NJ: Erlbaum.

Gay, G. (2000). *Culturally responsive teaching: Theory, research, and practice.* New York: Teachers College Press.

Gay, G. (2002). Dividing the pie more fairly: Improving achievement for students of color. *Journal of Thought, 37*(4), 51–64.

Geertz, C. (1973). *The interpretation of cultures.* New York: Basic Books.

Geisel, T. S. (1960). *Green eggs and ham.* New York: Random House.

Gonzalez, R. D., & Melis, I. (Eds.). (2001). *Language ideologies: Critical perspectives on the official English movement, Vol. 2: History, theory, and policy.* Mahwah, NJ: Erlbaum.

Goodlad, J. I., & McMannon, T. J. (Eds.). (1997). *The purpose of education and schooling.* San Francisco, CA: Jossey-Bass.

Goodwin, L. (2002). Low teacher expectation for children of color. *Journal of Thought, 37*(4), 83–104.

Graham, J. A., & Cohen, R. (1997). Race and sex as factors in children's sociometric ratings and friendship choices. *Social Development, 6,* 353–370.

Graham, J. A., Cohen, R., & Zbikowski, S. M. (1998). A longitudinal investigation of race and sex as factors in children's classroom friendships. *Child Study Journal, 28*(4), 245–266.

Graham-Bermann, S. A., Coupeet, S., Egler, L., Mattis, J., & Banyard, V. (1996). Interpersonal relationships and adjustments of children in homeless and economically distressed families. *Journal of Clinical Child Psychology, 25*(3), 250–261.

Greenfield, P. A., & Cocking, R. R. (Eds.). (1994). *Cross-cultural roots of minority child development.* Hillsdale, NJ: Erlbaum.

Greenfield, P. A., Raeff, C., & Quiroz, B. (1995). Cultural values in learning and education. In B. Williams (Ed.), *Closing the achievement gap: A vision for changing beliefs and practices* (pp. 37–55). Alexander, VA: ASCD.

Grimes, N. (1994). *Meet Damitra Brown.* New York: Lothrop, Lee & Shepard.

Gumperz, J. J. (1977). Sociocultural knowledge in conversational inference. In M. Saville-Troike (Ed.), *Linguistics and anthropology* (pp. 191–211). Washington, DC: Georgetown University Roundtable on Language and Linguistics.

Gumperz, J. J., & Hernandez-Chavez, E. (1972). Bilingualism, bidialectalism, and classroom interaction. In C. B. Cazden, V. P. John, & D. Hymes (Eds.), *Functions of language in the classroom* (pp. 84–108). New York: Teachers College Press.

Hall, E. T. (1959). *The silent language.* New York: Fawcett Books.

Hallinan, M. T., & Smith, S. S. (1987, April). *Classroom characteristics on the friendship cliques.* Paper presented at the Annual Meeting of the American Educational Research Association, Washington, DC.

Hallinan, M. T., & Teixeira, R. A. (1987). Opportunities and constraints: Black white differences in the formation of interracial friendships. *Child Development, 58,* 1358–1371.

Hartup, W. W. (1989). Social relationships and their developmental significance. *American Psychologist, 44*(2), 120–126.

Hartup, W. W. (1991). Having friends, making friends, and keeping friends: Relationships as educational contexts. *Early Report, 19,* 1–4.

Hartup, W. W. (1996). The company they keep: Friendships and their developmental significance. *Child Development, 67,* 1–13.

Haugen, E. (1953). *The Norwegian language in America: A study in bilingual behavior.* Philadelphia: University of Pennsylvania Press.

Haycock, K. (2001). Closing the achievement gap. *Educational Leadership, 58*(5), 1–8.

Heath, S. B. (1982). Questioning at home and at school: A comparative study. In G. D. Spindler (Ed.), *Doing the ethnography of schooling* (pp. 96–101). New York: Holt, Reinhart & Winston.

Helms, J. E. (1990). *Black and White racial identity development.* New York: Greenwood.

Henley, S. R. (2001). The two-edged sword. *Cesky' Hlas/The Czech Voice, 16*(2).

Hernandez, H. (2001). *Multicultural education: A teacher's guide to linking context, process, and content* (2nd ed.). Columbus, OH: Merrill Prentice Hall.

Hofstede, G. (1980). *Organizations and cultures: Software of the mind.* New York: McGraw-Hill.

Hollinger, J. D. (1987). Social skills for behaviorally disordered children as preparation for mainstreaming: Theory, practice and new directions. *Remedial and Special Education, 8,* 17–27.

Hollins, E. R. (1996). *Culture in school learning: Revealing the deep meaning.* Mahwah, NJ: Erlbaum.

Holmes, R. M. (1995). *How young children perceive race.* Thousand Oaks, CA: Sage.

Honig, W. (1985, November 18). "Last chance" to teach culture. Interview. *U. S. News and World Report, 99*(21), 82.

House, D. (2002). *Language shift among the Navajos: Identity, politics, and cultural continuity.* Tucson, AZ: University of Arizona Press.

Hurn, C. J. (1993). *The limits and possibilities of schooling: An introduction to the sociology of education* (3rd ed.). Boston: Allyn and Bacon.

Irvine, J. J. (1991). *Black students and school failure.* New York: Praeger.

Irvine, J. J., & York, D. E. (1995). Learning styles and culturally diverse students: A literature review. In J. A. Banks & C. A. M. Banks (Eds.), *Handbook of research on multicultural education* (pp. 484–497). New York: Macmillan.

Jackson, K. (2002). Meeting the special needs of GLBTQ youth of color. *Transitions, 14*(4).

Jahr, B. (2002). Harassment in school. *Transitions, 14*(4), 4.

Johnson, R. C., & Viadero, D. (2000). Unmet promise: Raising minority achievement. *Education Week* (pp. 1–10). Retrieved from http://www.edweek.org/ew/ewstory.cfm?slug=27pagintro.h10.

Jones, K., & Whitford, B. L. (2002). Let them eat tests: High-stakes testing and educational equity. *Journal of Thought, 37*(4), 35–50.

Josephs, A., & Caballero, J. (1988). *Yerma, tercera edicion.* Madrid, Espana: Catedra Letras Hispanicas.

Kaestle, C. F. (1983). *Pillars of the republic: Common schools and American society, 1780–1860.* New York: Hill &Wang.

Katz, P. A. (1987). Variations in family constellations: Effects on gender schemata. *New Directions for Child Development, 38,* 39–56.

Keating, D. P. (1990). Adolescent thinking. In S. S. Feldman & G. R. Elliott (Eds.), *At the threshold: The developing adolescent* (pp. 54–89). Cambridge, MA: Harvard University Press.

Kelley, R. D. (2001). Forward. In W. H. Watkins, *The white architects of black education* (pp. xi–xiii). New York: Teachers College Press.

Kennedy, M. M. (1999). The role of preservice teacher education. In L. Darling-Hammond & G. Sykes (Eds.), *Teaching as the learning profession: Handbook of policy and practice* (pp. 54–85). San Francisco: Jossey-Bass.

Kiang, P. N., Nguyen, N. L., & Sheehan, R. L. (1995). Don't ignore it: Documenting racial harassment in a fourth-grade Vietnamese bilingual classroom. *Equity & Excellence in Education, 28*(1), 31–35.

Kimmel, E. B., & Rudolph, T. (1999). Growing up female. In K. Borman & B. Schneider (Eds.), *The adolescent years: Social influences and educational challenges, Ninety-seventh yearbook of the National Society for the Study of Education, Part I* (pp. 42–64). Chicago: University of Chicago Press.

Kistner, J., Metzler, A., Gatlin, D., & Risi, S. (1994). Classroom racial proportions and children's peer relations: Race and sex effects. *Journal of Educational Psychology, 85,* 446–452.

Kluckhohn, C. (1949). *Mirror for man.* New York: Premier Press.

Knight, G. P., Bernal, M. E., Garza, C. A., & Cota, M. K. (1993). A social cognitive model of the development of ethnic identity and ethnically based behaviors. In G. P. Knight & M.

E. Bernal (Eds.), *Ethnic identity: Formation and transmission among Hispanics and other minorities* (pp. 213–234). Albany: SUNY.

Kochanska, G., Coy, K. C., & Murray, K. T. (2001). The development of self-regulation in the first four years of life. *Child Development, 72*(4), 1091–1111.

Kochman, T. (1981). *Black and white styles in conflict.* Chicago: The University of Chicago Press.

Kohlberg, L. (1966). A cognitive-developmental analysis of children's sex-role concepts and attitudes. In E. E. Maccoby (Ed.), *The development of sex differences* (pp. 82–173). Stanford, CA: Stanford University Press.

Kohn, A. (1999). *The schools our children deserve: Moving beyond traditional classrooms and "tougher standards."* Boston: Houghton Mifflin.

Kozulin, A. (2004). *Mediated learning experience and cultural diversity.* www.umanitoba.ca/unevoc/conference/papers/kozulin.pdf.

Krappmann, L. (1996). Amicitia, drujba, shin-yu, philia, freundschaft, friendship: On the cultural diversity of a human relationship. In W. M. Bukowski, A. F. Newcomb, & W. W. Hartup (Eds.), *The company they keep* (pp. 24–26, 30, 34). New York: Press Syndicate of the University of Cambridge.

Ladd, G. W. (1990). Having friends, keeping friends, making friends, and being liked by peers in the classroom: Predictors of children's early school adjustment? *Child Development, 61*(4), 1081–1100.

Ladd, G., & Oden, S. L. (1979). The relationship between peer acceptance and children's ideas about helpfulness. *Child Development, 50,* 402–408.

Ladson-Billings, G. (1994). *The dreamkeepers: Successful teachers of African American teachers.* San Francisco: Jossey-Bass.

Lave, J. (1988). *Cognition in practice.* Cambridge, UK: Cambridge University Press.

Lee, C. D. (2000). The state of knowledge about the education of African Americans. *Commission on Black Education.* American Educational Research Association.

Lennon, M. C., Blome, J., & English, K. (2001). *Depression and low-income women: Challenges for TANF and welfare-to-work policies and programs.* New York: National Center for Children in Poverty, Columbia University.

Losey, K. M. (1997). *Listen to the silences: Mexican American interaction in the composition classroom and community.* Norwood, NJ: Ablex.

Luria, A. R. (1928). The problem of the cultural development of the child. *Journal of Genetic Psychology, 35,* 493–506.

MacLeod, J. (1995). *Ain't no makin' it.* Boulder, CO: Westview Press.

Madaus, G., & Clarke, M. (2001). The adverse impact of high-stakes testing on minority students: Evidence from one hundred years of test data. In G. Orfield & M. Kornhaber (Eds.), *Raising standards or barriers? Inequality and high stakes testing in public education* (pp. 85–106). New York: Century Foundation.

Marcia, J. (1980). Identity in adolescence. In J. Adelson (Ed.), *Handbook of adolescent psychology* (pp. 159–187). New York: Wiley.

Martinez, G. A. (1997). Mexican-Americans and whiteness. In R. Delgado & J. Stefancic (Eds.), *Critical white studies: Looking behind the mirror* (pp. 210–213). Philadelphia: Temple University Press.

Maslow, A. H. (1968). *Toward a psychology of being* (2nd ed.). New York: Van Nostrand.

Massachusetts Department of Education. (1999). Massachusetts high school students and sexual orientation. Results of the 1999 youth risk behavior survey. Boston: Author.

McAdoo, P. H. (1993). *Family ethnicity strength in diversity.* Newbury Park, CA: Sage.

McLaughlin, B. (1995). *Fostering second language development in young children.* Washington, DC: National Center for Research on Cultural Diversity and Second Language Learning.

Mehan, H. (1987). Language and schooling. In G. Spindler & L. Spindler (Eds.), *Interpretive ethnography of education: At home and abroad* (pp. 109–136). Hillsdale, NJ: Erlbaum.

Merrow report: In schools we trust. (1997). VHS (available at http://www.pbs.org/merrow/tv/trust).

Mintz, S. W., & Price, R. (1992). *The birth of African-American culture: An anthropological perspective.* Boston: Beacon Press.

Moses, R. P., Kammi, M., Swap, S. M., & Howard, J. (1989). The algebra project: Organization in the spirit of Ella. *Harvard Educational Review, 59*(4), 423–443.

NAEYC (1995). NAEYC Position Statement: Responding to linguistic and cultural diversity—Recommendations for effective early childhood education. *Young Children, 51*(2), 4–12.

National Center for Children in Poverty. (1999). One in four: America's youngest poor. New York: Columbia School of Public Health.

National Center for Educational Statistics (NCES). (2001). *NAEP summary data tables* [online]. Washington, DC: U.S. Department of Education. Retrieved from: http://nces.ed.gov/Nationsreportcard.

National Commission on Excellence. (1983). *A nation at risk: The imperative for educational reform.* Washington, DC: U.S. Government Printing Office.

National Council of Teachers of Mathematics. (1989). *Curriculum and evaluation standards for school mathematics.* Reston, VA: National Council of Teachers of Mathematics.

Natrillo, G., & Dornbush, S. M. (1984). *Teacher evaluative standards and student effort.* New York: Longman.

Natrillo, G., Pallas, A., & McDill, E. (1986). Taking stock: Renewing or research agenda on the causes and consequences of dropping out. *Teachers College Record, 87*(3) 430–440.

Newmann, F. M. (1992). Conclusion. In F. M. Newmann (Ed.), *Student engagement and achievement in American secondary schools* (pp. 182–217). New York: Teachers College Press.

Nicholls, J. G. (1979). Quality and equality in intellectual development: The role of motivation in education. *American Psychologist, 34,* 1071–1084.

No Child Left Behind Act of 2001. (2001). Retrieved from http://www.ed.gov/nclb/landing.jhtml.

Ochs, E. (1997). Cultural dimensions of language acquisition. In N. Coupland & A. Jawroski (Eds.), *Sociolinguistics: A reader* (pp. 340–437). New York: St. Martin's Press.

Omi, M., & Winant, H. (1994). *Racial formation in the United States from the 1960s to the 1990s* (2nd ed.). New York: Routledge.

Orenstein, P. (1994). *Schoolgirls: Young women, self-esteem, and the confidence gap.* New York: Doubleday.

Orfield, G., & Kornhaber, M. (Eds.). (2001). *Raising standards or barriers? Inequality and high stakes testing in public education.* New York: Century Foundation.

Pai, Y., & Adler, S. A. (2001). *Cultural foundations of education* (3rd ed.). Upper Saddle River, NJ: Merrill Prentice Hall.

Paris, S. G., & Paris, A. H. (2001). Classroom applications of research on self-regulated learning. *Educational Psychologist, 36*(2), 89–101.

Parish, T. S. (1996). Examining the basic principles of friendships. *Education, 117,* 160.

Pasteur, A. B., & Toldson, I. L. (1982). *Roots of soul: The psychology of black expressiveness.* Garden City, NY: Anchor Press/Doubleday.

Paul, R., & Elder, L. (2001). *Critical thinking: Tools for taking charge of your learning and your life.* Upper Saddle River, NJ: Prentice Hall.

Perry, T., & Delpit, L. (1998). *The real Ebonics debate: Power, language, and the education of African American children.* Boston: Beacon.

Perry, W. S., Jr. (1970). *Scheme of intellectual and ethical development.* New York: Holt, Rinehart & Winston.

Philips, S. U. (1972). Participant structures and communicative competence: Warm Springs children in community and classroom. In C. B. Cazden, V. P. John, & D. Hymes (Eds.), *Functions of language in the classroom* (pp. 370–394). New York: Teachers College Press.

Piaget, J. (1952). *The origins of intelligence in children* (M. Cook, Trans.). New York: International Universities Press.

Pintrich, P. R. (1995). Understanding self-regulated learning. In P. R. Pintrich (Ed.), *Understanding self-regulated learning.* San Francisco, CA: Jossey-Bass.

Pollack, W. S. (1999). *Real boys: Rescuing our sons from the myths of boyhood.*

Portes, P. (1996). Ethnicity and culture in educational psychology. In D. C. Berliner & R. C. Calfee (Eds.), *The handbook of educational psychology* (pp. 331–357). New York: Simon, Schuster Macmillan.

Portes, A., & Hao, L. (1998). E pluribus unum: Bilingualism and loss of language in the second generation. *Sociology of Education, 71,* 269–294.

Portes, A., & Zhou, M. (1993). The new second generation: Segmented assimilation and its variances. *Annals of the American Academy of Political and Social Sciences, 530,* 74–96.

Putman, R. T., & Borko, H. (2000). What do new views of knowledge and thinking have to say about research on teacher learning? *Educational Researcher, 29*(1), 4–15.

Ramirez, M. (1992, September 6). Rhyme and reason: In this class, Spanish is an asset, not a hurdle. *Seattle Times/Seattle Post-Intelligencer Pacific Magazine,* 12–20.

Ramsey, P. G. (1986). Racial and cultural categories. In C. P. Edwards (Ed.), *Promoting social and moral development in young children: Creative approaches for the classroom* (pp. 78–101). New York: Teachers College Press.

Reese, D. (1997). Native Americans in children's literature. In V. J. Harris (Ed.), *Using multiethnic literature in the K-8 classroom* (pp. 155–192). Norwood, MA: Christopher-Gordon.

Resnick, L. B. (1991). Shared cognition: Thinking as a social practice. In L. B. Resnick, J. M. Levine, & S. D. Teasley (Eds.), *Perspectives on socially shared cognition* (pp. 1–20). Washington, DC: American Psychological Association.

Richardson, T. Q., & Silvestri, T. J. (1999). White identity formation: A developmental process. In R. H. Sheets & E. R. Hollins (Eds.), *Racial and ethnic identity in school practices: Aspects of human development* (pp. 49–66). Mahwah, NJ: Erlbaum.

Rizzo, T. A. (1988). *Friendship development among children in school.* Norwood, NJ: Ablex.

Rogers, C. R. (1970). *On becoming a person: A therapist's view of psychotherapy.* Boston: Houghton Mifflin.

Rogoff, B. (1990). *Apprenticeship in thinking: Cognitive development in social context.* New York: Oxford University Press.

Rogoff, B. (2003). *The cultural nature of human development.* New York: Oxford University Press.

Root, M. P. P. (Ed.). (1992). *Racially mixed people in America.* Newbury Park, CA: Sage.

Root, M. P. P. (1999). The biracial baby boom: Challenging constructions of racial identity in the twenty-first century. In R. H. Sheets & E. R. Hollins (Eds.), *Racial, ethnic, and cultural identity and human development: Implications for schooling* (pp. 67–90). Mahwah, NJ: Erlbaum.

Rosenshine, B. (2003). High-stakes testing: Another analysis. *Education Policy Analysis Archives, 11*(24). Retrieved from http://epaa.asu.edu/epaa/vlln24/.

Rothstein-Fisch, C., Greenfield, P., & Trumbull, E. (1999). Bridging cultures with classroom strategies. *Educational Leadership, 56*(7), 64–67.

Ryan, C., & Futterman, D. (1997). Lesbian and gay youth: Care and counseling. *Adolescent Medicine State-of-the-Art Review, 8*(2).

Sadker, M., & Sadker, D. (1994). *Failing at fairness: How America's schools cheat girls.* New York: Scribner's.

Sapon-Shevin, M. (1983). Teaching children about differences: Resources for teaching. *Young Children, 38*(2), 24–32.

Sarason, S. B. (1995). Some reactions to what we have learned. *Phi Delta Kappan,* 84–85.

Savan-Williams, R. C., & Cohen, K. M. (Eds.). (1996). *The lives of lesbians, gays, and bisexuals: Children to adults.* Orlando, FL: Harcourt Brace.

Schonert-Reichl, K. A. (1993). Empathy and social relationships in adolescents with behavioral disorders. *Behavior Disorders, 18,* 189–204.

Sheets, R. H. (1995a). From remedial to gifted: Effects of culturally relevant pedagogy. *Theory into Practice, 34*(3), 186–193.

Sheets, R. H. (1995b). *Student and teacher perceptions of disciplinary conflicts in culturally pluralistic classrooms.* Ann Arbor, MI: UMI Dissertation Services.

Sheets, R. H. (1996). Urban classroom conflict: Student-teacher perception: Ethnic integrity, solidarity, and resistance. *Urban Review, 28*(2), 165–183.

Sheets, R. H. (1997). Racial and ethnic awareness: Affirming identity. In J. Carnes and R. H. Sheets (Eds.) *Starting small: Teaching tolerance in preschool and the early grades* (pp. 16–21). Montgomery, AL: Teaching Tolerance Project.

Sheets, R. H. (1998a). A theoretical and pedagogical multicultural match, or unbridled serendipity. *Multicultural Education, 6*(1), 35–38.

Sheets, R. H. (1998b). *Ethnic identity behavioral displays and competence in an urban kindergarten: Implications for practice.* (Unpublished manuscript).

Sheets, R. H. (1999). Relating competence in an urban classroom to ethnic identity development. In R. H. Sheets & E. R. Hollins (Eds.), *Racial and ethnic identity in school practices: Aspects of human development* (pp. 157–178). Mahwah, NJ: Erlbaum.

Sheets, R. H. (2002a). *Multicultural pedagogical knowledge.* (Unpublished manuscript).

Sheets, R. H. (2002b). "You're just a kid that's there"—Chicano perception of disciplinary events. *Journal of Latinos in Education, 1*(2), 105–122.

Sheets, R. H. (2004). Multiracial adolescent perception: The role of friendship in identification and identity formation. In K. Wallace (Ed.), *Working with mixed heritage students: Perspectives on research and practice* (pp. 137–154). Greenwich, CT: Informational Age.

Sheets, R. H., & Hollins, E. R. (Eds.). (1999). *Racial and ethnic identity in school practices: Aspects of human development.* Mahwah, NJ: Erlbaum.

Sherman, A. M., de Vries, B., & Lansford, J. E. (2000). Friendship in childhood and adulthood: Lessons across the life span. *International Journal of Aging and Human Development, 51*(1), 31–51.

Sigelman, L., & Welch, S. (1993). The contact hypothesis revisited: Black-white interaction and positive racial attitudes. *Social Forces,* 795–803.

Signorella, M. L. (1987). Gender schemata: Individual differences and context effects. *New Directions for Child Development, 38,* 23–38.

Skinner, B. F. (1957). *Verbal behavior.* New York: Appleton-Century-Crofts.

Skinner, B. G. (1979). *The shaping of a behaviorist.* New York: Knopf.

Slavin, R. E. (1995). Cooperative learning and intergroup relations. In J. A. Banks and C. A. M. Banks (Eds.), *Handbook of research on multicultural education* (pp. 628–634). New York: Macmillan.

Spencer, M. B. (1983). Children's cultural values and parental child rearing strategies. *Developmental Review, 3*(4), 351–370.

Spencer, M. B. (1985). Cultural cognition and social cognition as identity factors in Black children's personal growth. In M. Spencer, G. Brookins, & W. Allen (Eds.), *Beginnings: The social and affective development of black children* (pp. 215–230). Hillsdale, NJ: Erlbaum.

Spring, J. (2001). *The American school 1642–2000* (5th ed.). New York: McGraw Hill.

Spring, J. (2002). *Political agendas for education* (2nd ed). Mahwah, NJ: Erlbaum.

Suarez-Orozco, M. M. (1991). Hispanic immigrant adaptation to schooling. In M. A. Gibson & J. U. Ogbu (Eds.), *Minority status and schooling: A comparative study of immigrant and involuntary minorities.* New York: Garland.

Sugrue, C. (1996). Student teachers' lay theories: Implications for professional development. In I. F. Goodson & A. Hargraves (Eds.), *Teachers' professional lives* (pp. 154–177). Washington, DC: Falmer Press.

Sutherland, R. (1985). Hidden persuaders: Political ideologies in literature for children. *Children's Literature in Education, 16,* 143–157.

Swanson, D. P., Spencer, M. B., & Petersen, A. (1998). Identity formation in adolescence. In K. Borman & B. Schneider (Eds.), *The adolescent years: Social influences and educational challenges, Ninety-seventh yearbook of the National Society for the Study of Education, Part I* (pp. 18–41). Chicago: University of Chicago Press.

Tatum, B. (1997). *Why are all the black kids sitting together in the cafeteria?* New York: Harper Collins.

Taylor, O. L. (1990). *Cross-cultural communication: An essential dimension of effective education.* Washington, DC: Mid-Atlantic Equity Center (ERIC Document Reproduction Service No. ED 325 593).

Tesch, S. A. (1983). Review of friendship development across the life span. *Human Development, 26*(5), 266–276.

Thorndike, E. L. (1910). The contribution of psychology to education. *Journal of Educational Psychology, 1,* 5–12. Retrieved from http://psychclassics.yorku.ca/Thorndike/education.htm.

Triandis, H. C. (1988). Collectivism vs. individualism: A reconceptualization of a basic concept in cross-cultural social psychology. In C. Bagley & C. K. Verma (Eds.), *Personality, cognition, and values: Cross-cultural perspectives of childhood and adolescence.* London: Macmillan.

Troiden, R. R. (1988). Homosexual identity development. *Journal of Adolescent Health Care, 9,* 105–113.

Tyson, C. A. (1999). "Shut my mouth wide open": Realistic fiction and social action. *Theory into Practice, 38*(3), 155–159.

U.S. Bureau of the Census. (1992). Report CPHL 133. Washington, DC: U.S. Government Printing Office.

Valdés, G. (2000). Introduction. Spanish for native speakers (Vol. 1). *AATSP Professional Development Series Handbook for Teachers K–16.* New York: Harcourt College.

Valdés, G. (2001). *Learning and not learning English: Latino students in American schools.* New York: Teachers College Press.

Valenzuela, A. (1999). *Subtractive schooling: U.S.–Mexican youth and the politics of caring.* New York: SUNY.

Van Ausdale, D., & Feagin, J. R. (2001). *The first r: How children learn race and racism.* New York: Rowman & Littlefield.

Verkuyten, M. (2001). National identification and intergroup evaluations in Dutch children. *British Journal of Developmental Psychology, 19,* 559–571.

Villanueva, V., Jr. (1999). Sophistry, Aristotle, contrastive rhetoric, and the student of color. In E. R. Hollins & E. I. Oliver (Eds.), *Pathways to success in school: Culturally responsive teaching* (pp. 107–124). Mahwah: NJ: Erlbaum.

Vygotsky, L. (1962). *Thought and language.* Cambridge, MA: MIT Press.

Vygotsky, L. (1978). *Mind in society: The development of higher psychological processes.* M. Cole, V. John-Steiner, S. Scribner, & E. Souberman (Eds. & Trans.). Cambridge, MA: Harvard University Press.

Vygotsky, L. (1986). *Thought and language.* Cambridge, MA: MIT Press.

Vygotsky, L., & Luria, A. (1930/1993). *Studies on the history of behavior.* Hillsdale, NJ: Erlbaum.

Walton, S. (1997). *Verve effects: The influence of cultural attributes, task variability, and background stimulation on the task performance of African American and European American children.* Paper presented at the annual meeting of the American Educational Research Association, Chicago, IL.

Watson, J. B. (1913). Psychology as the behaviorist views it. *Psychological Review, 20,* 158–177.

Watson, K. A. (1974). Understanding human interactions. *Topics in cultural learning, 2,* 57–66. (Available from the Culture Learning Institute, East-West Center, Honolulu, Hawaii).

Wellesley Center for Research on Women. (1992). *How schools shortchange girls: A study of major findings on girls and education.* Washington, DC: American Association of University Women.

Wideen, M., Mayer-Smith, J., & Moon, B. (1998). A critical analysis of the research on learning to teach: Making the case for an ecological perspective on inquiry. *Review of Educational Research, 68*(2), 130–178.

Wigfield, A., Eccles, J. S., & Pintrich, P. R. (1996). Development between the ages of 11 and 25. In D. C. Berliner & R. C. Calfee (Eds.), *The handbook of educational psychology* (pp. 148–184). New York: Simon, Schuster Macmillan.

Witkin, H. A. (1962). *Psychological differentiation.* New York: Wiley.

Woodward, A. (2003). Gender bias in education. *Gale encyclopedia of childhood and adolescence.* Retrieved from http://www.findarticles.com/cf_0/g2602/0002/2602000263/p1/article.jhtml.

Zimmerman, B. J. (1995). Self-regulation involves more than metacognition: A social cognitive perspective. *Educational Psychologist, 30,* 217–221.

Zimmerman, B. J., & Schunk, D. H. (Eds.). (2001). *Self-regulated learning and academic achievement: Theoretical perspectives.* Mahwah, NJ: Erlbaum.

AUTHOR INDEX

SUBJECT INDEX